METHODS OF TEACHING PHYSICS

By

Dr. M. Vanaja

M.Sc. Ed. (Physics), M.A., M.Ed., Ph.D.

Lecturer in Physical Science

St. Joseph's College of Education for Women

Guntur–522 001 (A.P.)

General Editor

Dr. Digumarti Bhaskara Rao

M.Sc., M.A., M.A., M.Ed., Ph.D.

Reader

R.V.R. College of Education

Srinivasa Nagar Colony

Guntur–522 006

Andhra Pradesh

India

DISCOVERY PUBLISHING HOUSE

NEW DELHI-110002

Published by:
Namit Wasan

DISCOVERY PUBLISHING HOUSE PVT. LTD.
4383/4B, Ansari Road, Darya Ganj
New Delhi-110 002 (India)
Phone : +91-11-23279245; 23253475; 43596065
E-mail : discoverybooksindia@gmail.com
discoverypublishinghouse@gmail.com
namitwasan9@gmail.com
web : www.discoverypublishinggroup.com

***Edition:* 2020**

ISBN: 978-81-7141-867-1

Methods of Teaching Physics

Printed at:
Infinity Imaging Systems
Delhi

Foreword

Teacher education is quantitatively marching ahead towards quality education. The central and state governments through the NCTE and the Directorates of School/Higher Education are rendering their legitimate service in improving the quality of teacher education by formulating and implementing various academic policies and educational programmes. Along with these policies and programmes, the teacher educators and the prospective teachers teaching and studying in teacher education institutions need good curriculum and quality books.

The methods of teaching each subject play a pivotal role in enhancing the efficiency of their practitioners. Identifying the very importance of the methods of teaching and the quality of books, a series of books on the methods of teaching different subjects have been developed by experienced teacher educators for the benefit of teachers in making in teacher education institutions. Thanks to the authors.

Valuable suggestions for the improvement of these books are welcome from fellow teacher educators, prospective teachers and other academicians involved in the arena of teacher education.

The authors and the editor dedicate this series of books on the methodology of teaching to Mr. Tilak Raj Wasan, Proprietor, Discovery Publishing House, New Delhi, for taking up this commendable task of publication to meet the felt needs of teacher education faculty and clientele.

Dr. Digumarti Bhaskara Rao

Research Director in Education

Nagarjuna University

br_digumarti@rediffmail.com

Preface

The movement of modern education in India is almost two century old. It has come of age now. Over the decades, great educationists have contributed towards the development and evolution of education, as a discipline. Thus, education in India has been enriched a lot.

As a result, the Indian education system can be placed at par with any advanced education system in the modern world. In fact, education is a vast sea and Teachers' Training is a stream in it. So, it makes it essential that the responsibilities of the faculty members are focused on the task of providing better training to the future teachers, for their better learning and proper development. And this responsible exercise can only be undertaken, if the trainers are equipped with all the needed skill and knowledge of the subject, they are supposed to teach. Hence, it becomes essential for making adequate provisions, for each course to the teacher-trainees. Methods of Teaching are very important for the successful training of teachers and for their career in future.

In order to provide all related material in one cover, here is this book, on this important subject. Of course there are several books on the subject in the market, but, every book has its own style and way of presentation. Similarly, the present one, too has its own merits and advantages.

During the course of the preparation of this book, the undersigned has done his best for the accomplishment of the job. He would be pleased and feel contented, if this book is acknowledged, as a textbook and a reference tool for the teachers and students, alike.

Author

Contents

1

Introduction

Science is taken to be the most important subject in school curriculum because the man's future depends to a large extent on scientific advances and development of productive activity. There is great feeling to teach science.

The International Congress on Science and Technology Education convened by Unesco in 1981 made numerous recommendations for Unesco's future role in this broad field of activity.

With the funds provided by Unesco studies were carried out regarding the place of science in curriculum in various countries. Following generalisations were made :

Africa

The data was provided by 21 countries of the region. It was found that in 'primary' classes in most of these countries time was allotted for teaching of science. The time allotted per week varied from 1 hour to 4.5 hours. Most of the countries adopted integrated approach for teaching of science. In middle classes also science forms a part of the curriculum and in secondary classes general science is a permitted alternative to integrated science. General science includes topics from physics, chemistry and biology only whereas integrated course includes elements of astronomy, geology, agricultural science, home science and economics in addition to physics, chemistry and biology.

Arab Nations

Ten countries of the region were surveyed. All countries put science firmly on time table of all grades from 1 to 6. The time allotted per week for science varies, between 1 to 35 hours. The 'intermediate' and secondary level courses in integrated science are provided and for classes 7, 8, 9 generally 2 hours per week are allotted. In grades 10,11 and 12 these are taught as separate subjects and 2 hours per week is allotted for each subject.

Asia and the Pacific

Seventeen countries of the region including India participated in survey. In almost every country, a course in integrated science is the one most favoured in the early secondary school years. The three traditional science disciplines physics, chemistry and biology, are almost invariably on offer as optional courses during the late secondary school years.

In India through the efforts of National Council of Educational Research and Training (NCERT) science has been made a compulsory subject through out the school stage. In this connection it would be in our interest to consider the views of Kothari Commission and Unesco's international commission on the development of education.

Kothari Commission

Kothari Commission was given the task of suggesting necessary improvements in educational system of the country. It worked during the years 1964-1966 and made a detailed study of educational system in India. It suggested various changes for improvement of education in India. Here we concentrate on the suggestions made by the commission about the science education. The commission suggested that great emphasis be laid on science education and that science be made a compulsory object of the school curriculum. Following lines from the commission report make the point clear:

"We lay great emphasis on making science an important element in the school curriculum. We, therefore, recommend that science and mathematics should be taught on compulsory basis to all pupil as a part of general education during the first ten years of schooling. In addition there should be provision of special course in these subjects at the secondary stage, for students of more than average ability."

International Education Commission

The recommendations made by Unesco's International Commission in 1972 are quite similar to those made by Kothari Commission (1964-1966) in India.

The recommendations nude by Unesco's Intenutional Commission about the teaching of science and technology are as under:

"Science and Technology must become essential components in any educational enterprise; they must be incorporated into all educational activity intended for children, young people and adults, in order to help the individual to control social energies as well as natural and productive ones — thereby achieving mastery over himself, his choices and actions —and finally, they must help man to acquire a scientific turn of mind so that he becomes able to promote science without being enslaved by it."

Furthermore this commission recommended that science be incorporated as a single science. In this respect the recommendation of the commission is as under:

"The natural science will one day incorporate the science of man, just as science of man will incorporate the natural sciences; There will be a *single sciences.*"

Science in Everyday Life

Present age is known as the age of science and so science is considered an important subject in the school curriculum. In this era of science larger number of people are being employed in scientific pursuits and for this they need a knowledge of science. The dawn of space age and explosion in knowledge have also necessitated the teaching of science to every student.

Science education is essential as it is of immense value in the students' individual life as also his life in society. Science education is important due to the following reasons:

Intellectual Importance

Science alongwith being a content of knowledge, is a method of acquiring knowledge. Scientific knowledge helps to sharpen our intellect and promotes intellectual honesty. It helps us to report about things and events without any bias. It makes us quite systematic in our reasoning. It helps us in acquiring the strength to face hardships and failures because the pursuit of science requires diligence and patience. The science education can develop the positive attitudes like open mindedness, reasoning etc. Such a positive attitude is quite helpful to an individual to understand, evaluate and solve many a social problems be faces in life and helps him to lead a happy, successful and satisfying life.

Vocational Importance

In the present age we do not find any vocation that does not need the knowledge of science more ever there are a large number of vocations for which study by science is a primary requirement, e.g., medicines, engineering, agriculture, paramedicines, computers etc. It thus becomes quite clear that to enter into any such vocational course an individual must have a knowledge of science and so the science education must be included in the school curriculum. In this age of science if we wish to prepare an individual for certain vocation it is essential that he be given a good education in science.

Aesthetic Importance

Knowledge of science develops in man a passion for truth and thus he has a passion for beauty. The English poet Keats has said, "Truth is Beauty." Science is basically unfolding of the mysteries of nature and nature is a store house of all the beautiful things. Thus we find that teaching of science of essential for developing an aesthetic sense in an individual. By enjoying the aesthetic aspects of his discoveries and inventions the scientist feel an intrinsic charm. The difference between a scientist and an artist is only superficial in that an artist aims more deliberately at beauty and a scientist attains and enjoys beauty through reasoning and truth.

Practical Importance

Scientific principles and laws find a large number of applications in our everyday life. For proper utility of such applications some knowledge of science is necessary. At present we depend on scientific discoveries to a very large extent. Even a cursory and casual look around ourselves shows a lot of applications of science. For example, electricity, electronics, communication, transport etc. We find that telephone has revolutionised the commercial world and has a profound effect on the market in general and stock market in particular. It has enabled us to talk to our friends or relatives sitting in remote comers of the world or even when they are a passenger on a liner and are in mid-sea. Aeroplane has reduced the distance and has helped to being countries together. Aeroplane has fulfilled the long cherished desire of man to fly like a bird.

The most important practical value of science is felt in the world of medicines and health. Science has discovered a large number of new medicines which are used to cure such diseases which were considered as incurable only a few decades ago. It has also given us new methods for prevention of diseases and we have been able to stop epidemics taking away a large number of human lives some contiguous disease have been completely eradicated and in this way science has reduced the miseries of humanity and lengthened the average life of ordinary poisons.

Science has also helped us overcome the problem of passing our leisure time and to make best use of it. Science has provided us with a large number of devices such as television, radio, cinema etc., which are a source of entertainment to all of us. These are also a source of knowledge and are used for spread of mass education and making the community aware of dangers of various ills. These devices are also used for eradication of various social evils. Science has also provided a large number of hobbies which we can usefully pursue in our leisure time, e.g. photography etc. The knowledge of science has also been found to a person whose hobby is gardening. Such a person will enjoy his hobby and will be benefitted more if he knows some thing about plant breeding, soil physics, chemical fertilizers etc.

Moral Importance

We have already learnt that a knowledge of science develops in us truthfulness and reasoning. Though such qualities may not make you a successful businessman or a successful politician according to present standards yet these are the very qualities which are desirable in all human beings. These qualities make the life worth living though they have lost their value in todays materialistic world. However none so far has said that training in truthfulness is bad.

Psychological Importance

Teaching of science is essential for developing scientific attitudes and scientific temper. Science helps us to develop positive attitudes such as open mindedness, reasoning etc., the learning of science is based on the fundamental principles of psychology i.e., 'learning by doing', 'learning by observing concrete and living specimens.' Being an activity oriented subject science helps to satisfy basic human desire of knowing about wonders of nature and so it satisfies common instincts as creative-ness, self-assertion, curiosity etc.

Cultural Importance

A study of the past scientists and their discoveries gives us an insight into the mode of their living, their spirit of sacrifice and their adventures. All such studies from the part of our cultural heritage and the study of this cultural past has a romance of its own. A knowledge of science develops in us a capacity to critically examining facts and arriving at logical conclusions. It also develops in us imagination power that is essential for propersolutions of various problems we actually face in our life.

Adjustment in Modern Life

Science develops in us a *scientific attitude.* It also develops in an individual a specific procedure for attacking any problem. Such a specific procedure is called *'scientific method.'* Such a method prepares an individual to face the problems of life boldly and to solve them successfully. A person having scientific attitude has an open mind, a desire for accurate knowledge and a confidence to solve a problem using his sense of reasoning. A person having scientific attitude lives a peaceful and successful life.

Scientific Conceptions

Science has long been taught in different branches such as Physics, Chemistry, Botany, Zoology etc., in a compartmentalised way. Each subject was taught separately and in isolation without bringing any correlation or integration between them. However in the later half of this century a new concept of science, with a completely compounded curriculum of all major branches has been evolved and courses were developed in integrated science (general science).

Concept of General Science

The first major international conference on the teaching of integrated science, sponsored by Unesco, was held in 1968 in Droujba (Bulgaria) in cooperation with the International Council of Scientific Unions (ICSU), Committee on the Teaching of Science (CTS).

Five main conclusions that emerged from it are :

(i) Teaching of integrated science contributes towards general education, emphasizes the fundamental unity of science and leads towards an understanding of the place of science in contemporary society.

(ii) It avoids unnecessary repetitions and permits the introduction of intermediate disciplines.

(iii) It is necessary to omit some details in such an integrated course of science and so the contents of the course be judiciously chosen and be carefully compiled by collaboration between different teachers and other specialists.

(iv) The extent of integration and the balance between integration and coordination will depend on the age of the students, the type of educational institutions and local conditions. At early stages of secondary education, a totally integrated course in experimental sciences is desirable.

(v) Science is an important part of primary education, particularly in arousing scientific curiosity and developing scientific attitudes and skills.

Another major conference for development of education in integrated science was held in Netherlands in 1978 which was organised by the International Council of Associations for Science Education (ICASE) in collaboration with Unesco.

The next significant international conference on integrated science teaching took place in Bangalore (India) in 1985. It was organised by ICSU — CTS and its major aim was to identify practical ways in which education jn science and technology can contribute to national development Eight areas selected for the conference were food and agriculture;
energy resources; land, water and mineral resources; health; industry and technology; the environment; information transfer and technology and ethics and social responsibility.

The most recent international gathering concerned with integrated science took place in Canberra (Australia) in July 1988. It made a distinction between 'Integrated' science and 'multi-disciplinary' science.

An integrated approach to scientific endeavour after characterizes the highest level of research, where the work involves the efforts of the two or more specialists or teams of specialists having different disciplinary backgrounds and training. The results resemble a chemical compound, where the individual constituents or elements can no longer be recognized or physically separated. In this respect integrated science, where collaboration, often in parallel, leads to physical mixture; here the ingredients can be seen and disengaged. The properties of a compound transcend those of its elemental parts, where as those of mixture never do.

Now this new subject has developed to impart a unitary knowledge of science as a whole. It has a broad scope and can be applied to a broad range of interests. It has its own body of subject matter which is chosen to meet the needs of the students.

With the spread of 'education for all' and the growing awareness of the role and importance of science in modern world; it is not surprising to find the teachingof science gaining prominence in schools. Thus the number of science courses available at the primary or elementary level has grown dramatically. Most of them use environment as an important source. Many of the integrated science courses developed for secondary schools reflect aspects of science and society, some of the courses incorporate technology but a majority still concentrate on two or more usually, all three of the traditional branches of science (i.e., biology, physics, chemistry). The impact of computer and information technology is quite evident in some courses of integrated science. But the extent of the use of computers and suitability of the software deserve closer study, especially in relation to the whole range of practical activities undertaken by students.

The main characteristics of an integrated science course as outlined above can be summarised as under :

(i) It is free of any traditional boundaries of different branches of science.

(ii) It is useful as a general education for every individual.

(iii) It covers Every Day Science for Every Body.

(iv) It helps common man in understanding his environment and help him to face his daily problems with confidence and solve them successfully.

John Murray has defined the general science as under :

"It is a course of scientific study and investigation which has its roots in common experiences of children and does not exclude any one of the fundamental special science."

In a recent review based on a study conducted by Unesco on *'The place of science and technology in school curricula.* The matrix proposed by Abraham Blum in 1973 has been used for purpose of definition. Blum's matrix has two axes; *scope* and *intensity.* Thus, for inclusion, courses must cover at least two scientific disciplines and provide evidence of a substantial amount interweaving.

The introduction of general science course in Indian schools was strongly recommended by Secondary Education Commission (1952-53). Introduction of such a course at school level was also favoured during All India Seminar on Science Teaching held at Taradevi (1956). Teaching of general science was introduced, in India, as a compulsory subject at primary, middle and secondary level. It was however discontinued in middle and high school because of the opposition by various quarters.

Views in Opposition

After introduction of General Science Course at various levels a genera] feeling was that the course has failed to achieve the objectives for which it was introduced. The following observations make the point clear.

A comprehensive report on science teaching in India was submitted by the Unesco planning mission under the leadership of Prof. S.G. Shepovalonko. The mission stayed in India from December 23,1963 to March 10,1964. It recommended the abolition of General Science at the middle level. The commission also recommended the introduction of Physics and Biology from class VI and of Chemistry from class VII.

The view expressed by Kothari Commission (1964-66) are as under:

"The General Science approach to teaching of science...., has not proved successful as it tends to make science appear somewhat formless and without structure and runs counter to its methodology. A disciplinary approach to science learning would, it is felt, be more effective in providing the necessary scientific base to young people."

Disciplinary Approach

Keeping in view the opposition faced by the general science teaching the National Council of Educational Research and Training (N.C.ER.T.) introduced disciplinary approach to teaching of science at middle school stage on an experimental basis. However even this experimental replacement of general science was not suitable aqnd was being replaced by Integrated Science. As has already been discussed the Integrated Science and a significant internal conference to give attention to Integrated Science took place in Bangalore (India) in 1985. The main aim of this conference was to identify practical ways in which education in science and technology can contribute to national development.

The most recent international gathering of science educators to be concerned with integrated science took place in Canberra (Australia) in July, 1988. Here a seminar, jointly sponsored by ICASE and Unesco received the place of integrated science course in education systems worldwide.

Integrated Curriculum

Integrated approach to scientific endeavour in different from *multi-disciplinary Science.*

The Journal *Interdisciplinary Science Reviews* contain, in the editorial of Vol. I, No. 1, the following reference to inter-disciplinary science.

Increasing orientation towards interdisciplinary topics with in the scientific community requires an understanding by specialists in one field of the needs, problems and terminology of another field. Here the examples of Robert Boyle (1627-1691) and Alexander von Humboldt (1769-1859) are worth mentioning. These two scientists excelled in more than a single field of science and modern scientists may well be able to learn from their experience.

In recent times interdisciplinary research found its most widespread use in operations research or operational research as it is called in United Kingdom, where it was originated by A.P. Rowe in 1937. He and his colleagues started teaching the intricacies of radar and they succeeded to such a large extent that by 1945 operational research activities had become a truly interdisciplinary effort of scientists and industrialists. Operations research is defined as the application of scientific method to the management of organized systems in which human behaviour plays an important part.

Systems engineering also use an interdisciplinary approach and tends to concentrate on technological innovations with less emphasis on the human factor. Systems analysis includes humanity in all its aspects and differs little from operations research as both fields have developed and matured through their outstanding achievements in industrial, military and space activities. The essence common to all is Interdisciplinary thinking and a fusion of efforts.

This understanding of integration can be widened to embrace many more scientific and human activities in wide variety of fields, including education.

Abraham Blum in 1973 proposed a Matrix as a criterion for including or excluding particular courses. This matrix has two axes : *Scope* and *Intensity.*

The *scope* of a course is the range of disciplines; scientific or social which it includes.

The *Intensity* measures the extent to which the subjects have been blended together to give a deliberate synthesis of the material.

Four discemibly different approaches are named as 'concept', the 'topic', the 'process' and the 'environmental' approach. There appears a trend towards adopting the 'process' approach and also for more courses to be oriented towards the 'environment'. The latter development no doubt reflects the growing concern with science and society issues.

In most of the integrated science courses the curriculum has been developed keeping the following objectives in view :

(i) It should help develop a scientific attitudes.

(ii) It should be able to explain the relevance of science to every day life.

(iii) It must be able to create a feeling of reliance in the use of principles and practices of science.

(iv) It places due emphasis on the experimental work in science.

(v) It emphasises the unity of methods of various disciplines of science.

Nature of Curriculum

Curriculum development frequently originates within the confines of the country for which the learning material is devised, but it often borrows from extraneous sources. The courses in integrated science have been developed in such a way so as to integrate science with the environment of child and not as an artificial integration of disciplines.

In Integrated science courses devised so far three categories of *intensity* can be identified: *coordinated, combined* and *amalgamated.*

In *coordinated courses* it is possible to identify distinct sections of chemistry, biology and physics. In *combined* courses, separate sciences are the starting point and the course in so designed that the three sciences are blended together.

In *amalgamated courses,* the ideas associated with separate sciences are used as required to give unified whole or a high degree of integration.

That amalgamated courses will be the hardest to devise and coordinated courses the easiest can be easily assumed.

Questions

1. Discuss and differentiate between the integrated approach and disciplinary approach adopted for the teaching of science. Which one is at present being adopted in our schools?

2. What is the position of teaching physical sciences today in our schools?

3. "The study of physical sciences as a compulsory subject is useful." Justify the statement.

4. Write short notes on the following :

   (i) Values of teaching physical sciences,

   (ii) Concept of physical sciences.

   (iii) Integrated v/s disciplinary approach to science education.

2

The Correlation

In the modern nations of the world, the primary school curriculum bears little relation to that of fifty years or so ago. Then the subjects were reading, writing and arithmetic. Now the curriculum is achieved much more as a whole. The primary school curriculum has to a considerable extent become integrated and a large number of good primary school teachers possess a broad background, which enables them to guide their pupils' learning on a variety of topics as often based as the surroundings of the school.

However, secondary school curriculum generally consists of a number of separate subjects having little or no coordination between them. This may largely be due to the training received by secondary school teachers and to the public examination system which a strongly subject bounded. An attempt has been made in recent years to bring about an integrated curriculum which has helped to bring various science subjects closer but no effort has been made to consider other areas such as languages, mathematics and social sciences.

The major aim of education is the unification of knowledge existing in different branches of learning. To achieve such a unification a conscious effort has to be made by teachers teaching various subjects. It is only by such a joint venture that we will be able to achieve the goal of unification of knowledge and bridge the gap that separates them.

The Importance

No subject can be taught in isolation and so is the case with teaching of chemistry. For an effective learning all advantage must be taken of correlations and applications of chemistry and physics. In addition to correlation of chemistry and physics with other school subjects and daily life, a lot of correlation is possible with other science subjects. Artificial division of science into various branches is a matter of convenience and not of necessity. Based upon this premise, many educators advocate the implementation of curricula based upon the correlation between various subjects. These kinds of curriculum give more meaning to our class-room instructions. Various inventions in chemistry and physics have contributed a lot to the social and physical advancement of our society. Chemistry and physics has contributed a lot to development of some other subjects. In the following pages we will take up the correlation of chemistry and physics with other subjects.

Various Types

The three important type of correlations are:

1. Correlation with daily life.
2. Correlation of various science subjects with one another.
3. Correlation with other subjects.

Correlation of Science with Daily Life

Though the main aim of science is to impart a training in scientific methods yet the study of science also aims to provide an insight into many of natural phenomenon and also teaches us the various scientific principles that lie at the bottom of many simple rules of life. For fostering a love for science study among children teacher should bring home to his students the useful and interesting application of principles of science in daily life. Every principle of science has some useful application in daily life and it is the duty of the teacher to emphasise these while teaching the principle. It is likely to make his lesson more interesting, stimulating and realistic. Teacher is free to include those phenomenon which are matters of every day experience even if these are not prescribed in the syllabus. Teacher should make a conscious effort to arouse the interest of his students in such applications of science in every day life. Science teacher can find many applications of science in daily life and it would be much better if he quotes examples with rural background in rural schools and examples having urban background in urban schools. For correlating science with every day life an effort be made to make use of available community resources. For example, a teacher can plan a visit to a power station or hydro-electric generator while teaching the generation of electric current. The topic on levers can be correlated with their functioning in human body and their use in agricultural implements etc.

Correlations of Science with other Subjects

It is not possible to divide study of science into water-tight compartments of physics, chemistry, biology etc., because we find that there are many a principles and facts that are common to different science subjects. Because of this difficulty at present we find that subjects such as Bio-chemistry, Bio-physics, Physical-chemistry, Geophysics, General science etc., are emerging.

We can thus see that the science teacher can correlate his lesson in any one branch of science with some other branches of science using suitable examples. There are a plenty of topics which are common to two or more branches of science. For example.

Atom and Atomic Structure: It is quite common both in the study of chemistry and physics.

Electrolysis and Electrochemical Cells: The study of these topics is also included both in physics and chemistry.

Chemistry of Life or Living Bodies: It forms the subject-matter of both chemistry and biology.

Various Topics: In physics, chemistry and biology these also help in the study of *Hygiene.* For example

Physics

During study of light in physics we can tell the students about the effects of light on health and can discuss the topics as light and germs;
light and vitamins; artificial sun light; sun-bathing; Eye as camera etc.

The study of heat can be correlated to body temperature, heat and energy, humidity, treatment of heat burns etc.

While discussing a lesson on sound we can discuss the functioning of ear, effects of noise on health etc.

Similarly discussion of various other topics in physics can be suitably correlated with health and hygiene.

Chemistry

There a large number of topics in chemistry which actually revolve sound the chemistry of life. For example, chemistry of cell, chemistry of food and digestive system, chemistry of blood and blood circulation, poisons etc. The effects of hard and soft water on our health, ozone and importance of ozone layer, the effects of U.V. light, fission of atom and atomic energy etc.

Biology

Biology is intimately connected with health and hygiene. In study of biology is included the study of development, structure and functions of body, breathing, circulation of blood, digestive system and various other systems of human body. It also includes the study of bacteria and the dependence of man on animals and plants.

Note: In addition to relating the study of science to physics, chemistry, biology and hygiene it can also be correlated to other science subjects such as astronomy, geography, geology, home-science etc.

In the study of home science, we find various topics which could be taught as applications of various branches of science. For example, nutrition, laundry work, cleaning etc., are explained on the basis of knowledge of chemistry.

It is possible to correlate teaching of science with the study of almost any other subject. It can be correlated easily with mathematics.

Mathematics

Mathematics is considered as the mother of all sciences. A knowledge of mathematics is essential for understanding a topic in science. Science can be easily correlated with mathematics. The solution of practical problems, physical measurements, graphs of temperature, rainfall and pressure, laws of reflection, laws of refraction etc., all could be understand only with the help of knowledge of mathematics. In derivation of various equations in different branches of science an adequate knowledge of some fundamentals of mathematics is essential. Algebraic equations, graphs, geometry, calculus, coordinate geometry, statistics etc., arc a few important branches of mathematics whose knowledge is used while teaching certain branches of science. The use of logarithms is gaining importance and science and mathematics teachers should cooperate and coordinate their teaching.

Mathematics and science teachers can supplement each other if the study of graphs in mathematics is illustrated by drawing graphs of some experimental data obtained by the students in a science practical class.

Similarly useful data for trignometry (a branch of mathematics is provided by sextant (an instrument *used* to measure heights).

Geography

The teaching of science can be easily correlated with geography. There are a number of topics which are common to science and geography. For example, the study of rock and soils, study of plant and animal life etc. Physical geography requires an elementary knowledge of science for its foundation. For example, principles of facts on which climate depends, instructions in use of a barometer, thermometer, sundial, magnetic needle etc. In all these fields such as the actual recording of atmospheric pressure, temperature, wind direction, rain-fall etc., lies in the realm of geography but the study of recording instruments used forms the subject-matter of other branches of science. Geography interprets the results obtained by science. The study of various types of soil formed by weathering of different types of rocks is common to both science and geography. Not only in this but in various other topics the study of geography and science supplement each other. Of the various branches of science geology is quite akin to geography.

Art Subjects

There is a close relationship between the study of science and study of art. In biology a student is required to draw a large number of diagrams which he cannot draw in the absence of a good deal of practice in art lessons. A large number of drawings are also found in physics and chemistry and for these also some practice in art of making drawings is essential.

Drawing and band work are thus correlated to the study of science. Charts and diagrams for display in science laboratory should be good looking and quite durable. For this lettering should be done in script. Thus for drawing and lettering such charts the students needs the help of art.

The making models of scientific instruments, polishing articles of wood, soldering etc., can be encouraged among science students. In this way hand work can be easily correlated with the study of science. Such a correlation between science and work experience (SUPW) can be utilised in developing various improvised apparatus.

It is not only the science that needs the help of arts but arts also needs the help of science. A knowledge of chemistry of pigments, chemical properties of various types of dyes etc., is quite useful to art.

Music

In science a student gets the knowledge of reasonance, reverberations, vibrating systems in strings and air columns, musical scales etc., which is quite useful to him to endergo the study of music. In music, he comes across various types of instruments and equipments which are based on one or the other principle of sciences.

Social Studies

There is a lot of correlation between science and social studies. Knowledge of science produces a great impact on our life style, way of thinking, our behaviour etc. A great change occurs in our outlook because of the influences of scientific knowledge. Science has revolutionised the civilisation. The advancement in technology and science have brought about a tremendous change in our social behaviour. The role of television, radio and other means of communication should be emphasised in the social science class and the science teacher should emphasise the fact there is only conceptual change in beliefs about God and life. In this way, we find that a study of science can be easily correlated with the study of social science and vice-versa.

Languages

Science can be correlated to a language *e.g.* English. A science teacher also acts as an English teacher when he corrects the oral and written description of his students. While making such correlations he makes correction from scientific point of view as also from point of view of language. Not only English teacher but any language or composition teacher has to correct essays dealing with scientific topics. For a better correlation the language teacher may suggest essays on scientific topics and can also give passages for translation from historical scientific works, There are a lot of science books that deal with history of science, biographies of great scientists and important science works in various languages. All these are a valuable contribution to the literature in that particular language and are excellent and interesting reading material for the students.

History

We can correlate important historical events with discoveries in science and in this way write a history of science. The history of science is very interesting. In the history of science, we can find and correlate the fact of a certain discovery of science with the rule of certain kings. We can also mention the fact of some kings having patronised the teaching of science and some of the scientific discoveries can be attributed only to such a patronage; Some such personalities are the king of Syracuse and Archimedes, the king of Italy and Von Guericke.

A correlation existing between science and history can made more clear while discussing topics like the *story of earth, story of wheel, story of man's endeavours to fight* against diseases etc and find a solution to the perils.

Questions

1. What do you understand by the term correlation ? Discuss its need and importance in relation to seeking correlation of science teaching with other subjects and daily life.
2. Discuss the place of correlation in teaching of science.
3. In what ways the teaching of science be correlated with every day life ?
4. Discuss with the help of examples, how the study of science be correlated with the following subjects.

   (i) Mathematics.

   (ii) Social Studies.
5. Write short notes on the following:

(i) Types of correlation in science teaching.

(ii) Correlation of science with every day life.

3
The Attitudes

Inculcation of scientific attitude among its learners through its study. However, the credit of development of such attitude through the study of science goes to scientific method adopted by science both in the development and in the application. In the following pages an attempt has been made to discuss both these i.e. *scientific attitude* and *scientific methods.*

Scientific Attitude

One of the major aims of teaching science is the development of *scientific attitude* in the pupil. Following are some of the various aspects included in the scientific attitude:

(i) Making pupils open-minded.

(ii) Helping pupils make critical observations.

(iii) Developing intellectual honesty among pupils.

(iv) Developing curiosity among pupils.

(v) Developing unbiased and impartial thinking.

(vi) Developing reflective thinking.

NSSE (National Society of the Study of Education) has defined scientific attitudes as "open mindedness, a desire for accurate knowledge, confidence in procedures for seeking knowledge and the expectation that the solution of the problem will come through the use of verified knowledge."

The views regarding scientific attitude expressed at a workshop conducted by the National Council of Educational Research and Training (NCERT) at Chandigarh in 1971 can be summarised as follows. A pupil who has developed scientific attitude :

(i) is clear and precise in his activities and makes clear and precise statements;

(ii) always bases his judgement on verified facts and not on opinion;

(iii) prefers to suspend his judgement if sufficient data is not available;

(iv) is objective in his approach and behaviour;

(v) is free from superstitions;

(vi) is honest and truthful in recording and collecting scientific data;

(vii) after finishing his work takes care to arrange the apparatus, equipments etc., at their proper places;

(viii) shows a favourable reaction towards efforts of using science for human welfare.

Developing Scientific Attitudes

In the previous pages an effort was made to define the term *'scientific attitude.'* By developing scientific attitude in a person certain mind-sets are created in a particular direction. Such mind-sets may be developed either by direct teaching in schools or by out of school experiences gained by the pupil. Though out of school experiences contribute to a large extent yet according to *Curtis* direct teaching does modify the attitude of young pupil.

Tyier also made some suggestions for planning learning experiences in order to inculcate scientific attitude in the pupil. These are summarised below:

(i) The increase in the degree of consistency of the

environment helps in developing and inculcating scientific attitude in the pupil.

(ii) The scientific attitude can be inculcated ia a pupil by providing him more opportunities for making satisfying adjustments to attitude situations.

(iii) The scientific attitude can also be developed in the pupil by providing him opportunity for the analysis of problem or situation so that a pupil may understand and then rest intellectually in desirable attitude.

Role of Teacher

The major role can be played by the science teacher in developing scientific attitudes among bis students and this he can do by manipulating various situations that infuse among the pupils certain characteristics of scientific attitudes. He can also help in developing a scientific attitude among his students if he possesses and practices various elements of these attitudes. The practical examples given by the teacher leaves an indelible mark on the personality of his students.

Teacher can use one or more of the ways for developing scientific attitude among his pupils.

Making Use of Planned Exercises: A large number of exercises for development of certain scientific attitudes are reported by various journals and magazines. Teacher can frequently use such exercise for developing certain scientific attitudes among the pupils. He can also make use of cuttings from newspapers and science magazines and can display such materials on bulletin board so that It Is used again and again for direct teaching.

Exercises which are always included in good text books can also be used by the teacher for developing scientific attitude among his pupils.

Wide Reading : On the basis of a study conducted by him, *Curtis* reported, that those pupil who engage, themselves in wide reading in science, develop scientific attitudes more than those who study only one textbook. Thus a teacher should encourage his students to read library books and supplementary books on science. For this it is essential that each school at least has a science journal in its library. The teacher himself must be in ha bit of making proper use of science library so that his students get encouragement for use of science library. The teacher himself be familiar with the latest new titles in his subject and he willing to share his joys of new readings with his pupils. He should refer some suitable books to his students.

Writing about teachers, Dr. Rabinder Nath Tagore has observed, "A teacher can never truly teach unless he is still learning himself. A lamp can never light another unless it continues to burn its own flame. The teacher who has come to the end of his subject, who has no living traffic with his knowledge, but merely repeats his lessons to his students, can only load their minds. He cannot quicken them."

Proper Use of Practicals Period : A student of science gets many an opportunities for learning scientific attitudes during his practical periods. It is for the teacher to properly use such opportunities for developing scientific attitudes amongst his pupils. Teacher should take extra care to state the problem of the experiment and should present hypotheses onsolution. He should practice the proper method of testingthe hypothesis. He should actively participate in discussion and interpretation of results after the experiment. He must inculcate in his students the habit to postpone judgements in the absence of sufficient evidence to support a hypothesis.

Personal Example of the Teacher : Personal example of the teacher is perhaps the single greatest force that is helpful in inculcating the scientific attitudes amongst his pupils. Psychologists have found a great tendency amongst the students to copy their teachers. In this regard some have stated, "As is the teacher, so is the student." It is therefore essential that science teacher is free from bias and prejudices while dealing with his pupils. He should have an open mind and be critical in thought and action in his everyday dealings. He should be totally free from superstitions and unfounded beliefs and should be objective and impartial in his approach to his everyday problems. He should be truthful and should have faith in cause and effect relationship.

Study of Superstitions :There are dilfercent types of supersitions that still prevail in Indian society. Simply talking of these superstitions and calling them bad and out of date, will not leave a lasting impression on the minds of the pupils. It will be more useful in the teacher can encourage at least a few of his students to carry out practicals on some popular superstitions such as that the presence of a broken minor in any home leads to disharmony in that home or that if a cat crosses your way when you are going out for some work, then your work will not be done on that day etc. etc.

Such beliefs can easily be discarded by a student if he keeps a broken mirror at his home and finds to his satisfaction that it has not created any type of disharmony in his home. Similarly, other supersitions and misbeliefs can be tested and easily discarded by a student of science. Various researches carried out in the field have drawn the same conclusion i.e., by practical survey and study of such common beliefs, students have developed permanent mind-sets orattitudes towards such supersitions.

Co-curriculum Activities in Science : Various co-curricular activities such as organising science club, hobbies club, science society, photographic club, organising scientific tours and excursions etc., can be taken up by science teacher. Such activities should be properly organised by science teacher under his direct supervision but students be given enough freedom to plan their activities. It will help inculcate in students some desirable scientific attitudes. Co-curricular activities may include making of scientific charts and modes, making of improvised science apparatus etc.

Atmosphere of the Class: A proper atmosphere in the class room provided a desirable atmosphere for inculcating of certain scientific attitudes in the pupils. By a proper class atmosphere we mean that the room is properly arranged and suitably decorated in such a manner that it provides an incentive to the pupil to inculcate the habit of cleanliness and orderliness. In addition to such a congenial physical atmosphere of the class room, the teacher's behaviour also contributes to the development of proper class room atmosphere. For inculcating the scientific attitudes amongst his pupils teacher should encourage them in their various activities. He should also take care to see that his lessons contain such matter as to encourage the students to ask a large number of intelligent questions. He should feel pleasure in answering and explaining such questions and must not snub his pupils for asking so many questions.

Scientific Method

It has already been pointed out that two basic aims of teaching science are:

(i) development of scientific attitude, and
(ii) training in scientific methods.

In previous section we have discussed same ways for developing scientific attitude and in this section our aim is to concentrate mainly on training in scientific methods.

A 'scientific method is a method which is used for solving a problem scientifically'. It is also referred to as 'the method of science' or 'the method of a scientist.' Sometimes it is called as 'problem solving method'. So far it has not been possible to arrive at any commonly agreed definition of scientific method.

The scientific method of teaching science is based upon the process of finding out results by attacking a problem in definite steps, therefore, there cannot be any one 'particular method' but such methods have certain common characteristics.

According to Fitzpatrick, "Science is a cumulative and endless series of empirical observations which result in the formation of concepts and theories, with both concepts and theories being subject to modification in the light of further empirical observation. Science is both the study of knowledge and the process of acquiring and refining knowledge." From this it because quite clear that student of science be exposed to the scientific method of finding out. Scientific method helps to develop in a student the power of reasoning, critical thinking and application of scientific knowledge. It also helps in developing positive attitudes amongst the pupils. A list of such traits as given by Woodburn and Obum is as under:

(i) A scientist must have an unsatiable curiosity, inquisitiveness and a spirit of adventure.
(ii) He should be capable of independent thinking and be ready to abandon the disproved.
(iii) He should be knowledgeable, enlightened and informed.
(iv) He should possess a power of sound judgement and prudent foresight.
(v) He should possess a high degree of perseverance.

Various Steps

Since we don't have any single well-defined scientific method so we cannot have any well-defined fixed steps for a scientific method. However in general the scientific method of teaching science proceeds in the following steps:

(i) Problem in an area of science learning is identified and well-stated.
(ii) Relevant data is collected.
(iii) Certain hypothesis are proposed for testing.
(iv) Experiments are set and done to test the proposed hypothesis.

(v) Prediction of other observable phenomenon are deduced from the hypothesis.

(vi) Occurrence or non-occurrence of predicted phenomenon is observed.

(vii) From observations, the conclusions are drawn to accept, reject or modify the proposed hypothesis.

Thus, the scientific method is a sequenced and structured way of finding out the results through experiments. Various steps of scientific method are discussed here.

Statement of the Problem: A student comes across so many things which arouse his curiosity and he has a large number of questions to ask. A good science teacher always encourages his students to ask questions and tries to answer them in a simple and understandable manner. However in answering a particular question the teacher brings to fore many new problems and it has rightly been said that, "when we double the known, we quadruple the unknown."

Most of the question asked are about 'what?', 'why?' or 'how?' type and these can be conveniently classified as under :

(a) 'what' type of questions are predictive,

(b) 'why' type of questions are explanatory, and

(c) 'how' type of questions are inventory.

The most important things in a scientific method is a simple and well-defined statement of the problem. The statement of the problem be such that it clearly defines the scope of the problem as also its limitations.

Data Collection: When the problem has been stated in clear terms an effort be made to collect the data from as many different sources as is possible. Such data may be available in books in science, library which are an important source for data collection. Data may be collected by use of certain instruments etc., and observations. In data collection an effort be made to minimise the errors that are likely to be caused due to apparatus and instruments used (*mechanical errors*) and those which are likely to be caused due to personal bias (*personal errors*).

Proposing a Hypotheses : On the basis of collected data a tentative hypothesis is proposed for testing. A hypothesis is in fact a certain tentative solution to the problem. The hypothesis should be proposed only after an objective analysis of the available data because any number of hypothesis can be proposed for a problem. For an objective analysis the student be given a training so that he is free from all his bias towards the problem.

Conducting Experiments : After a hypothesis has been proposed suitable experiments are designed to test the validity of the hypothesis. From the observations of such experiments the validity of the hypothesis is tested. The experiments will show the occurrence or non-occurrence of the expected phenomenon and from this we will be able to accept or reject or modify the hypothesis.

The Advantages

Some of the advantages of scientific method are :

(i) Students learn science by their own experiences and the teacher is just a guide who provides them an opportunity and proper environment for learning science.

(ii) It trains the students to identify and formulate scientific problems.

(iii) It gives enough training to students in techniques of information processing.

(iv) It develops in students the power of logical thinking as he is required to interpret data in a logical way.

(v) It helps to develop an intellectual honesty in the student because he is required to accept or reject the hypothesis on the basis of evidences available.

(vi) It helps the students to learn to see relationships and patterns amongst things and variables.

(vii) It provides the students a training in the methods and skills of discovering new knowledge.

The Disadvantages

Some important disadvantages of scientific methods are as under:

(i) It is a long drawn out and time consuming process.

(ii) It can never be a full-fledged method of learning science.

(iii) Majority of science teachers cannot implement it successfully because of their back of exposure to such a method.

(iv) It is suitable for only bright and creative students not ordinary ones.

Questions

1. What is scientific attitude ? Discuss the characteristics that are essential for naming a person as a man of scientific attitude.
2. Define scientific attitude and explain it with the help of concrete situations.
3. What is scientific attitude ? Discuss its importance in daily life.
4. What is scientific method ? Discuss its nature, meaning and significance.
5. Training in scientific methods is considered as an important aim of teaching science. Give practical suggestions to realize this aim in our schools.
6. Write short notes on :

   (i) Elements of scientific attitude.

   (ii) Steps involved in scientific method.

   (iii) The characteristics of the person having scientific attitude.

4

The Concept

Since his advent man has been trying to understand the changes going on around him and has been constantly receiving a great number of impressions through his various senses such as hearing, sight, smell, taste and touch. Making an effective use of his senses and using his communicative ability he accumulated information about his surroundings, organised this information and sought regularities in it and tried to find out why the regularities exist and finally transmitted his findings to the next generation.

This systematised store of human knowledge gained after generalising and interrelating the various isolated facts is known as science .

The word science has its origin from a Latin word 'Scientia' meaning 'to know'. Science in universal but has been defined in different ways, e.g.

"Science is a systematised body of knowledge." "Science is nothing but organised common sense." "Science is a heap of truth."

John Woodbum and E.O. Obourn consider *science as that human endeavour that seeks to describe with even increasing accuracy, the events and circumstances which occur or exist within our natural environment.*

The definition of science found in report on Policies for Science Education is *'Science is a cumulative and endless series of empirical observations which result in the formation of concepts and theories, with both concepts and theories being subject to modification in light of further empirical observations. Science in both a body of knowledge and the process of acquiring and refining knowledge.*

Thus science is simultaneously a *body of knowledge* and also a *self-evaluative process of enquiry.*

Science thus has two important approaches:

(a) Science as a Product.

(b) Science as a Process.

Various laws, theories, principles etc., are included in the category of *science as a product* where as scientific attitude, scientific method etc. form part of *science as a process* though both aspects arc important in their own way but to attain the aims of science education in School more emphasis will be placed on process approach.

From the above discussion it can be concluded that:

(i) Science is a process as well as the product of that process. In process form it suggests the ways and means of exploring truth and in its product form it presents a systematic and organised body of useful knowledge.

(ii) The process form of knowledge is more important than its product form as the way of exploring truth and acquiring knowledge is always given more preference in sciences than were memorisation of the accumulated facts.

(iii) The Science always remains in search of truth and the scientific truths can never be taken as absolutely and permanently true. Thus science by nature is dynamic and not static.

(iv) The method or process adopted by science in the explanation of truth is quite unique and distinct from the methods adopted in such a study by other subjects. It is known as *scientific method.* A scientific method is characterised by such qualities as soundness, validity, reliability, impartiality, objectivity etc.

(v) The study of science brings a typical change in the attitude of its reader and development of such attitude is known as *scientific attitude*. The person with scientific attitude is found to have love for the explanation of truth by adopting true means for such exploration and 'believing in results of such true findings'.

It appears that science performs two types of responsibilities :

(i) Investigation and exploration of facts, and

(ii) Building of a systematic and organised body of facts based on such explanations.

Thus science provides us a systematic and organised information *comprising scientific facts, concepts, generalisations, laws* and *theories* which may prove helpful to all of us in increasing our knowledge and also in solving our problems. Science also help us to make our lives happier.

What Scientific Facts are ?

Man is always eager to know more and more about what happens and exists around him. He makes use of all his resources to know all about such happenings and the conclusions drawn as a result of his findings are called *facts*. Thus, we can define a fact as something that is known to exist or happen, the existence or happening of which is supported through some source. The next question now is whether every fact so known can be called a *scientific fact* or not. The answer is a definite 'No'. A *fact can be called a scientific fact only when it has been arrived at through the scientific method*. For this reason we consider scientific facts to be highly reliable, valid and objective.

It is not out of place here to emphasise here that idea or information collected from whatever source should not be accepted as scientific fact unless it has been observed personally by our sense organs or unless it has been tested and verified experimentally. In this way we find scientific fact to be quite distinct and different from the general notions and facts common to masses.

To conclude we can say that scientific facts are neither too far from the reality and pure truth like the general notions and simple facts nor they are absolutely eternal, fixed and static like the naked truth.

What Concepts are ?

Concepts are nothing but the generalised ideas or notions formed by us towards an object, person or event. These are based on our previous experiences—direct or indirect. Scientific concepts (e.g. solids, liquids, dewpoint, reflection, refraction etc.) do not represent merely in object, person or event but extend to whole class of that particular object, person or situation. The knowledge of various scientific concepts helps a child to develop his scientific vocabulary. Concepts are not eternal, they are liable to be changed, modified or replaced on account of the further experiences, scientific researches and innovations. An attempt be made to gaurd against acquiring faulty concepts and if acquired such faulty concepts should be replaced by proper concepts as soon as possible.

Impact of Physical Sciences

The two important constituents of physical sciences are Physics and Chemistiy. To understand the impact of physical sciences let us discuss the impact of physics and chemistry.

Impact of Physics

In the present age called "Age of Science" knowledge of physics is essential to take up certain professional and applied courses. The knowledge of physics is essential for such courses as engineering, medicines, technology, space etc. The knowledge of physics is essential for every body because of its immense value in our every day life, importance of physics can be summarised as under:

> ***Interest in Wonders of Physics :*** Physics teaching-learning process provides more possibilities of involving children in such activities as are liked by the students. Physics teaching provides more opportunities of carrying out practical work in comparison to social sciences which are less practical

in nature. We can say that basically physics in a very interesting subject and teaching physics involves a lot of fun.

Help in Thinking Process : Physics is one of those subjects which helps in the improvement of the thinking skills in the students. This development of thinking skill takes place because of the fact that in physics students come across a large number of problems which provide them opportunities for thinking. Thus physics has an immense educational value.

Application in Life : Knowledge of physics is applied in various ways in our daily life. You can look around yourself and you will find a very large number of electrical and electronic goods which all utilise one or the other principle or law of physics. For example. Radio, T.V., V.C.P., Electronic watches, Washing machines, Mixers and Juicers etc., all utilise the knowledge of physics. Thus, physics has a utilitarian value in life.

Development of Intellectual Honesty: The study of physics not only improves the academic knowledge of the student but also develops an intellectual honesty in the student. Since it is a subject which involves a lot of practical work so the students acquire the habit of making reports without bias and thus, it develops in them the habit of intellectual honesty.

Helps Develop Positive Attitude : A proper teaching of physics develops in the student not only the scientific attitude and scientific temper but also certain positive attitudes such as open mindedness, unbiased thinking, power of reasoning etc.

Satisfaction of Curiosity and Creativity: Physics is a highly activity oriented subject and these activities taken up by the students in learning physics help a lot to satisfy the basic human " desire of knowledge about the wonders of nature. It helps develop a creative thinking in them.

Insight into Scientific Processes : Students learn a lot of a knowledge by the study of physics and this knowledge becomes a very valuable tool for him in acquisition of new knowledge. Most of the knowledge of physics is gained by students while passing through various steps of acquisition of scientific knowledge i.e. statenrnt of problem, perfonnncc of experiments, developing a hypothesis and testing the hypothesis. Thus, he gets an insight into the scientific process.

Trains for Adjustment in Modern Life: The present day life, as pointed out earlier is highly dependent on various instruments, appliances which are based onone or the other principle of physics. To work with these appliances and to make a proper use of these a basic knowledge of physics is essential for every one of us. It is only such knowledge of physics that will make us less dependent on others for proper functioning of these items of daily use. Thus, it is only by acquiring a basic knowledge of physics that we can adjust ourselves to the modem style of living.

Development of Social Skills: The discoveries of Telephone, Fax, Telex etc., can be attributed to the knowledge of certain branch of physics. All such discoveries which have made the life comfortable, have decreased the distance between nations and thus they have provided the basis for a corporate living, coexistence and better human relations. All these lead to development of social standards both in personal and professional life.

Vocational Value : Like any other field of knowledge, a knowledge of physics forms the basis of some vocational and professional courses. For example, computers, electronics, space science etc.

Impact of Chemistry

Chemistry is considered an important subject in school curriculum as many professional and applied courses, directly or indirectly use the knowledge of chemistry. Moreover, the present age is the era of science and more number of people are being employed in scientific pursuits which require knowledge of chemistry.

Chemistry education is also necessary because of its immense value in the students' individual life as well as in society.

Chemistry is essentially a secondary school subject. At this level, it may be taught as a subject in its own right or as part of a broader science course identified by a variety of titles, e.g., integrated science, general science and modular science. The discipline may also feature as a component of courses in physical or biological sciences.

The most significant aspect of modern science is the impact it has had in solving a variety of problems of practical and technological importance as well as those related to the pressing problems of mankind. A large number of these problems require a proper understanding and application of chemical principles and processes.

The major threats to the present day civilisation are population explosion, hunger and disease, environmental pollution, depletion of sources of energy as well as natural resources. The growth of population is probably the greatest problem facing us.

In solving most of these pressing problems, chemists have a lot to do. Paracclus (1493-1541) said, 'the true use of chemistry is not to make gold, but to prepare medicines'. The problem of atmospheric pollution, if and when it is solved will only be done through an understanding of chemical dynamics.

Chemistry has made a significant contribution in the fields of drugs, fuels, agriculture, animal farming, fibres etc. In addition to these there are many inter-disciplinary areas where the contribution of chemists is significant. In the area of *environmental pollution,* chemists are finding better methods of analysis and solutions to get rid of pollutions. There is the entire area of *marine chemistry* to investigate new sources of food and fuel.

Questions

1. What is science ? Discuss fully.
2. "Science is a process as well as a product." Discuss this statement.
3. What are scientific facts ? Discuss their nature and differentiate them from simple facts.
4. What are concepts ? How are the scientific concepts formed ? Discuss their significance.
5. Explain the difference between science as a process and science as a product.
6. Write an essay on impact of physics.
7. Write an essay on impact of chemistry.

5

Objectives and Aims

In order to accomplish the task of teaching physical sciences. It is essential for us to understand clearly the purpose of teaching physical sciences. This clarity of purpose could be helpful to teach any prescribed course and also in measuring the effectiveness of teaching that course. Many educational reform committees have emphasised spelling out aims and objectives of teaching a particular subject.

The purpose of physical science teaching in secondary schools is to enable students to grasp systematically the basic knowledge of physical sciences needed for the further study of modern science and technology and to understand its applications. In addition, it should help them to acquire experiment skills, develop the ability to think and to use mathematics to solve physical problems, cultivate a dialectical materialist view point and make them aware of need to study hard and to struggle for the modernization, along socialist lines, of industry, agriculture, national defence and science and technology. For clarity of purpose of physical science teaching an emphasis have been placed by many educational reform committees to spell out the aims and objectives of a course of study.

The Aims

Physical sciences can claim an honourable place in school curriculum if it can produce desirable changes in students.

The specific objectives of teaching physics must be based on some criterion in any society.

The Criteria

Thurber and Collette have proposed the following criteria for selection of aims:

(i) *Usefulness* : The knowledge gained should be useful to the students in their lives.

(ii) *Timeliness* : The knowledge given should be concerned with materials/objects with which student is familiar.

(iii) *Fitness:* The knowledge must fit into a sequence that leads him to broad objectives.

(iv) *Appropriateness* : The learning should be appropriate for maturity and background of the students.

(v) *Practicability* : It means that experiences required for the development of learning should be possible.

Aims of physics curriculum should be as follows :

(i) To make students interested in physics.

(ii) To familiarise the students with the important role played by physics in their daily life.

(iii) To develop in students a scientific culture.

(iv) To provide a training to students in methods of science.

(v) To emphasise upon students the role of physics on social behaviour.

(vi) To prepare students for those vocations which require a sound knowledge of physics.

(vii) To increase students understanding to such a level that he can understand various concepts and theories which unify various branches of physics.

The Objectives

By educational objectives, we mean explicit formulation of the ways in which students are expected to be changed by educative process. Objectives are not only the goals towards which the curriculum is shaped and towards which instruction is guided, but they are also the goals that provide the detailed specification for the construction and use of evaluative techniques.

Probably the most common educational objective is the *acquisition of knowledge*. By knowledge, we mean that the student can give evidence that he remembers, either by recalling or by recognizing, some idea or phenomenon, which he has had experience in the educational process. Knowledge may also involve more complex processes of relating and judging.

Another important objective is development of *intellectual abilities* and *skills.* This has been labelled as *'critical thinking'* by some, *'problem solving'* by others.

Arts or skills + knowledge = ability.

'Arts and skills' refer to modes of operation and generalised technique for dealing with problem. The arts and skills emphasize the mental processes of organising and resorganising material to achieve a particular purpose. *Intellectual abilities* refer to situations in which the individual is expected to bring specific technical information to bear on a new problem.

Objectives are the specific and precise behavioural outcomes of teaching a particular topic or lesson of physical science. Objectives actually control other factors of physics teaching to a great extent, therefore more emphasis be laid on writing the objectives in behavioural terms for each unit of class room instructions in physics.

Bloom's Taxonomy

Taxonomy: "Classification especially of animals and plants according to their natural relationships."

Taxonomy of educational objectives is intended to provide for classification of the goals of our educational system. It is expected to help in discussion of curricular and evaluation problems with greater precision. It is expected to facilitate the exchange of information about curricular developments and evaluation devices.

Bloom's taxonomy is a classification of instructional objectives in a hierachy. It is found quite useful in communicating the objectives of a physics lesson as also as a criteria for evaluation of physics teaching. Under this scheme the specific objectives are classified as falling into the following three domains :

1. Cognitive domain objectives.
2. Affective domain objectives.
3. Psychomotor domain objectives.

Cognitive Domain

Probably the most common educational objective is acquisition of knowledge. Knowledge, as defined here, involves the recall of specifies and universals, the recall of methods and processes of the recall of a pattern, structure or setting.

The cognitive domain can be summarised as under :

Classes	*Instructional Coverage*
1	2
Knowledge	Recall and recognition of facts, information, principles, laws and theories of physics.
(i) Knowledge of specifics	The recall of specific and isolable bits of information.
(ii) Knowledge of terminology	Knowledge of the referents for specific symbols (verbal and nonverbal) e.g., to define technical terms.
(iii) Knowledge of specific facts	Knowledge of dates, events, persons, places etc.
(iv) Knowledge of ways and	Knowledge of the ways of organising, studying,

1	2
means of dealing with specifics	judging and criticizing.
(v) Knowledge of conventions	Familiarity with the forms and conventions of scientific papers.
(vi) Knowledge of trends and sequences	Knowledge of the processes, directions and move ments of phenomenon with respect to time.
(vii) Knowledge of classification and categories	To recognise the area encompassed by various kinds of problems and arguments.
(viii) Knowledge of criteria	Knowledge of criteria by which facts, principles, opinions and conduct are tested or judged.
(ix) Knowledge of methodology	Knowledge of scientific methods for evaluation.
(x) Knowledge of principles and generalisations	Knowledge of important principles.
Comprehension	It represents the lowest level of understanding.
(i) Translation	The ability to understand non-literal statements.
(ii) Interpretation	The ability to grasp the thought of the work as a whole at any desire level of generality.

1	2
(iii) Extrapolation	The ability to deal with the conclusions of a work in terms of the immediate inference made from the explicit statements.
Application	Application to the phenomena discussed in one paper of the scientific terms or concepts used in other papers.
Analysis	The breakdown of a communication into its constituent elements or parts such that the relative hierarchy of ideas is made clear and/or the relations between the ideas expressed are made explicit.
(i) Analysis of Elements	The ability to recognise unstated assumptions skills in distinguishing facts from hypotheses.
(ii) Analysis of relationship	Ability to check the consistency of hypotheses with given information and assumptions.
(iii) Analysis of organisational principles	The organisation, systematic arrangement, and structure which hold the communication together.

1	2
Synthesis	The putting together of elements and parts so as to form a whole.
(i) Production of a unique communication	Skill in writing, using an excellent organisation of ideas and statements. Ability to tell a personal experience effectively.
(ii) Production of a Plan	Ability to propose ways of testing hypotheses.
(iii) Derivation of a set of Abstract Relations	Ability to formulate appropriate hypothesis based upon an analysis of factors involved and to modify such hypothesis on the basis of new factors and considerations.
Evaluation	Judgement about the value of material and methods for given purposes.
(i) Judgement in terms of internal evidence	The ability to indicate logical fallacies in arguments.
(ii) Judgement in terms of	Judging by external standards, the ability to comp-
external criteria	are a work with the highest known standard in its field.
Psychomotor	Development of skills such as of handling

1	2
	pieces of apparatus, their assemblies, drawing diagrams and circuits, repair of apparatus and appliances. A brief discussion of the objectives is given below:

Knowledge

To impart knowledge is the basic aim of education and so it naturally is the basic aim of teaching of any subject including physics. By imparting knowledge of physics to the student it is expected that he acquires the knowledge of:

(i) Natural phenomenon.

(ii) Terminology in physics.

(iii) Scientific concepts and formulae.

(iv) Moderm inventions of physics.

(v) Importance of physics for animal life and plant life.

(vi) Manipulation of nature by man.

(vii) Correlation and inter-dependence of physics with various branches of science.

(viii) Environment.

Knowledge objective is considered to have been achieved if the student is able to recall and recognise terms, facts, symbols, concepts etc.

Comprehension

This objective considered to have been achieved if the student is able to:

(i) interpret charts, graphs, data, concepts etc., correctly,

(ii) illustrate various terms, concepts, facts, phenomenons etc.,

(iii) explain facts, concepts, principles etc.,

(iv) discriminate between different facts, concepts etc., that are closely related to each other,

(v) identify relationships between various facts, concepts, phenomenon etc.,

(vi) Change tables, symbols, terms etc., from any given form to some other desired form,

(vii) find faults, if any, in statements, concepts etc.

Applications

This objective seems to be the most neglected one in our educational system. The common observation that supports it is that a physics graduate fails to insert even a fuse wire in the electric circuit of his house. This objective is considered to have been achieved to a great extent if the pupil can:

(i) analyse a given data,

(ii) explain giving reasons various physics phenomenon,

(iii) formulate hypothesis from his observations,

(iv) confirm or reject a hypothesis,

(v) correctly infer the observed facts,

(vi) find cause and effect relationship,

(vii) give new illustrations,

(viii) predict new happenings,

(ix) find relationships that exist between various facts, concepts, phenomenon leamt by him.

Skills

This objective can be considered to have been achieved if a pupil learns:

(i) handling pieces of apparatus,

(ii) assembling pieces of apparatus for experiment,

(iii) drawing diagrams and illustrations,

(iv) constructing things, and

(v) carrying out repairs of apparatus and appliances.

Thus, here we aim to develop three types of skill in the pupil. These are:

(a) drawing skill,

(b) manipulative skill, and

(c) observational and recording skill.

The drawing skill is considered to have been achieved if pupil is able to draw labelled sketches and diagrams quickly.

The manipulative skill is considered to have been achieved if pupil is able to

(i) keep and handle the apparatus properly,

(ii) improvise models and experiments,

(iii) observe various precautions while handling apparatus and doing experiments.

The observational and recording skill is considered to have been achieved if the pupil can

(i) read correctly the instrument or apparatus,

(ii) record observations faithfully,

(iii) make calculations correctly, and

(iv) draw inferences correctly.

Interests

To achieve this objective the pupil is provided with physics hobbies and other leisure time activities. By providing such activities our aim is to inculcate, among pupils, a living and sustaining interest in environment in which he lives.

This aim is considered to have been achieved if the pupil

becomes curious and develops such an interest in physics that he is always eagpr and is on look out to:

(i) take to some interesting physics hobby,

(ii) visit places of interests for physics,

(iii) undertake some physics projects,

(iv) meet and interact with some reputed person in the field of physics,

(v) read literature of physics,

(vi) collect specimen, photographs, biographies etc., concerned with physics,

(vii) participate in fairs, science exhibitions, clubs etc., concerned with physics,

(viii) actively participate in debates, declamation contests, quiz etc., held in connection with various topics connected with physics.

Attitudes

Development of proper scientific attitude is one of the major objectives of teaching physics. The development of scientific attitude makes pupil open-minded, helps him to make critical observations, develops in him intellectual honesty, curiosity, unbiased and impartial thinking etc.

This objective is considered to have been achieved if a pupil:

(i) becomes free of superstitions and prejudices,

(ii) depends for his judgement only on verified facts and not on opinion,

(iii) is readily willing to reconsider his own judgement when some more facts are brought to his notice,

(iv) has an objective approach,

(v) is honest in recording and collecting scientific data.

Abilities

By the teaching of physics we expect to develop the following abilities in the pupil:

(i) ability to use scientific method,

(ii) ability to use problem solving method,

(iii) ability to process information,

(iv) ability to report things in a technical language,

(v) ability to collect data from suitable source and to interpret it correctly,

(vi) ability to organise fair, exhibition, etc.

Appreciation

To achieve this objective the teaching of physical science has to be done in an evolutionary way. For this the curriculum should include such topics where it is possible to reveal stirring biographical anecdotes, some stories having some incidents of adventure, charm and romance. It is possible to achieve this objective by teaching history of physical science including life stories of some physicists. This objective can also be achieved by telling the impact of physics on modern life.

The objective of teaching physics may be considered to have been achieved if the pupil:

(i) appreciates the contributions of various physicists and chemists to human progress,

(ii) appreciates the history of development of physics and chemistry,

(iii) realises the importance of physics in modem civilisation,

(iv) take pleasure in understanding the progress made by physics and chemistry.

Providing Vocational Career

In the modern world majority of career courses depend to a

large extent on the basic knowledge of physics and chemistry. Some vocational courses can be taken up only by students of physics, e.g., Engineering, Agriculture etc. For various courses offered by I.T.I's the knowledge of physics in the basic requirement. Thus physics opens a vast field of opportunities for taking up any vocational course and choose a career. Not only this the knowledge of physics develops in a pupil the manipulation skills and he can easily improvise apparatus and experiements and can use his knowledge and skill to make many a common things which provide the pupil with a profitable leisure time work.

Some Committees

This very objectives of teaching science have been emphasised by various commissions. A brief summary of Tara Devi Report and Kothari Commission is given here.

Tara Devi Report

The important seminar on an all India basis was held at Tara Devi (H.P.) in 1956. The following is the summary of aims and objectives of teaching science as recommended at this seminar :

The aims and objectives of teaching science at primary, middle and secondary level are as under

(i) *Primary Level.* The main aims of teaching of science at primary level are :

(a) to arouse and maintain interest in nature and physical environment;

(b) to arouse love for nature and the habit of conserving nature and natural resources;

(c) to inculcate habitof observation, exploration, classification and a systematic way of thinking;

(d) to develop manipulative powers and creative and inventive faculties;

(e) to inculcate habits of healthful living.

(ii) *Middle School Level.* At middle school level, teaching of science aims at the following in addition to the aims given above:

(a) it aims at acquisition of a lot of information about nature and science;

(b) it aims at developing ability of make generalisations and use them for solving problems in every day life;

(c) it aims at understanding the impact of science on ourway of life;

(d) it aims to develop an interest in various scientific hobbies; and

(e) inspire pupils by telling them stories of some great scientists and their discoveries.

(iii) *High and Higher Secondary Level.* At this stage the aims of teaching science are:

(a) to familiarise the student with his surroundings and to make him understand the impact of science on society and thus enable him to adjust himself with his environment;

(b) to familiarise him with 'scientific method' and thus to help him to develop the scientific attitude;

(c) to make him understand the evolution of science in the historical perspective.

Kothari Commission

An education commission was constituted under the chairmanship of Dr. D.S. Kothari and it made the following recommendations in its report:

(i) The teaching science in primary schools should aim at developing proper understanding of main facts, concepts, principles and processes in physical and biological environments.

(ii) The science education be imparted making use of both

deductive and inductive approaches, however more emphasis be given to deductive approach.

Following recommendations were made by Kothari Commission (1964-1966) for different school stages:

Lower Primary Stage

(i) Af this stage emphasis be put on the child's environment— social, physical and biological.

(ii) In classes (I) and (II) more attention be paid to cleanliness, formation of healthy habits and development of power of observation.

(iii) In classes (III) and (IV) more emphasis be given on personal hygiene and sanitation.

(iv) In class (IV) Roman alphabets be taught to the students as these are the internationally accepted symbols for units of scientific measurements. Moreover, the symbols of elements and compounds also make use of Roman alphabets.

(v) At this stage an effort be made to develop proper understanding of important facts, concepts, principles etc., that we come across in physical and biological sciences.

Higher Primary Stage

The teaching of science at this stage should emphasize on the acquisition of knowledge alongwith the ability of logical thinking and drawing conclusions for taking decisions at a higher level. At this stage a disciplinary approach of teaching science is favoured instead of an integrated science teaching. The teaching of physics, chemistry, botany, etc., is likely to develop more effective scientific, base.

Secondary Stage

(i) At this stage science be taught as a discipline of mind and a preparation of higher education.

(ii) In lower secondary classes (classes IX and X) the subjects of physics, chemistry, biology and earth sciences be made compulsory.

(iii) At higher secondary stage diversification of courses and provision for specialisation be allowed.

Recommendations of N.C.E.R.T.

The objectives of teaching science according to various recommendations of N.C.E.R.T. may be summarised as under:

(i) To explore immediate environment of the pupil.

(ii) To observe, record, report accurately in oral, written and graphic form.

(iii) To formulate precise questions about various things in environment.

(iv) To collect information from various sources and use it in a given situation.

(v) To classify objects, events, phenomenon.

(vi) To arrange objects and data in a sequence so as to ascertain a pattern.

(vii) To analyse data and make inference.

(viii) To find some cause — effect relationship from the data available.

(ix) To make predictions.

(x) To design simple experiments.

(xi) To solve problems.

(xii) To develop an objective attitude towards experimental evidences and to make decisions on the basis of facts and data.

(xiii) To understand the role of Indian scientists in the development of science.

(xiv) To make a judicious use of national resources after their proper identification.

(xv) To be careful to avoid any wastage of natural resources and to take necessary steps for prevention of pollution.

(xvi) To correlate the knowledge of science and technology to economic and social development of the community.

(xvii) To place due emphasis on scientific knowledge in every day life.

(xviii) To make proper use of scientific knowledge for development of desired social and moral values.

(xix) To develop instrumental, conununicational and problem solving skills.

(xx) To develop scientific attitude, spirit of cooperation, scientific temper and scientific approach.

Instructional Objectives

What can be achieved by a teacher within the normal class-room period with the help of various resources available to him by teaching of a particular lesson is called *class-room instructional objective.*

Though writing of such an objective will differ from topic to topic and situation to situation, yet the format remains almost same. Generally no consideration is given to change ineffective domain because it is quite difficult to bring as also to plan for their assessment in the short duration of the class-room period and that too with only limited resources available to teacher. In writing instructional objectives'care is taken to include such objectives as knowledge, understanding, skill, application etc. To illustrate it following example will suffice :

Topic: Preparation and properties of oxygen gas.

Knowledge Objectives

(i) Pupil recalls

(a) the occurrence of oxygen gas in air,

(b) general properties of some other gases.

(ii) Pupil can differentiate between physical properties and chemical properties.

Understanding Objectives

(i) Pupil understands the nature of chemical reactions that takes place i. e. $2KCl0_3 + MnO_3$ -» $2KCl + 30_2$.

(ii) Pupil knows how to write a balanced chemical equation.

(iii) Pupil understands the role of catalyst.

Skill Objectives

(i) Pupil can fit up the apparatus for preparation of oxygen gas.

(ii) Pupil can draw a labelled diagram for the preparation of oxygen gas.

(iii) Pupil can arrange various things on the table in a proper way.

Application Objectives

(i) Pupil can write 3 physical and 4 chemical properties of oxygen.

(ii) Pupil can write equations for various chemical properties.

General Objectives

It should be clearly understood that there is a close interrelationship between objectives, learning experiences and evaluation. The objectives can be achieved through learning experiences and the extent of success to achieve the objectives is measured by evaluation. To evaluate any achievement in a better way it is desirable to set out the objectives in such a way which can be evaluated in terms of some kind of activity or performance. Thus we should strive for performance based objectives and not general objectives. This is essential for us to be definite and objective in imparting learning experiences as well as in evaluating them.

It is possible to transform general objectives into performance based objectives if we give due consideration to essential characteristics of performance based objectives. The statement of a performance based objective must involve following steps :

(i) *Specification of the learner:* The performance based objective must specify whose performance is to be evaluated at the end of the instructions.

(ii) *Specification of the learner's performance in the observable behavioural terms.*

In it, we write about our expectations from the child in terms of his performance as a result of the process of instructions. For this appropriate action verb such as recall, recognition, differentiate, explain, compare, contrast etc., for each objective has to be chosen.

(iii) *Specification of conditions in which the learners performance occurs.*

In it, we mention the definite conditions and environmental situations wherein the pupil will be demonstrating his performance after going through the desired instructions.

(iv) *Specification of the minimum expected level of performance of the learner.*

In it, we mention what we essentially expect from the child in terms of minimum level of his performance as a result of the instructional process.

Following example illustrates it:

Topic: Properties of carbon dioxide gas.

At the end of instructions the pupil is expected to identify two physical and three chemical properties of the gas from the list of various properties told to him.

In this example, the first condition is covered by mentioning the *void pupil.* To cover second condition we should write the word; *mention name* etc. (i.e. mention 2 physical and 3 chemical properties of carbon dioxide). The third condition is covered by mentioning the word 'list of properties' (i.e. mention 2 physical and 3 chemical properties of carbon dioxide gas out of the 'list of properties' provided). The fourth step is covered by mentioning 2 physical and 3 chemical properties of carbon dioxide.

Questions

1. What should be the objective of teaching physical sciences at the high school stage. Discuss with suitable examples.
2. Discuss the general aims of teaching physical sciences at the school stage.
3. Differentiate between aims and objectives.
4. Discuss the Bloom's taxonomy of objectives.
5. Enumerate the specific objectives of teaching physical sciences at higher secondary stage.

6

Role of Teacher

A good teacher is a congenial and conscientious person who leads an ordinary normal life. He is respected and intelligent person. He possesses a sense of humour and also an aptitude for teaching.

Another requirement for a good teacher is that he should have a high sense of principle and an aptitude for creative work and scientific curiosity.

In this chapter, we will try to make a distinction between a good teacher and a good chemistry teacher. We will also discuss the kind of training required to produce a good chemistry teacher.

The training of a good chemistry teacher, to a large extent, depends on the following factors:

(i) The careful selection of the candidates.

(ii) The educational process.

(iii) The efficacy of retraining programmes.

Selection of Candidates

The search for potential teachers should begin with future candidates are at school. For such a selection very useful role can be played by university and college teachers in taking part, with school teachers and pupils, in chemistry competitions, evening get-togethers, science clubs etc. It is essential because only personal contacts and close acquaintance with potential teacher-training candidates can ensure success in the search of boys and girls who are sufficiently talented and gifted to become good teachers.

This process of selection should continue through out the academic career of the prospective candidate and should not end even at the end of university education.

For any one who opts to become a teacher the basic requirement is that he must be dedicated and sincerely interested in communicating knowledge. He must also be willing to undertake the ardous task of educating younger generation.

While looking for potential teachers we must ensure that only such boys and girls are selected, for being trained as chemistry teachers, who are sufficiently talented and motivated to become 'good', teachers the search for such 'good' teachers should be carried out by teachers at all levels, among secondary pupils, undergraduates and graduates. The number of teachers depend directly on the number of young people choosing this difficult career.

Education and Training

The preparation of a secondary school chemistry/physics teacher involves three elements i.e.:

(i) The academic study of the subject,

(it) Educational and professional studies, and

(iii) School experience.

In most of the countries those who obtain their M.Sc. degree in physics/chemistry or subjects in which chemistry plays a major role and who opt for teaching profession are trained for a year or so in special institutions (e.g. College of Education) and awarded a degree in teaching (i.e. B.T., B.Ed. etc). It is a general belief that a thorough knowledge of chemistry/physics is first and foremost for becoming a good pnysics/ chemistry teacher. It is also desirable for a chemistry/physics teacher to become acquainted with those aspects of physics, biology and other natural sciences which chemists need and use.

Secondary school chemistry/physics teachers are in short supply in most countries and even developed countries also face difficulties in recruiting specialised teachers. A serious shortage of teachers inevitably entails additional concern about quality. Not surprisingly, therefore, both these concerns, together with the need to respond to innovation in school curricula, have been important in promoting a reconsideration of the structure and content of teacher training programme in many countries.

Teachers for primary classes are usually trained in colleges of education, which may or may not be attached to the university. Teachers for senior secondary classes have followed a science course in a university.

These days there is an increasing number of university courses devoted to chemistry and education and students have to choose before going to university whether or not they wish to teach. In Malaysia B.Sc. course was introduced in four universities. Such a system with slight varieties can be seen in a wide range of developed and developing countries.

In some universities an inter-linked study scheme has been introduced e.g., in Yugoslavia. This type of structure is also seen in U.K. At one university in U.K., a chemistry-with-education course allows students to spend about 65% of their time working alongside chemistry undergraduates, taking the same classes and examinations. The remaining 35% of the curriculum time is used for educational studies but students still have to take a fourth-year, post-graduate course of training for the teaching profession.

In Sri Lanka some elements of chemical education have been introduced into university chemistry courses. Chemical education is also available as an optional study for a small proportion of the chemistry undergraduates in United Kingdom.

In the United States, 4-year courses of concurrent study of chemistry and other sciences and of education is the common pattern. This leads to coures of approximately 60% science, 20% education and 20% general education.

In 1980's yet another approach of teacher education has emerged. It is based on Schon's notion of 'reflective practitioner'. This approach is committed to analysing how 'professionals think in action' and it seems to hold much promise for teacher education in general.

Recently some initiatives have been taken in United Kingdom to increase the role of schools in the teacher training process. This is quite evident in the 'articled teacher' scheme, which requires student teachers to spend most of a 2-year training period working under supervision in a school that shares responsibility for students' professional development with a training institution.

Thus we can see that the three elements of training described earlier must be inter-related : the acquisition of knowledge in the sciences; the foundation in education; and teaching methods and practices. The relative importance attached to the three parts and degree of integration between them varies from country to country.

One aspect of moving the balance in favour of methodology is the need to arrange as much teaching practice as possible. Methodology courses include not only methods of teaching but also a study and evaluation of curricula being studied at schools. The content of methodology part of the course must also include an appreciation of assessment techniques because these will be crucial part of their pupils work and thorough training in setting questions and marking answers is needed.

Appropriate Working Conditions

Appropriate working conditions for a good chemistry teacher should include the following:

(i) Provision of graduates with certainty of employment.

(ii) Encouragement of society by giving them the esteem they deserve.

(iii) Providing them the material conditions necessary for their work, e.g., chemistry laboratory, library etc.

(iv) Providing them opportunities for strengthening the education and training received by them in their pre-service training.

Various ways in which school teachers can receive further training are :

By Self-improvement : It requires reading books, pamphlets and journals, consulting specialists etc. In this self-improvement process T.V. programmes can contribute a lot. For success of self-improvement programme the teacher must have the time and money to buy books and pay for subscription of journals. However, secondary school teachers have seldom been found interested to utilise this opportunity of self-improvement

Organisation of Refresher Courses : Refresher courses are organised by universities for the improvement in the quality of their teachers. Such refresher courses provide an opportunity to secondary school teachers to establish working links with scientific groups, obtain first hand knowledge and become immersed in main stream of modern scientific thought

Participation in Revision and Improvement of Text-books : By such a participation teachers get an opportunity to come in close contact with each other and discuss their problems and elicit their concrete suggestions for further training.

Curriculum Development

The type and extend of educations that training institutions can offer to their students depends on various factors. A need is felt to identify the skill areas which the trainee-teacher ought to develop.

A survey was conducted in United Kingdom and it revealed that the seven most important skills out of a list of twenty-seven in which trainee science teachers should gain competance are :

(i) Lesson planning and preparation.

(ii) Lesson presentation.

(iii) Practical work organisation.

(iv) Teacher demonstrations.

(v) Safety in the laboratory.

(vi) Discipline and class-room.

(vii) Class-questioning skills.

These areas are concerned with the short-term aim of pre-service training. Thus they aim to prepare and equip the student for first few years of class-room teaching. They ignore the long-term aspects of the teacher's job. They also assume that the teacher has a mastery in his subject.

For a long-term aim such prospective teachers must be acquainted with the history, philosophy, sociology and economics of educational system.

Various curriculum development projects in teacher education have been started in different parts of the world. The aims of such projects are:

(i) Indentification of those aspects of science teaching methods which must be covered in pre-scrvice training.

(ii) Pooling up the experience and expertise of leading teacher trainer and to share them with others.

At the university of Monash in Australia, the Australian Science Teachers Project (1976) was coordinated with science teacher educators across Australia participating. ASTEP introduced fourty-seven units of activities and experiences in six sections.

1. Understanding science (7 units),
2. Understanding pupils (6 units),
3. Models of teaching (12 units),
4. Considering the curriculum (8 units),
5. The laboratory as a teaching resource (9 units), and

6. The Australian context (5 units).

The Thai Science Teaching Project (Thai-STEP) is another such projects which aims at improving the pre-service training in all higher educational institutions with teacher training responsibility across Thailand.

In United Kingdom, the Nuffield Foundation provided funds for the Science Teacher Education Project (STEP). STEP pooled the ideas of over fifty science tutors in training institutions and developed and tested materials.

Such projects have been found useful even beyond their countries of origin as they provide range of activities and materials that be used selectively or modified and also provide guidelines for curriculum development in teacher education.

STEP has devised many activities in different areas such as aims and objectives; the nature of science and scientific enquiry; the pupil's thinking; language in science lessons; teacher-pupil-interaction; methods and techniques; resources for learning; adapting to the pupil; feedback to teacher and pupil; curriculum design; safety; laboratory design and management and the social context of science teaching.

We find that emphasis is laid on devising such activities which not only cover the identified skill areas but also give due consideration to what is likely to motivate the student teacher.

In-service Education and Training

It is now universally accepted that in-service education is a career-long necessity, although the means of carrying it out are not readily available. The in-service training is quite expensive and be provided most economically.

In many countries, in-service training is a semi-voluntary activity, often taking place during school holidays. Sometimes such training is compulsory. In Malaysia such a training was made compulsory when the new integrated science curriculum was introduced. Similar was the situation in Thailand when IPST chemistry was introduced.

In the east while USSR, all teachers were required to attend refresher courses every five years.

In Yugoslavia, in-service-training, of at least 3 days annually is compulsory since 1972.

In United States, chemistry, physics teachers are expected to earn a Master's degree of its equivalent with in their first 5 years of teaching.

In India, NCERT (New Delhi) has conducted courses for over 500 teachers to help them with new senior secondary school curriculum.

In Japan there is a provision which allows groups of teachers to study abroad for upto a month.

Similar arrangements can be found in many other countries.

Science teacher's associations are also actively participating in such in-service-training programmes. National chemical societies also make some distinctive contribution to promote the professional development of chemistry teachers. Institutions of higher education and universities are also participating in such programmes.

The following advantages accrue to the teacher by in-service-training:

(i) He can reorient himself with the latest knowledge and developments in chemistry.

(ii) He gets acquainted and acquires the latest strategies, techniques and methodology of teaching chemistry.

(iii) He can develop proper scientific attitude, temper and interests and learn scientific method for solving the problems and discovering scientific facts.

(iv) He can acquire necessary competency in motivating the students for learning chemistry and applying it to their day to day life.

(v) He can acquire necessary skills to guide his students in the form of educational, personal and vocational guidance.

(vi) He can be in a position to take active part in

reconstruction and revision of curriculum, in preparation and revision of textbooks, instructional material, teaching aids, evaluation scheme etc.

Making Teaching More Interesting

It is a compulsory subject in curriculum of secondary schools in many countries. It is a must for further education required by many a socially attractive occupations (medicines, engineering etc.). In view of this we should expect no problem in motivation for learning but it has been found by majority of chemistry teachers that their students consider as hard, dull and boring. To change this attitude teacher and curriculum developers made an attempt by concentrating on the materials to be learnt. Changes in curriculum occur slowly and to avoid any frustration due to these slow changes teachers should find other ways to tackle the problem.

To make chemistry learning more interesting there should be a clear linkage between the affective and cognitive aspects of learning on the concerned culture.

Johnstone proposed the model for the situation of a learner confronted with the heavily conceptual content of chemistry. If information content does not over-load the concept understanding, perceived difficulty will be low and feeling will be positive.

For its success the teacher should explicitly explain 'Chunking' strategies. Teacher should use a consistent language and should avoid providing any unessential information. The effective use of chemistry laboratory and chemistry practicals be made by the teacher to make chemistry learning more interesting.

Effective Use of Laboratory

There are various types of activities that could be taken up in the laboratory. However, in some countries we lack laboratory facilities and in some others where such facilities are available they have not been put to proper use.

Researches have proved beyond any doubts that the pupil's time in laboratories does contribute positively to their enjoyment of the subject, thus any increase in the component of a course should make it more interesting.

Karplus *et al.* developed a series of laboratory exercises for teacher in-service education that are based on Piagetian research and theory.

Gagne and White have developed a model of ways in which memory can aid or inhibit learning. Two of these postulates are more relevant for making effective use of laboratories. The first are called *images.* They are figural representation in memory of diagrams, pictures or scenes. This type of memory can be built up by chemistry teacher in the class-room or laboratory.

The second are called *episodes.* There are representation in memory of part events in which the individual was personally involved.

Both *images* and *episodes* are useful aids for recall of knowledge associated with them. Generally we have those episodes which have less emotive associations but which provide a stock of concrete experiences from which meaning can be attached to new information.

Teacher should use opportunities to link the laboratory experience of the students to the learning process. He should choose images and episodes carefully and associate them with key topics in the course of study. By such an association teacher can give meaning to the abstractions of chemical knowledge.

Duties and Responsibilities of a Teacher

The duties and responsibilities of a teacher can be summarised as under:

1. He should be fully acquainted with and should have a full knowledge of school time table, the ideals of school and the social environment of the school.
2. He should be regular and show eagerness in performing his duties of teaching chemistry to various classes assigned to him.

3. He should take special interest in arranging and performing demonstration relevant to chemistry teaching in his classes.
4. He should help the students of his class to carry out practical work in the laboratory.
5. He is responsible for organisation of chemistry laboratory, chemistry library etc.
6. He is also expected to organise various co-curricular activities such as science fair, science exhibition, hobbies etc.
7. He is expected to help and organise the evaluation of students' progress and their achievements specifically ia terms of realisation of aims and objectives of chemistry education.
8. He is also required to help in preparation and production of quality books in chemistry.
9. He is expected to select and recommend good text-books to his students,
10. He should provide active assistance in improving chemistry curriculum.
11. He should assign appropriate and relevant home-work and assignments to his students and to check such assignments regularly.
12. He should keep a proper record of the progress of his students. Such record would be quite useful for better results.
13. He is expected to make proper use of various audio-visual aids in teaching of chemistry.
14. He is expected to help in setting up of audio-visual room in the school.
15. He is expected to help in preparation and collection of audio-visual materials and improvised apparatus.
16. He must strive hard for bis own personal growth and keep himself acquainted with :

(i) the latest knowledge and development in the subject and methodology of teaching chemistry,

(ii) chemistry journals and instructional material,

(iii) new trends and experiments in teaching chemistry,

(iv) attending work-shops, summer institutes etc.,

(v) joining chemistry teachers associations,

(vi) keeping himself in touch with schemes and provisions for progress of students like science scholarship, NTSE etc.

17. He should maintain a diary and make proper records in it.

18. He is expected to help in school administration and in carrying out the inspection of school specifically concerned with chemistry department.

Questions

1. Discuss the duties and responsibilities of physics/ chemistry teacher.
2. Write short notes on the following:
   (i) Qualities of physics/chemistry teachers,
   (ii) Functions of physics/chemistry teachers.
3. What considerations should be kept in mind while selecting a physics/ chemistry teacher?
4. Discuss in brief the qualities that are desirable to become a successful physics/chemistry teacher.
5. Write a short essay on importance of teacher in our educational set up.

7

Teaching Aids

The teaching aids are required by a teacher of physical science like teachers of other subjects, for effective teaching of subject and to realise various objectives of teaching the subject. Teaching aids help the teacher to communicate with his students in more desirable and effective way. Some barriers of communication can be overcome by using special aids appealing to the senses of the receiver alongwith managing the communication along certain principles. Class-room instructions or teaching a curriculum transaction is also a special kind of communication and it is helpful in achieving the instructional goals of a course of study. Effective communication requires a mastery of managerial skills of handling various teaching aids like audio-visual aids, visual aids, audio aids, activity aids etc.

The Classification

Teaching aids are classified, for convenience of study, into the following categories:

(i) Audio aids,

(ii) Visual aids,

(iii) Audio-visual aids, and

(iv) Activity aids.

Examples of various types of teaching aids generally used to make class-room teaching of chemistry more effective are given below:

Audio Aids : In this type of aids fall the teaching aids like radio, tape recorder etc. This type of aids help the process of learning as they help the learner to acquire knowledge through his auditory sense.

Visual Aids : This type of aids arc very common e.g, charts, pictures, models, film strips etc. These aids the learner to acquire the learning experiences through his visual senses.

Audio-visual Aids : These are sensory aids which help to make teaching concrete, effective and interesting. Examples of this type of aids are television, motion picture, video films, living objects etc. By use of these aids we provide the learner an opportunity to utilise both his auditory and visual senses for gaining the desired learning experiences.

Activity Aids : In this type of aids we include all those teaching aids in which the learner is required to be engaged in some useful activity e.g.

(a) Excursions and visits.

(b) Exhibitions and fairs.

(c) Experimentation in the laboratory and work-shop.

The Significance

Teaching aids make the teaching-learning process interesting and more meaningful as we are required to make use of our senses. While commenting on the desirability of making use of one's senses the Indian Education Commission has remarked, "for acquiring right and proper knowledge and experiences regarding the objects and processes must be gained through one's senses."

The importance of teaching aids can be summarised as under

(i) Teacher can win the interest and attention of the pupils by making use of teaching aids.

(ii) They are effective motivating agents.

(iii) They help to bring clarity to the subject-matter.

(iv) The same time and energy of the students and teachers and make learning more effective and durable. A fact, principle or phenomenon that cannot be understood properly with verbal explanation or experience can be easily comprehended by use of teaching aids. In this way the time and energy of both the students and teacher is saved.

(v) Proper use of teaching aids helps to develop in the pupils scientific attitudes and provide them with a training in scientific method.

(vi) They provide the pupils with the first hand experience by looking at concrete things and actual demonstrations.

(vii) They provide a solution to a number of educational and administrative problems.

(viii) They provide permanent and effective learning.

The importance of teaching aids can be summarised as under in the words of Edgar Dale—Because audio-visual materials supply of concrete basis for conceptual thinking, they give rise to meaningful concepts—the words enriched by meaningful associations. Hence they offer the best anti-date available for disease of verbalism.

Principles for Selection

Following principles be kept in mind while making a selection of teaching aids for use in teaching a particular topic:

(i) The aids should have a relevance to the topic to be taught.

(ii) The aid must be such so as to suit the topic and help to make the study of the topic interesting.

(iii) Any teaching aid used should not only be interesting and motivating but it also have some specific educational value.

(iv) The aid to be used should be a best possible substitute in terms of reality, accuracy and truthful representation of object or the first hand experiences.

(v) The aid should be simple.

(vi) The aid should suit the physical, social and cultural environment of the pupils.

(vii) The teaching aid be easily available.

(viii) The teaching aid must help in proper realization of stipulated learning or instructional objectives of topics in hand.

Principles for Effective Use

Teaching aids should be used properly to make teaching more effective. Teaching can become more effective if such aids are used widely but the use of such aids cannot provide a guarantee of good teaching. Following points are important for a proper use of teaching aids :

(i) Teaching aids should be woven with class-room teaching and these aids should be used only to supplement the oral and written work being done in the class.

(ii) While making use of any teaching aid an effort be made that the teaching aids being used inany class are in confirmity with the intellectual level of the student and is in accordance with the previous experience of the students.

(iii) Only such aids be preferred which provide a stimulus to the students for greater thinking and activity.

(iv) If possible actual specimens be preferred to a photograph or a slide of a specimen.

(v) The teaching aid used should be exact, accurate and real as far as practicable.

(vi) The teacher should use a teaching aid only when he is quite sure about handling a specific teaching aid. For handling some aids (e.g. operating a projector etc.) training is provided by various authorities. For this purpose more information can be obtained from local SCERT or directly from NCERT, New Delhi.

(vii) Teaching aids used be such as are closely related to pupils experiences.

(viii) The teacher should use a teaching aid only after a proper planning so that the aid is used exactly at the point; in the process of teaching, where it best fits in the process of teaching.

(ix) Teacher should see that a follow up programme follows the lesson wherein a teaching aid has been used.

(x) Teacher should carry out occasional evaluation about the use, function and effect of a teaching aid on the learning process.

Types of Teaching and Materials

For convenience of discussion the teaching aids may be grouped as under:

1. Visual aids,
2. Audio aids,
3. Audio-visual aids,
4. Activity aids, and
5. Memory aids.

Visual Aids : Under this head we will take of following types of teaching aids:

(a) Displayboards such as Chalkboards or Blackboards, Flannelboards, Bulletinboards, Magneticboards etc.

(b) Charts, pictures and models.

Visual aids are those which can be appreciated and understood by seeing them only.

Displayboards: It is any flat surface that can be used to white information to be communicated. At present for this purpose the use is made of *blackboard* or *chalkboard, bulletinboard, flannelboard, magnetic board* etc.

Though material for display on such a board can be collected from any source even from a text book but for being effective the material should be displayed in such a way that it is eye catching, colourful and purposeful.

Blackboard or Chalkboard: It is one of the most common visual aids in use. It is slightly abrasive writing surface made of wood, ply, hardboard, cement, ground glass asbestos, state, plastic etc., with black, green or bluish green paint on it. Details of various types of chalkboards and their arrangement for a science laboratory have been given in the lessons dealing with these topics. A chalkboard is generally installed facing the class which is either built into the wall or fixed and framed on the wall and provided with a ledge to keep the chalk sticks and duster. Portable chalkboards are also available these days. Such chalk boards can be placed on a stand with adjustable height. Generally white chalk sticks arc used for writing on the blackboard or chalkboard but sometimes coloured chalk sticks are also used. The coloured chalk sticks are used for better illustration.

Characteristics of a Good Chalkboard : Some of the characteristics of a good chalkboard arc as follows :

(i) Its surface should be rough enough so that it is capable of holding the writing on the board.

(ii) Its surface should be dull so that it can eliminate glare.

(iii) Its surface should be such that the writing on the board can be easily removed by making use of a cloth or a foam duster.

(iv) Its height should be so adjusted that it is within the easy reach of the teacher and is easily visible to the students.

Effective use of Chalkboard : We find that chalkboard is the most common teaching aid used by the teacher for writing important points, drawing illustrations, solving problems etc. The chemistry teacher should keep the following points in mind to use the chalkboard effectively :

(i) Write in a clear and legible handwriting the important points on the chalkboard but avoid over crowding of information on the chalkboard.

(ii) The size of the words written on blackboard should be such that they can be seen even by the back-benchers. The letters should not be less that one inch in height. The recommended height of letters on a chalkboard in between 6 cm to 8 cm. For this the teacher should frequently inspect his own chalkboard writing from the view point of the back-bench on a corner seat.

(iii) There should be proper arrangement of light in the class-room so that the chalkboard remains glare free.

(iv) To emphasise some pbints or parts of a sketch or a diagram coloured chalks be used.

(v) Rub off the information already discussed in the class and noted down by the students.

(vi) Draw a difficult illustration before hand to save the class time.

(vii) Stand on one side of the chalkboard while explaining some points to the students.

(viii) Make use of a pointer for drawing attention to the written material on the chalkboard.

(ix) Students may be allowed to express their ideas on chalkboard, or to make alterations or corrections. Sometimes teacher may intentionally draw some incorrect diagram and ask the students to make necessary correction, alteration etc.

(x) For maintenance of proper discipline in the class the teacher should always keep an eye on his class while writing on the blackboard.

(xi) For proper writing on chalkboard the chalk stick be broken into two pieces and the broken end of the piece be used to start writing.

(xii) While writing on a chalkboard keep your fingers and wrist stiff and move your arm freely.

Disadvantages of Chalkboard: Some of the advantages of chalkboard over other visual aids are as follows :

(i) It is a very convenient teaching aid for group teaching.

(ii) It is quite economical and can be used again and again.

(iii) Its use is accompanied by the appropriate actions on the part of the teacher. The illustrations drawn on the blackboard captures students attention.

(iv) It is one of the most valuable supplementary teaching aid.

(v) It can be used as a good visual aid for drill and revision.

(vi) These boards can be used for drawing enlarged illustrations from the textbooks.

(vii) It is a convenient aid for giving lesson notes to the students.

Limitations of the Chalkboard: Some of the important limitations of a chalkboard are as under:

(i) The use of chalkboard makes students very much dependenton the teacher.

(ii) It makes the lesson teacher-paced.

(iii) It makes the lesson dull and of routine nature.

(iv) It gives no attention to the individual needs of the students.

(v) Due to constant use chalkboards become smooth and start glaring.

(vi) While using chalk-sticks to write on chalkboard the teacher spreads a lot of chalk powder which is inhaled by teacher and students and it may affect their health.

Bulletinboards : It is a display board on which learning material on some scientific topic is displayed. It is generally of the size of a blackboard but sometimes even bigger depending on the wall space available. It is generally in the form of a framed softboard or strawboard or corkboard or rubber sheets. Such bulletin boards can be specified for individual branches of chemistry or even for some specified chemistry topics e.g., chemistry puzzles, chemistry news, chemistry cartoons etc. such a board can also be used for displaying the best work of students. However for a all purpose bulletinboard the following type of display material is recommended :

(i) Interesting science news.

(ii) Book Jackets of recently published chemistry books.

(iii) Brochures.

(iv) Cartoons.

(v) Poems.

(vi) Sketches.

(vii) Pictures.

(viii) Photographs.

(ix) Thoughts.

(x) Announcements etc.

An effort be made to change the material on bulletinboard as frequently as in practicable. Whenever, the teacher starts a new topic he may ask the students to display the concerned material on the bulletinboard and the teacher should specifically mention to the students the display material on the bulletinboard while teaching a topic to the class. Students be asked to take the charge of bulletinboard by rotation.

How to use a Bulletinboard: To make use of bulletinboard as a useful teaching aid the bulletin board be used for creating interest amongst students an specific topics. For effective use of bulletinboard as a teaching aid following points be kept in mind :

(i) Effort be made jointly by the teacher and the students to procure material from various sources on a given subject or topic.

(ii) Before displaying the material on the board sort out the material relevant to a specific subject or topic.

(iii) Make best use of your aesthetic sense to display the material on the bulletinboard.

(iv) Do fix a title for the specific subject/topic of display material on the top centre of the bulletinboard.

(v) It is desirable if a brief description about the specific subject or topic is fixed below to title.

(vi) The height of bulletinboard from ground level be about 1 m.

(vii) The bulletinboard be fixed in an area where enough lighting can be provided.

(viii) The material displayed should be large enough and should be provided with suitable headings.

(ix) Overcrowding of material on bulletinboard be avoided.

Advantages of Bulletinboard : Some of the advantages of bulletinboard as a teaching aid are as follows :

(i) It is good supplement to class-room teaching.

(ii) It helps in arousing the interest of students in a specific subject/ topic.

(iii) It can be effectively used as follows up of chalkboard.

(iv) Such boards add colour and liveliness and thus also have decorative value in addition to their educational value.

(v) Such boards can be conveniently used for introducing a topic and for its review as well.

Limitations of Bulletinboard : Some limitations in the use of bulletinboards as teaching aids are as follows :

(i) They cannot be used for all inclusive teaching.

(ii) They can be used only as supplementary aids to some other teaching aid.

(iii) At times it becomes very difficult to make proper selection of the display material for certain topic.

Flannelboard : It is also sometimes referred to as *flannel graph or felt board.* It is made of wood, cardboard or strawboard covered with coloured flannel or woollen cloth. It is one of the latest devices effectively used for science teaching. Display materials like cut-outs, pictures, drawings and light objects backed with rough surfaces like sand paper strips, flannel strip etc., will stick to flannelboard temporarily.

For display purposes a flannelboard of 1.5 x 1.5 m is generally used. It can be fixed next to the blackboard or can be placed on a stand about one metre above the ground.

How to use a Flannelboard: Following points be kept in mind for effective use of flannel board as a teaching aid :

(i) The teacher should collect a large number of pictures or wall cut diagrams etc., and back them with sand paper pieces. He may then make use of these by displaying there on the board one by one, after proper selection.

(ii) Display the material on the flannelboard in a sequence to develop the lesson.

(iii) Make proper use of flannelboard for creating properscenes and designs relevant to the lesson.

(iv) Change the display material on the board as frequently as required.

(v) Flannelboard can be used quite effectively for showing relationship between different parts or steps of a process.

Advantages of Flannelboard : Some of the advantages of using flannelboard as a teaching aid are as follows :

(i) It is quite economical and easy to handle and operate.

(ii) The pictures or cuttings can be easily fixed and removed when required, without spoiling the material. Thus same material can be used for display many a times.

(iii) Any display material on the board holds the interest of students and arrests their attention.

(iv) Such boards enable a teacher to talk along with changing illustration to develop a lesson.

Magnetic Chalkboard : It is a framed iron sheet having porcelain coating in black or green colour. Such a board can be used either to write with chalk sticks, glass marking pencils and crayons or to display pictures, cut-outs and light objects with disc magnets or magnetic holders.

Thus such a board functions both as a chalkboard and as a flannelboard. We can display visual learning material on such a board while writing key points on it. Such a board provides the flexibility of movement of visual material. It is possible to display even a three dimensional object on such a board using magnetic holders.

Since the magnetic chalkboard functions both as a chalkboard and as a flannelboard so various points discussed for the effective use of these boards be kept in mind while using magnetic chalkboard as an effective teaching aid.

Advantages of Magnetic Chalkboard : Some of the advantages of magnetic chalkboard are as follows :

(i) It is a versatile teaching aid that combines the advantages of both a chalkboard and a flannelboard.

(ii) It is possible to move visual material by sliding it along the surface of the board such a movement is not possible on a flannelboard.

(iii) It is very light and can be easily taken from one place to another.

(iv) Such a board can be easily got prepared in the school from an iron sheet and printing with some good paint.

Charts, Pictures and Models : Charts, pictures and models also are an important teaching aids.

Charts : Sometimes charts are needed by the teacher to supplement his actual teaching. There are certain charts where in the interior of something is depicted e.g., various system of human body, internal combustion engine, motor car etc.

Following points be kept in view while using charts as teaching aids :

(i) An effort be made to use charts prepared by students under the guidance of the teacher, however some charts may be purchased.

(ii) Duly such charts be purchased which have bold lines and in which such colours are used as could be seenand distinguished even by the back-benches.

(iii) Charts should give only the essential details.

(iv) Charts should be properly and clearly labelled in block letters.

Sources for Procurement of Charts

(i) Charts can be prepared by students and teacher.

(ii) Charts can be purchased.

(iii) Charts can be procured on a very normal cost from the following sources :

(a) Ministry of Education, Govt. of India, Delhi.

(b) NCERT, New Delhi.

(c) Director, Extension Service of College of Education in the State.

(d) SCERT of the state.

(e) District Public Relation Officer.

Advantages of Charts

(i) They can be made quickly.

(ii) They have a better appeal.

(iii) Only bare essentials can be shown in the chart and unnecessary details can be avoided.

(iv) Charts are available from various sources.

Pictures : Pictures of gas-works, steamships, and

locomotives and portraits of great men of chemistry—chemists will be of great help in teaching of chemistry provided a reference in made to them. Portraits of great scientists if displayed in chemistry room give it the proper scientific atmosphere. These pictures, portraits etc., can be used as teaching aids and they are quite useful in a demonstration lesson. Everything a child learns can be presented graphically with the aid of pictures and brightly coloured diagrams which will excite his interest.

Following points be given due consideration while using pictures as teaching aids:

(i) Pictures should be bold, direct and sufficiently large.

(ii) Pictures should not be overloaded with information rathe they should stick to the maxim, *one picture, one idea.*

Models : In teaching of science models are very frequently used. Various costly models are available and some of these may be available and in school laboratory. However the cost of such models should not be any hindrance of the use of models as teaching aid because a science teacher can prepare almost all types of models by making use of ingenuity. It is also possible to take some very costly models on loan or such models can even be hired. Models are very helpful in making the subject clear to the students and they also give the student an idea of the actual shape/size etc., of the article under discussion.

In using charts, pictures and models as teaching aids the teacher should be careful to plan their proper display. These should be displayed in such a way and at such a height that each student can have a detailed view of it.

Following is the list of some firms from whom scientific charts and models can be procured :

1. M/s Scientific Instruments Stores, J-355, NewRajinder Nagar, New Delhi.
2. M/s Educational Aids and Charts, 20,1 Block, Kumara Park, West Extension, Bangalore-20.

3. M/s Variety Teaching Aids, Bagalkot, Distt. Bijapur.
4. M/s Educational Emporium, 15-A, Chittranjan Avenue, Calcutta-7.
5. M/s Oxford University Press, Apollo Bunder, Bombay.
6. M/s School Aids Manufacturing Co., 12-Gum Boot Street, Fort, Bombay-1.
7. The Director, Survey of India, Hathi Barkala Road, Dehradun (UP).
8. M/s Hobby Centre, Mount Road, Madras-2.

Audio Aids

In this type the following aids are considered :

(i) Broadcast talks,

(ii) Gramophone lectures, and Tape recordings.

Broadcast Talks : All-India Radio has in its regular feature some programmes meant for school children. In such a programme generally talks on educational matters or on scientific topics are broadcasted. Such a talk in quite useful for students as also for chemistry teacher. The topic, date and time of broadcast of such talks are given an advance by All-India Radio. A school can take benefit of such talks only if it possesses a good radio set and a period is provided in the school time-table for listening such talks. Such an arrangement can be worked out by the school authorities and then teacher can refer to such talks while teaching his class. It is also possible to synchronise the broadcast talk as some topic with the actual teaching of that topic in a class.

Some handicaps of such broadcast task are listed here:

(a) Sometimes when the receiving set is not working satisfactorily; there prevails a sense of strain in the class-room.

(b) Some students are poor listeners and may not be benefited by such talks although they benefit by normal teaching through questions, demonstrations and reading.

For the maximum utility of such talks following points be kept in view:

(a) The students with bad hearing be seated on front seats.

(b) To keep students interest alive in such talks teacher should tell his students in advance a few questions which they have to answer after the talk.

(c) Only short duration talks be arranged.

Such talks cannot be a substitute to the actual teaching and such a talk is only to help in teaching.

(ii) **Gramophone Lectures and Tape Recording :** Another teaching aid available to a science teacher is records of short talks an interesting scientific topics by eminent scientists, doctors etc. Magnetic tapes of such recorded talks are now available and the talk can be easily reproduced in the class-room. These talks provide an inspiration to the students and such a talk once recorded can be used again and again. Such recording can either be used to introduce a topic or to develop a topic.

Audio-visual Aids

In this category those teaching aids are included which involve the use of two of our senses i.e., hearing and seeing. These are classified as:

(i) optical aids, and

(ii) television.

Need for A.V. in Teaching : Audio-visual aids are very important in teaching of chemistry because of the following reasons:

(i) Sensory experience is the foundation of intellectual activity. Verbal symbol, which is meaningless becomes meaningful when it is associated with visual symbols. For example, meaning of precipitate is understood only when it is seen in test-tube.

(ii) A.V. aids are needed to stress facts and concepts in chemistry teaching.

(iii) Mental growth is the outcome of two antithetical processes i.e., differentiation and integration. Differcntiation develops out of integration. Audio-visual aids are more useful in process of differentiation.

(iv) Generalisation attains a meaning and it becomes concrete experience only with the help of A.V. Aids.

(v) A.V. aids also help in increasing the vocabulary of pupils.

Optical Aids

Some such aids are discussed here.

Magic Lantern (or Glass slide projector). Psychologists have now confirmed that a child grasps abstract facts slowly and can only remember a name which recalls some definite reality. Thus he should be confronted with visual teaching aids to broaden his experience.

A *magic lantern* is a simple device used to project pictures from a glass slide on a screen or wall. Teacher can make use of this device when he intends to show some small figure or illustration to whole class. Many a schools have a *magic lantern* in their laboratories as it is not very costly. Slides are readily available in the market on various chemistry topics. These can also be got prepared on demand and the cost of such a slide is quite reasonable. Such slides can even be prepared by science teacher himself after some practical training which can be provided by extension service department of training colleges.

Epidiascope : Epidiascope is a more costly instrument but it can project opaque objects as well as transparent objects. The pictures projected by epidiascope arc much brighten and need, a less powerful light so that room need not be absolutely dark. Epidiascope can be used to project any picture, map, diagram, photograph or small object. No slide is needed for projection with an epidiascope.

The name *epidiascope* is given to this machine because of the fact that it works, as an *episcope* when it is used to know the image of an opaque object. This machine can be used to project slides and this is possible just by moving a lever provided for the purpose. When it is used to project a slide then at serves as a *diascope.* Thus *epidiascope* is a combination of these two i.e. *episcope* and *diascope.*

Advantages of Epidiascope. In comparison to other projection machines *epidiascope* has some advantages. Some of these are as follows:

(i) It can be operated in a room which may not be absolutely dark.

(ii) With the help of this machine original colours of the picture or photograph can be projected.

(iii) The projection on the screen can be kept for sometime during which teacher can explain and discuss it in the class.

(iv) It provides teacher an option to handle the lesson according to himself.

Following points provide useful hints for the proper handling of an epidiascope:

(i) The apparatus works well in a dark room.

(ii) While projecting with an epidiascope an effort be made to keep exposed to the head of the lamp for minimum time delicate pictures, photographs or other such objects.

(iii) The person handling the apparatus must be given some. practical training before he is allowed to handle the machine.

Film Projector, Film-strip Projector, Micro-projector

There are further improvements on the teaching aids discussed so far. These have brought about a revolution in teaching of science. Science films are shown to the students to illustrate various applications and uses of science as also to supplement the class-room teaching. Both type of films have some basic objectives to serve.

Film-strip Projector

It is an improvement on magic lantern and this machine can be used to project many topics on a single strip. One such strip generally consists of 40-100 separate pictures and such films strips are available on loan from Central Film Library, NCERT, New Delhi. On such a film strip pictures concerning one topic are arranged in a definite order.

This machine can be easily handled by the chemistry teacher. The machine is operated by hand and thus can be stopped at the discretion of the teacher whenever he wants to explain some aspect of a topic being shown on machine.

Micro Projector

This is less commonly used in chemistry teaching. This projector is generally operated in a dark room. The projection can be taken on vertical screen if whole class is expected to see it. However such a film cannot be distinctly seen by a student if he is sitting at a distance more than 12 feet from the screen.

Film Projector

This machine is used for showing chemistry films. Some good science films on various topics are available and these can be had a loan sometimes even free of charge from the source, given below:

(i) Central Film Library, NCERT, New Delhi.

(ii) U.S. Information Service, New Delhi.

(iii) British High Commission Office, New Delhi.

(iv) Some Other Embassies, New Delhi.

For projecting this films in school generally 16 mm projector ('RCA', 'Bell and Havell') are used. These 16 mm projectors are less costly and easier to transport as compared to a 35 mm projector.

Advantages of Motion Pictures : There are some definite advantages of motion pictures to be used as teaching aids, some of these are as follows:

(i) They draw attention of the students.

(ii) They help to bring past to the class-room.

(iii) It is possible to reduce orenlarge the size of the object by using the machine.

(iv) They can be used to show a process which a naked human eye cannot see without its aid.

(v) They can be used to show a record of an event.

(vi) They can serve a large class at a time.

(vii) They provide a good aesthetic experience.

(viii) They help in understanding relationship between things, ideas and events.

Precautions : The teacher should take the following precautions whenever he wants to use a film projection as a teaching aid:

(i) He should satisfy himself about the lighting management and seating arrangement in the room where such a Him show is to be given.

(ii) He should himself see the film before hand.

(iii) He should give a complete background of the film to the students before the actual screening of the film.

(iv) He should see that complete calm and peace is maintained during the screening of the film.

(v) Immediately after the film show, he should invite comments, questions etc., from the students and try to answer all the quarries of the students.

(vi) He should encourage some of his students to write articles etc., based on the film show and such articles etc., may be shown on well-magazine, may be printed in school magazine.

Television

The rok of television in the present day world is becoming more and more important and it is one of the most important teaching aids. It combines the advantages of a radio (broadcast) and of a film. This can be used for mass education and now U.G.C. programmes are a regular feature on "Door Daishan". The topics of discussion are announced in advance and lesson from well-qualified reasons and specialists in their fields are shown on T.V. Teacher can easily plan his work accordingly and in this way he can make use of TV as a teaching aid.

The Limitations : The use of A.V. aids in teaching of chemistry has the following limitations:

(i) The use of A.V. aids is not a guarantee of successful teaching.

(ii) A.V. aids are not a clear substitute for oral or written methods of gaining knowledge.

(iii) Visual instructions are sometimes confused with entertainment.

(iv) Visual aids vary in their effectiveness in direct proportion of their degree of reality.

Some other Teaching Aids

Visits and Excursions : There are certain things which cannot be explained to students very effectively without observing them in real setting. This makes it necessary for the science teacher to arrange visits and excursions to the places of scientific interest quite relevant to the syllabus in physical sciences e.g. for a thorough understanding of the lesson on Telephone/ Telegraph etc. Visit to telephone exchange/ telegraph office will be quite helpful.

Uses of Field Trips

(i) It offers first hand experience,

(ii) It enables intimate contact with environment,

(iii) It improves the power of observation and exploration,

(iv) It helps in the correlation of school subjects,

(v) It makes pupils active participants,

(vi) It effects a real socialisation of school work,

(vii) It develops problem solving skill, and

(viii) It facilitates collection of specimen for school museum.

Purpose of Field Trips : The specific purposes for which the field trips may be conducted are :

(i) Serving as a perview of a lesson and for gathering instructional materials.

(ii) For creating teaching situations.

(iii) Serving as a means of arousing specific interest.

(iv) Supplementing class-room instructions and securing definite information for a specific lesson.

(v) Verifying previous information, class discussion and conclusion.

Conditions to be Borne in Mind in using Field Trip as Teaching Aid : In using field trips as an aid to teaching physical sciences following points be bome in mind :

(i) Previewing the place and determining the purpose.

(ii) Making necessary arrangements with school authorities.

(iii) Preparing the students physically and mentally for the trip.

(iv) The teacher should be prepared to act asa guide during the trip.

(v) To evaluate the trip in terms of specific educational games.

Science Fairs and Exhibitions

Holding of science fairs by individual institutions and also by several institutions in a district jointly have proved quite useful in creating interest in scientific studies and in encouraging the students to make their contributions making full use of their creative and inventive faculties.

A visit to such fairs and exhibitions is also quite rewarding. It helps to wider the knowledge of the progress of science in the present age and also inspires the young students to contribute something from their side for the enhancement of this progress.

Science Museum

In science museum we have various scientific instruments, preserved articles etc. which are quite useful in teaching of physical sciences. For the establishment of science museum teacher may seek active cooperation of his students and they may be asked to make collections from whatever source possible.

For establishment of physics section of the museum the students may be asked to collect small gadgets both electrical and mechanical, instruments and apparatus used in various industries, charts, pictures etc., explaining various principles of physics.

The establishment of a science museum helps not only in providing the valuable information but also helps to create a genuine interest in comprehensive study of physical sciences.

Questions

1. Give a list of audiovisual aids that may be used in teaching of physical sciences. Discuss one in detail.
2. Describe briefly the use and importance of the following in teaching of physical sciences.
   (i) Films.
   (ii) Television.
   (iii) Radio.

3. Discuss the need and importance of audio-visual aids in teaching of physical sciences.
4. What are audio-visual aids? Discuss their utility for teaching of physical sciences.
5. "Teaching aids are designed to enhance the teacher's art of communication." Comment.
6. Discuss the educational value of following aids in teaching of physical
   - (i) Diagrams.
   - (ii) Models.
   - (iii) Charts and pictures.
7. Briefly discuss the use of following aids in teaching of physical sciences.
   - (i) Field trips and excursions.
   - (ii) Science museum.

8

Teaching Methods - 1

By teaching physical sciences we aim at bringing about a desirable behavioural changes among pupils. Teaching is thus a most difficult task and every body is not fit to be a teacher. Some persons may have a 'flair' for teaching and such persons have the ability to awaken interest and arrest the attention of the students. Some others who are not so fortunate can improve their teaching through practice if they are fully acquainted with various methods of teaching. In order to make children leam effectively, the teacher has to adopt the right method of teaching. For choosing right method for a given situation the teacher must be familiar with different methods of teaching. In this chapter an effort will be made to discuss common methods used for teaching of science.

Lecture Method

Lecture method is the most commonly used method of teaching physical science. This method is most commonly followed in colleges and in schools in big classes. This method is not quite suitable to realise the real aim of teaching science. In lecture method only the teacher talks and students are passive listneis. Since the students do not actively participate in this method of teaching so this method is a teacher controlled and information centred and in this method teacher works as a sole resource in class-room instructions. Due to lack of participation students get bored and some of them sometimes may go to sleep.

In this method students is provided with readymade knowledge by the teacher and due to this spoon feeding the students loses interest and his powers of reasoning and observation get no stimulus.

In this method the teacher goes ahead with the subject matter at his own speed. The teacher may make use of black board at times and may also dictate notes. This teacher oriented method in its extreme from does not expect any question or response from the students.

Advantages : It has the following advantages:

(i) It is quite economical method. It is possible to handle a large number of students at a time and no laboratory, equipment, aids, materials are required.

(ii) Using this method the knowledge can be imparted to the students quickly and the prescribed syllabus can be covered in a short time.

(iii) It is quite attractive and easy to follow. Using this method teacher feels secure and satisfied.

(iv) It simplifies the task of the teacher as he dominates the lesson for 70-85% of the lesson time and students just listen to him.

(v) Using this method it is quite easy to impart factual information and historical anecdotes.

(vi) By following this method teacher can develop his own style of teaching and exposition.

(vii) In this method teacher can easily maintain the logical sequence of the subject by planning his lectures in advance. It minimises the chances of any gaps or overlappings.

(viii) Some good lectures delivered by the teacher may motivate, instigate, inspire a student for some creative thinking.

Disadvantages : The disadvantages of lecture method can be as under:

(i) In this method the students participation is negligible and students become passive recipients of information.

(ii) In this method we are never sure if the students are concentrating and understanding the subject-matter being taught to them by the teacher.

(iii) In this method knowledge is imparted so rapidly that weak students develop a hatred for learning.

(iv) It does not allow all the faculties of the student to develop.

(v) In this method there is no place of "learning by doing' and thus teaching by this method strikes at the very root of science.

(vi) It does not take into account the previous knowledge of the student.

(vii) It does not provide for corrective feed back and remedial help to slow learners.

(viii) It does not cater to the individual needs and differences of students.

(ix) It does not help to inculcate scientific attitudes and training in scientific method among the pupils.

(x) It is an undemocratic and authoritarian method in which students depend only as the authority of the teacher. They cannot challenge or question the verdict of the teacher. This checks the development of power of critical thinking and proper reasoning in the student.

Conclusions : After considering various merits and demerits of method it may be concluded that this method may be suitable for teaching in higher classes (XI, XII) where we aim to cover the prescribed syllabus quickly. In these classes this method can be used successfully for imparting factual knowledge, introducing some new and difficult topics, make generalisation from the facts already known to the students, revision of lessons already learnt etc.

Teaching by this method these students of classes XI and XII will also help those students who intend to join college so that they can prepare themselves for college where lecture method of teaching is a dominant method of imparting instruction.

This method of teaching can be made more ber-ftficial if the teacher encourages his students to take notes during the lesson. After the lesson teacher can give his students sometime for asking questions and answers their queries without any hesitation. While delivering his lesson the teacher may see that the lesson is delivered in good tone, loudly and clearly. He should use only simple and understandable words for delivering his lesson. If a teacher can introduce some humour in his lesson it would keep students interested in his lesson.

Demonstration Method

This method of teaching is sometimes also referred to as *Lecture-cum-Demonstration Method*. This is considered to be a superior method of teaching in comparison to lecture method. In lecture method the teacher speaks and students listen so it is a one way traffic of flow of ideas and students are only passive listeners. This one-sidedness is the major drawback of lecture method. A teaching method is considered better if both teacher and taught are active participants in the process of teaching. This particular aspect is taken care of in demonstration method.

This lecture-demonstration method is used by good science teachers for imparting science education in class-room. By using this method it is possible to easily impart concrete experiences to students during the course of a lesson when the teacher wants to explain some abstract points. This method combines the instructional strategy of 'information imparting' and 'showing how'. This method combines the advantages of both the lecture method and the demonstration method.

In this method of teaching the teacher performs experiment before the class and simultaneously explains what he is doing. He also asks relevant questions from the class and students are compelled to observe carefully because they have to describe each and every step of the experiment accurately and draw inferences. After thorough questioning and cross-questioning the inferences drawn by the students are discussed in the class. In this way, the students remain active participants in the process of teaching. The teacher also relates the outcomes of his experiment to the content of the on-going lesson. Thus while in lecture method teacher merely talks in demonstration method he really teaches.

This method is based on the principle : Truth is that which works.

Requirements for a Good Demonstration

For success of any demonstration following points be always kept in mind:

(i) It should be planned and rehearsed by the teacher before hand.

(ii) The apparatus used for demonstration should be big enough to be seen by the whole class. It would be much better if a large mirror is placed at a suitable angle above the teacher table which will enable the pupils to have a view of everything that the teacher is doing while performing the experiment.

Alternately, if the class is well-disciplined the teacher may allow the students to sit on the stools placed on the benches to enable them to have a better view.

(iii) Adequate lighting arrangements be made on demonstration table and a proper background be provided.

(iv) All the pieces of apparatus be placed in order before starting the demonstration. The apparatus likely to be used should be placed on the left hand side of the table and it should be arranged in the same orderin which it is likely to be used. After an apparatus is used it should be transferred to right hand side. Only things relevant to the lesson be placed on demonstration table.

(v) Before actually starting the demonstration, a clear

statement about the purpose of demonstration be made to the students.

(vi) The teacher must make sure that the demonstration-cum-lecture method leads to active participation of the students in the process of learning. This he can achieve by putting well-structured questions.

(vii) The demonstration should be quick and slick and should not appear to linger on unnecessarily.

(viii) The demonstration should be interesting so that it captures the attention of the students.

(ix) The teacher must be sure of success of the experiment to be demonstrated and for this he should rehearse the experiment under the conditions prevailing in the class-room. However, even after all the necessary precaution the experiment fails in the class-room due to one reason or the other, the teacher should not get nervous instead he should make an effort to find the reasons forthe failure of the experiment. Sometimes in this process a good teacher may draw very useful conclusions.

(x) No complaints about inadequate and faulty apparatus he made by the teacher. In such a situation a good teacher finds an opportunity to show his skill.

(xi) It would be much better if the teacher demonstrates those experiments which are connected with common things which are seen and handled by students in their everyday life.

(xii) There should be a correlation between the demonstrations and the sequence of experiments performed by the students in their practical classes.

(xiii) For active participation of students, the teacher may call individual student, in turn, to help him in demonstration work.

(xiv) During lecture-cum-demonstration session, teacher must act like a 'showman' and a 'performer'. He should know different ways of arresting the attention of the students.

(xv) He should write, a summary of the principlesarrived at because of demonstration, on the blackboard. The blackboard canalso be used for drawing necessary diagrams.

How to Demonstate a Lesson ?

We commonly find science teachers making use of demonstration method for teaching of science. The conduct of a demonstration lesson is very difficult and here we will try to discuss some of the essential steps that should be followed in a demonstration lesson.

Planning and Preparation : *A* great care be taken by the teacher while planning and preparing his demonstration lesson. He should keep the following points in mind while preparing his lesson:

(a) subject matter;

(b) questions to be asked;

(c) apparatus required for the experiment.

To achieve the above stated objective the teacher should thoroughly go through the pages of the text book, relevant to the lesson. After this he should prepare his lesson plan in which he should essentially include the principles to be explained, a list of experiments to be demonstrated and the type of questions to be asked from the students. These questions should be arranged in a systematic order that has to be followed in the class. Before actually demonstrating the experiment to a class the experiment be rehearsed under the conditions prevailing in the classroom. Inspite of this, some thing may go wrong at the actual lesson, so reserve apparatus is often useful. The apparatus should be arranged in a systematic order on the demonstration table. Thus, for the success of demonstration method a teacher has to prepare himself as thoroughly as a bride prepares herself for the marriage.

Introduction of the Lesson : As in every other subject so also in case of science the lesson should start with proper motivation of the students. It is always considered more useful to introduce the lesson in a problematic way which would make students realise the importance of the topic. The usual ways in which a teachers could easily introduce his lesson is by telling some personal experience or incident a simple and interesting experiment, a familiar anecdote or by telling a story.

A good experiment when carefully demonstrated is likely to leave an everlasting impression on the young mind of the pupil and it would set his pupils talking in school and out of it, about the interesting experiment that had been demonstrated to them in the science class. This should be kept in mind not only to start the lesson but be used, on every suitable occasion, during the lesson.

It is not possible to give an exhaustive list of such interesting experiments but as an illustration we can consider the opening of soda water bottle in the class-room, by the teacher, following by a direct question to his pupil, have they seen any gas coming out of the bottle? At this stage the teacher can introduce the topic of carbon dioxide. Similarly, a lesson on magnet and magnetism may be introduced by telling the story of the shephered boy and his crook. The simple way to introduce a lesson about human heart is to prick in the finger of one of the students which will result in blood coming out. The teacher can now introduce the lesson by asking the question, from where has this blood come?

Presentation : The method of presenting the subject-matter is very important. A good teacher should present his lesson in an interesting manner and not in a boring way. To make the lesson interesting the teacher may not be very rigid to remain within the prescribed course rather he should make the lesson as much broad based as is possible. For widening of his lesson the teacher may think of various useful applications of the principle taught by him. He is also at liberty to take examples and illustrations from other allied branches of science to make his lesson interesting. The life history and some interesting facts from the life of the great scientist whose name is associated with the topic under discussion can also be cited to make the lesson interesting. Thus every effort be made to present the matter in a lively and interesting manner and a lesson should never be presented as 'dry bones' of an academic course. Thus in a lesson dealing with Archimedes principle the teacher should not feel satisfied just by stating the principle and then demonstrating it with one or two experiments rather he should discuss its applications in daily life such as ships, floating bodies, diving and rising of submarines, the use of balloons and air ships etc. It is also advisable to make use of pictures, posters, diagrams, slides, films etc., in addition to experiments to illustrate the topic in hand.

Constant questions and answers should from part of every demonstration lesson. Questions and cross questions are essential for properly illuminating the principle being discussed. Questions be arranged in such a way that their answers from a complete teaching unit Though an effort be made to encourage the students to answer a large number of questions but if students fails to answer some questions teacher should provide the answers to such questions. It is unwise to expect all toe answers from the pupil and a teacher should feel satisfied if he has been able to create a desire in a student to know what he does not know.

The lesson the presented in a clear voice and the teacher should speak slowly and with correct pronunciation. He should avoid the use of any bombastic and ambiguous terms. The continuous talk is likely to monotony and to avoid it experiments be well-spaced throughout the lesson.

Performance of Experiments : A good observer has been described as a person who has learned to use his senses of touch, sight, smell and hearing in an intelligent and alert manner. We want children to observe what happens in experiments and to have ample opportunities to state their observations carefully. We also want them to tiy to explain what happens in reference to their problem, but we want to make certain. There is separation between observations and generalization and conclusions. We will be violating the true spirit of science if we allow children to generalise from one experiment or observation.

The following steps are generally accepted as valuable in developing and concluding science experiments with the children;

1. Write the problems to be solved in simple words so that every one understands.
2. Make a list of activities that will be used to solve problems.
3. Gather material for conducting experiments.
4. Work out a format of the steps in the order of procedure so that every one knows what is to be done.
5. The teacher should always try the experiment himself to become acquainted with the equipment and procedure.
6. Record the findings in ways commensurate with the maturity level and purposes of the student.
7. Assist students in making generalisations from conclusions only after sufficient evidence and experiences.

The demonstration experiment be presented by the teacher in a model way. He should work in a tidy, clean and orderly manner while demonstrating an experiment. Some of the important points to be kept in mind while demonstrating an experiment are as under:

(i) Experiments should be simple and speedy.

(ii) The experiments must work and their results should be clear and striking.

(iii) Experiments be properly spaced throughout the lesson.

(iv) Keep some reserve apparatus on the demonstration table.

(v) Keep the demonstration apparatus in tact till it has to be used again.

Black Board Summary : *A* summary of important results and principles be written on the black board. Use of black board should also be frequently made for drawing necessary sketches and diagrams. The black board summary should be written in neat, clean and legible way. Since black board summary is an index to a teacher's ability he should keep the following points in mind while writing on black board :

(i) Proper space be left between different letters and words.

(ii) Always start writing from left hand corner of the black board.

(iii) Start a new line only when the first one has extended across the black board.

(iv) Take care not to divide the words at the end of a time.

(v) Make all efforts to keep all the paragraphs and similar signs in calculations under one another.

(vi) While drawing sketches and diagrams preferably use 'single lined' diagrams.

(vii) All the diagrams drawn on the board be properly labelled.

Supervision : Students be asked to take the complete notes of the black board summary including the sketches and diagrams drawn. Such a record will be quite helpful to the student for learning his lesson. Such a summary will prove beneficial only if it has been copied correctly from the black board and to make sure that students arc copying the black board summary properly the teacher should check it by frequently going to the seats of the students.

Common Errors : A summary of common errors committed while delivering a demonstration lesson is given below:

(i) The apparatus may not be ready for use.

(ii) There may not be an apparent relation between the demonstration experiment and the topic under discussion.

(iii) Black board summary is not upto the mark.

(iv) Teacher may be in a hurry to arrive at generalisation without allowing sufficient time to arrive at these generalisation from facts.

(v) Teacher may sometimes fail to ask right type of questions.

(vi) Teacher sometimes may use a difficult language.

(vii) Teacher sometimes takes to talking more which may mar the enthusiasm of the students.

(viii) Teacher may not have allowed sufficient time for recording data etc.

(ix) Teacher has not given proper attention to supervision.

The Advantages : Following are the merits of this method :

(i) It is an economical method as compared to purely student centred approaches.

(ii) It is a psychological method and students take active interest in teaching-learning process.

(iii) It leads students from concrete to abstract situations and thus is more psychological.

(iv) It is a suitable method if the apparatus to be handled is costly and sensitive. Such an apparatus is likely to damage if handled by students.

(v) This method can be more safe if the experiments to be demonstrated are dangerous.

(vi) In comparison to Heuristic method, project etc., it is time saving but lecture method is too speedy.

(vii) It can be used successfully for all types of students.

(viii) In this method such experiments which are difficult for students can be included.

(ix) This method can be used to impart manual and manipulative skills to students.

The Disadvantages : Some of the disadvantages of this method are as under:

(i) It provides no scope for 'learning by doing' for students as students just observe what the teacher is performing. Thus students fail to relish the joys of direct personal experience.

(ii) Since the teacher performs the experiment in his own pace, many students cannot comprehend the concept beingclarified.

(iii) Since the method is not child-centred so it makes no provision forindividual differences. All types of students includingslow learners and genius have to proceed with the same speed.

(iv) It fails to develop laboratory skills in the students. It cannot work as a substitute for laboratory work by students in which they are required to handle the apparatus themselves.

(v) It fails to impart training in scientific attitude.

(vi) In this method students many a times fail to observe many finer details of the apparatus used because they observe it from a distance.

Conclusion : It is thoroughly accepted that success is greater with experiments in elementary schools if they start with a real purpose, are simply done with uncomplicated apparatus, are done by children under careful direction of the teacher, and help the children think and draw valid, tentative conclusion.

This is considered as one of the best methods of teaching science to secondary classes. An effort be made to involve a larger number of students by calling them in batches to the demonstration table.

Science teachers should encourage more direct experimentation by children in order to help children broaden their range of fact-finding skills beyond three T's- teacher, textbook, television.

Heuristic Method

Heuristic method is a pure discovery method of learning science independent of teacher. The writings and teachings of H.E. Armstrong, Professor of Chemistry at the City and Guilds Institute, London have had much influence in promoting since teaching in schools. He way a strong advocate of a special type of laboratory training—heuristic training ('heuristic' is derived from the Greek word meaning 'to discover'). In Heuristic method, the student be put in the place of an independent discover. Thus no help or guidance is provided by the teacher in this method. In this method the teacher sets a problem for the students and then stands aside while they discover the answer.

In words of Professor Armstrong, "Heuristic methods of teaching are methods which involve our placing students as far as possible in the attitude of the discoverer—methods which involve their finding out instead of being merely told about things."

The method requires the student to solve a number of problem experimentally. To almost every one—especially children—experiments and science arc synonymous. Once an idea occurs to a scientist he immediately thinks in terms of ways of trying out his ideas to see if he is correct. Trying to confirm or disprove some thing, or simply to test an idea, is the backbone of the experiment. Experiments start with questions in order to find answers, solve problems, clarify ideas or just to see what happens. Experiments should be part of the elementary school science programme as an aid to helping children find solutions to science problems as well as for helping them to develop appreciation for one of the basic tools of science.

The Procedure : The method requires the students to solve a number of problems experimentally. Each student is required to discover everything for himself and is to be told nothing. The students are led to discover facts with the help of experiments, apparatus and books. In this method the children behaves like a research scholar.

In the stage-managed heuristic method, a problem sheet with minimum instructions is given to the student and he is required to perform the experiments concerning the problem in hand. He must follow the instructions, and enter in his notebook an account of what he has done and results arrived at. He must also put down his conclusion as to the bearing which the result has on the problem in hand. In this way he is led to reason from observation.

Essentially therefore, the heuristic method is intended to provide a training in method. Knowledge is a secondary consideration altogether. The method is formative rather thn informational.

The procedures and skills in science problem solving can only be developed in class-rooms where searching is encourged, creative thinking is respected, and where it is safe to investigate, try out ideas, and even make mistakes.

Teachers Attitude : One of the most important aspects of the problem-solving approach to children's development in scientific thinking is the teachers attitude. His approach should be teaching science with a question mark instead of with an exclamation point. The acceptance of and the quest for unique solutions for the problem that the class is investigating should be a guiding principle in the teacher's approach to his programme of science. Teachers must develop sensitiveness to children and to the meanings of their behaviour. Teachers should be ready to accept any suggestion for the solution of problems regardless of how irrelevant it may seem to him, for this is really the true spirit of scientific problem solving. By testing various ideas it can be shown to the child that perhaps his suggestion was not in accord with the information available. It can then be shown that this failure gets us much closer to the correct solution by eliminating one possibility from many offered by the problem.

In this method teacher should avoid the tempetation to tell the right answer to save time. The teacher should be convinced that road to scientific thinking takes time. Children should never be exposed to ridicule for-their suggestions of possible answers otherwise they will show a strong tendency to stop suggestions.

For success of this method a teacher should act like a guide and should provide only that much guidance as is rightly needed by the student. He should be sympathetic and courteous and should be capable enough to plan and devise problems for investigation by pupils. He should be capable of good supervision and be able to train the pupils in a way that he himself becomes dispensable.

The Merits : This method of teaching science has the following merits:

(i) It develops the habit of enquiry and investigation among students.

(ii) It develops habit of self-learning and self-direction.

(iii) It develops scientific attitudes among students by making them truthful and honest for they learn how to arrive at decisions by actual experimentations.

(iv) It is psychologically sound system of learning as it is based on the maximum, "learning by doing."

(v) It develops in the student a habit of diligency.

(vi) In this method most of the work is done in school and so the teacher has no worry to assign on check home task.

(vii) It provides scope for individual attention to be paid by the teacher and for closer contacts. These contacts help in establishing cordial relations between the teacher and the taught.

The Limitations : Main limitations of this method are as under:

(i) It is a long and time consuming method and so it becomes difficult to cover the prescribed syllabus in time.

(ii) It pre-supposes a very small class and a gifted teacher and the method is too technical and scientific to be handled by an average teacher. The method expects of the teacher a great efficiency and hard work, experience and training.

(iii) There is a tendency on the part of the teacher to emphasize those branches and parts of the subject which lend themselves to heuristic treatment and to ignore important branches of the subject which do not involve measurement and quantitative work and are therefore not so suitable.

(iv) It is not suitable for beginners. In the early stages, the students needs enough guidance which if not given, may greatly disappoint them and it is possible that the child may develop a distaste for studies.

(v) In this method too much stress is placed on practical work which may lead a student to form a wrong idea of the nature of science as a whole. They grow up in the belief that science is some thing to be done in the laboratory, forgetting that laboratories were made for science and not science for laboratories.

(vi) The gradation of problems is a difficult task which requires sufficient skill and training. The succession of exercises is rarely planned to fit into a general scheme for building up the subject completely.

(vii) Sometimes experiments are performed merely for sake of doing them.

(viii) Learning by this method, pupils leave school with little or no scientific appreciation of their physical environment. The romance of modern scientific discovery and inventionremains out of picture for them and the humanizing influence of the subject has been kept away from them.

(ix) Evaluation of learning through heuristic method can be quite tedious.

(x) Presently enough teachers are not available for implementing learning by heuristic method.

Conclusion : This method cannot be successfully applied in primary classes but this method can be given a trial in secondary classes particularly in higher secondary classes. However, in the absence of gifted teachers, well-equipped laboratories and libraries and other limitations this method has not been given a trial in our schools. Even if these limitations are removed this method may not prove much useful under the existing circumstances and prevailing rules and regulations. Though not recommending the use of heuristic method for teaching of science it may be suggested that at least a heuristic approach prevails for teaching of science in our schools. By heuristic approach we mean that students be not spoon fed or be given a dictation rather they be given opportunities to investigate, to think and work independently alongwith traditional way of teaching.

Assignment Method

The heuristic method is based exclusively on laboratory work where as the lecture method and demonstration method do not give any opportunity for laboratory work. For teaching of science, assignment method is best suited because it involves a harmonious combination of training at the demonstration table and individual laboratory work. In this method of teaching science, the given syllabus is split into well planned assignments with a set of instructions about solving the assignments. It is also possible to plan assignments based on the individual needs of the students.

Procedure : The whole of the prescribed course is divided into so many connected weekly portion or assignments. One topic is taken and a set of instructions regarding the study is drawn up. The printed page containing instructions or the assignment is handed to the pupil a week in advance of their practical work. They are then required to read the pages of the text book referred to in the assignment and write answers to a few (generally not more than three or four) questions in a note-book. The students then hand over these answers to the teacher a day before the practicals. The teacher corrects the answer. If there are a lot of mistakes in the assignments then the teacher sets the remedial and corrective assignments.

The second part of every assignment consists of laboratory work. Full instructions about laboratory work i.e., fitting up of apparatus, recording of results, precautions to be taken etc. On the day of the practical work the students are returned their note-books and those students whose preparatory work is found satisfactory by the teacher are allowed to proceed with the practical work.

Teaching by this method demands a lot of careful planning by the teacher and generally two out of six periods allotted to science in time table are reserved for demonstration work and remaining four for practical work. During periods reserved for demonstration work teacher gives a demonstration on a topic that is considered to be a difficult one by the pupils. These periods can also be utilized by the teacher to clarify some facts which are not very clear to the pupils. For the success of assignment method the teacher should prepare a list of experiments to be demonstrated by him and another list of experiments which are to be done by the students. The success of this method mainly depends on properly drawn assignments. If the teacher keeps a progress chart he can easily distinguish between a good and an average or dull student. He can then prepare special assignments according to the needs of the student. An assignment chart may be of the following type :

Aims : Aims of assignment method are as follows :

(i) To provide a synthesis of various methods of learning.

(ii) To provide students a training in information processing.

(iii) To develop a habit of self-study among the students.

(iv) To develop scientific attitude and a habit of critical thinking among students.

(v) To expose students to various resources of learning.

To achieve these aims the following points be kept in mind while drawing up an assignment:

(i) The assignment must be based on one textbook.

(ii) The assignment should clearly state what portion of textbook are to be read.

(iii) It should draw attention to particular points and give explanation of difficult points.

(iv) It should also indicate those portions of matter which can be omitted by the students.

(v) Questions are an essential part of the assignment and the questions be so designed that:

   (a) they test whether the student has read and understood the portion assigned;

   (b) their answers are short;

   (c) their answers require diagrams to be drawn;

   (d) they ask for a list of apparatus for coming laboratory work.

(vi) In each assignment the teacher should indicate portion of book dealing with the same or allied topics.

(vii) The assignment should include detailed instructions about the experiment. This portion of instruction should include :

   (a) the procedure of the experiment;

   (b) the method of recording results;

   (c) the precautions to be observed;

   (d) a diagram illustrating the set up of apparatus.

Features of a Good Assignment

(i) It should be related to subject-matter under study.

(ii) It should be concise and balanced which can be finished by student easily and quickly.

(iii) Its purpose should be clear and its objective be made known to the students.

(iv) It should be so worded that it fosters thinking and independent learning.

(v) It should be such so as to suit to the age, aptitudes and interest of the student.

(vi) It should be able to combine various methods of teaching.

Teacher's Role : The teacher has to do the following for the success of assignment method of teaching.

(i) He should split up the prescribed course in science into successive and progressive assignments.

(ii) He should list down the objectives for each assignment which students must achieve.

(iii) He should prepare a progress chart for each student.

(iv) He must prepare and provide a list of reference material required for each assignment.

(v) To cover up the learning gaps he should prepare remedial assignments.

(vi) He should also prepare activity sheets for laboratory work and experiments.

Merits of Assignment Method : This method of teaching has the following advantages :

(i) It provides the students an opportunity for self-study.

(ii) It synthesizes various methods of teaching of science and makes the learning process very effective.

(iii) It provides an opportunity to the student to learn at his own pace and thus the progress of the brighter students is not hindered by weaker students.

(iv) In this system teacher gets the central role of contingency manager and facilitator of learning. The teacher acts as a guide and interferes least in the student's work.

(v) It places more emphasis on practical work and provides students a training in skill of information processing.

(vi) It provides a feel for the scientific methods to students.

(vii) In this process the learning process can be individualized to a great extent by having differential assignment.

(viii) It provides for corrective feed back and remediation.

(ix) The progress chart with the teacher shows the progress of each student at a glance which gives the teacher an idea of a gifted and weaker students.

(x) In this process the student learns to work himself because in laboratory he is not provided with any laboratory attendant.

(xi) Habit of extra study is developed because a number of books for extra study are recommended by the teacher. Such a study helps in widening the outlook of the pupil.

(xii) Since the burden of work lies on pupil so he learns to take responsibility.

(xiii) Since the students perform experiments at their own speed so owing to their different speeds they do not perform the same experiment at the same time. Thus a large quantity of same kind of apparatus is not required.

Disadvantages of Assignment Method : Some of the disadvantages of assignment methods are as follows :

(i) It burdens the teacher with a lot of planning and thus increases his work load to a large extent. It requires the teacher to prepare a well-thought out scheme for the year before starting the method.

(ii) No source material is available in the market for assignments preparation of assignments for different students becomes an uphill task for the teacher. For teaching science beginner is advised to use the book "Assignments in Practical Elementary Science" by Df. Whitehouse. However, if a book other than "Experimental Science" by Gregory and Hodges is being used as a textbook then the above book of assignments should only be used after making necessary alteration in connection with references.

(iii) The success of method depends on the availability of rich library and laboratory facilities. It makes the method very expensive.

(iv) Before starting with this method teacher must satisfy himself that the apparatus and chemicals required for practical work are available in the laboratory. He should also satisfy himself about the availability of text books, laboratory manual, note book etc., and see that each student possesses them.

(v) Teacher should also be vigilant to see that weak students do not get a chance to copy the answers from the note books of brighter students.

(vi) Weakers students need a lot of help and guidance at individual level and it becomes an unnecessary drain on the teacher's energies.

(vii) This method is suitable only for a small group of students.

Conclusion : Though the method has some limitations but can be used successfully if following points are given due consideration :

(i) The teacher should prepare a well-thought out plan for the year.

(ii) He should find some good resource book and use the same after necessary changes.

(iii) He should be very particular to check copying by weaker students. As remedial measures the teacher should clearly explain difficult topics and principles to the students during demonstration class and set only a limited number of questions in his assignment.

(iv) The availability of apparatus and chemicals needed for experiment be confirmed before hand.

(v) Only those students who have text book, laboratory

manual and note book whose preparatory work has been found to be satisfactory be allowed to do the practical work.

(vi) A new experiment be allowed to a student when be has completed his previous experiment and has shown it to the teacher.

(vii) Students be asked to record all their observations directly inthe fair note book. They should be asked to complete their practical note book in the class itself.

(viii) Teacher can provide necessary help to needy students and for this he should move from one table to another when the students are performing the experiment.

Project Method

This method was given by Dewey—the American philosopher, psychologist and practical teacher. The project method is a direct outcome of his philosophy. According to Dr. Kilpatrick "A project is a unit of whole hearted purposeful activity carried on preferably, in its natural setting." According to Stevenson "A project is a problematic act carried to its completion in its natural setting". According to Ballard, "A project is a bit of real life that has been incorporated into the school."

The project method is not totally new. Project equivalents are advocated for the adolescent period by Rousseau in Emile. A project plan is a modified form of an old method called "concentration-of-studies". The main features of concentration-of-studies plan" is that some subject is taken as the core or centre and all other school subjects as they arise are studied in connection with it.

Project method is based on the following principles :

(i) Learning by doing.

(ii) Learning by living.

(iii) Children leam better through association, cooperation and activity.

What is an Educational Project ? Various definitions of project have already 'been considered. A modified definition of project is given by Tomas and Long. They define it as "a voluntary undertaking which involves constructive effort or thought and eventuates into objective results."

Considering various definitions of project we may consider it as a kind of life experience which is an outcome of a craving or desire of the pupils. This is a method of spontaneous and incidental teaching. "Learning by living" may be a better meaning of project method, because life is full of projects and individuals carry out these projects in their every day life.

The projects may broadly be classified as :

(i) Individual projects, and

(ii) Social projects.

Individual projects are to be carried out by individuals where as social projects are carried out by a grant of individuals.

Steps in a Project : For completing a project we have five stages in actual practice. These are :

(i) Providing a situation.

(ii) Choosing and proposing.

(iii) Planning of the project.

(iv) Executing the project.

(v) Judging the project.

Recording the project is also essential.

Providing a Situation : A project should arise out of a need felt by pupils and it should never be forced on them. It should be purposeful and significant. It should look important and must be interesting. For this the teacher should always be on the look out to find situation that arise and discuss them with students to discover their interests. Situations may be provided by different methods. Some such methods may include talking to students on the topics of common interest e.g., how did they spend their holidays, what did they see in Delhi etc.

Choosing and Proposing : From various definition of an educational project we get the same underlying ideas:

(a) school tasks are to be as real and as purposeful as the tasks of wider life beyond the school walls,

(b) they are of such a nature that the pupil is genuinely eager to carry them out in order to achieve a desirable and clearly realised aim.

Accordinng to Kilpatrick, "the part of the pupil and the part of the teacher, in most of the school work, depends largely on who does the proposing." The teacher should refrain from proposing any project otherwise the whole purpose of the method would be defeated. Teacher should only tempt the students for a particular project by providing a situation but the proposal for the project should finally come from students. The teacher must exercise guidance in selection of the project and if the students make an unwise choice, the teacher should tactfully guide them for a better project. The essentially of a good projects are :

(a) It should have evident worth forthe individual or the graph that undertakes them.

(b) The project must have a bearing on a great number of subjects and the knowledge acquired through it may be applicable in a variety of ways.

(c) The project should be timely.

(d) The project should be challenging.

(e) The project should be feasible.

It is for the teacher to see that the purpose of the project is clearly defined and understood.

Planning : The students be encouraged by the teacher to plan out the details of the project. In the process of planning teacher has to act only as a guide and he should give suggestions at times but actual planning be left to the students.

Execution : Once the project has been chosen and the details of the project have been planned, the teacher should help the students in executing the project accoridng to the plan. Since execution of a project is the longest step in the project method so it need a lot a patience on the part of the students and the teacher. During this step the teacher should carefully supervise the pupils in manipulative skills to prevent waste of materials and to guard accidents. The teacher should assign work to different students in accordance with their tastes, interests, aptitudes and capabilities. Teacher should see that every member of the grasp gets a chance to do something. Teacher should constantly check up the relation between the chalked out plans and the developing project and as far as possible at the spot changes and modification be avoided. However, if such changes become unavoidable these should be noted and reasons explained for future guidance.

Evaluation : The evaluation of the project should be done both by the pupils and the teachers. The pupils should estimate the qualities of what they have dotie before the teacher gives his evaluation. The evaluation of the project has to be done in the light of plans, difficulties in the execution and achieved results. Let the students have self-criticism and look through their own failings and findings. This step is very useful because as a result of the project, the pupils can know the values of the information, interest, skills and attitudes that have been modified by the project.

Record : A complete record of the project be kept by the students. The record should include every thing about the project. It should include the proposal, plan and its discussion, duties allotted to different students and how far were they carried out by them. It should also include the details of places visited and surveyed, maps etc., drawn, guidance for future and all other possible details.

Role of Teacher

(i) In project method of teaching the role of a teacher is that of a guide, friend and philosopher.

(ii) He helps the students in solving their problems just like an elder brother.

(iii) He encourages his students to work collectively, amicably in the group.

(iv) He also helps his students to avoid mistakes.

(v) He makes ita point that each member of the group contributes something to the completion of the project and in this process helps the sky and weaker students to work along with their classmates.

(vi) If the students face failure during execution of some steps of the project the teacher should not execute any portion of the project but should only explain to his students the reasons of their failure and should suggest them some better methods of techniques that may be used by them next time for the success of the project.

(vii) During the execution step teacher also learns something.

(viii) Teacher should always remain alert and active during execution, step and see that the project goes to completion successfully.

(ix) During execution of the project teacher should maintain a democratic atmosphere.

(x) Teacher must be well-read and well-informed so that he can help the students to the successful completion of the project.

The Project Method has Following Merits :

(i) It is a method of teaching based on psychological laws of learning. The education is related to child's life and he acquires it through meaningful activity.

(ii) It imbibes the spirit of cooperation as it is a cooperative venture. Teacher and students join in the project.

(iii) It stimulates interest in natural as also man made situations. Moreover, the interest is spontaneous and not under any compulsions.

(iv) The method provides opportunities for pupils of different tastes and aptitudes with in the frame work of the same scheme.

(v) It upholds the dignity of labour.

(vi) It introduces democracy in education.

(vii) It brings about a close correlation between a particular activity and various subjects.

(viii) It is a problem solving method and places very less emphasis on cramming or memorising.

(ix) It helps to inculcate social discipline through joint activities of the teacher and the taught.

(x) A project can be used to arouse interest in a particular topic as it blends school life with outside world. It provides situations in which the students come in direct contact with their environment.

(xi) It develops self-confidence and self-discipline.

(xii) A project tends to illustrate the real nature of the subject.

(xiii) A project affords opportunity to develop keenness and accuracy of observation and produces a spirit of enquiry.

(xiv) It puts a challenge to the student and thus stimulates constructive and creative thinking.

(xv) It provides the students an opportunity for mutual exchange of ideas.

(xvi) This method helps the children to organise their knowledge.

The Demerits : This method has few demerits as follows :

(i) Projects require a lot of time and this method can be used as a part of science work only.

(ii) Though the method provides the student superficial knowledge of so many things it provides insufficient knowledge of some fundamental principles.

(iii) In the project planning and execution of the project the teacher is required to put in much more work in comparison to other methods of teaching.

(iv) The teacher has been assumed as master of all subjects which is practically not possible.

(v) Good textbooks on these lines have not yet been produced.

(vi) It is an expensive method as it involves tours, excursions, purchase of apparatus and equipment etc.

(vii) The method of organising instruction is unsystematised and thus the regular time table of work will be upset.

(viii) The method may fit those who cannot listen but it is very questionable if it has the same value for those who can listen.

(ix) The method leaves a gap in pupils knowledge.

(x) It underestimates man's power of imagination which enables him to savour the full experience of another without the necessity of undergoing the experience himself.

(xi) Sometimes the projects may be too ambitious and beyond pupils capacity to accomplish.

(xii) Larger projects in hands of an unexperienced teacher lead to boredom.

(xiii) The education given by projects is likely to emphasise relationships in breadth than in depth.

Conclusions : The project method provides a practical approach to learning of both theoretical and practical problems. If it is difficult to follow this method of teaching it would be better at least not to ignore the spirit of this method.

This method has been found to be more suitable for primary and middle classes and is of restricted use for high and higher secondary classes. This method may be tried alongwith formal class-room teaching without disturbing the school time-table. With this in view some projects may be undertaken by the students to be completed on certain fixed days of a week. Alternately first half of the day may be devoted to class-room teaching and the project work be carried out in toe remaining half day. To help solve the problem of fund's shortage such projects be chosen which are self-supporting or the projects selected be such that their final products can be sold to partially support the funds. Some such projects are improvising science apparatus, growing a vegetable garden etc. Costly projects should be avoided. As it is not suitable for drill and continuous and systematic teaching, it is not very desirable to use it freely.

9

Teaching Methods - 2

This is a system of organising a course rather than a method of teaching. It is therefore better to call it *concentric system or approach.* It implies widening of knowledge just as concentric circles go on extending and widening. It is a system of arrangement of subject matter. In this method the study of the topic is spread over a number of years. It is based on the principle that subject cannot be given an exhaustive treatment at the first stage. To begin with, a simple presentation of the subject is given and further knowledge is imparted in following years. Thus beginning from a nucleus the circles of knowledge go on widening year after year and hence the name concentric method.

Procedure : A topic is divided into a number of portions which are then allotted to different classes. The criterion for allotment of a particular portion of the course to a particular class are the difficulty of portion and power of comprehension of students in that age group. Thus it is mainly concerned with year to year teaching but its influence can also be exercised in day-to-day teaching. Knowledge can be given today should follow from knowledge given yesterday and should lead to teaching on following day.

The Merits

(i) This method of organisation of subject-matter is decidedly superior to that in which one topic is taken up in particular class and an effort is made to deal with all aspects of the topic in that particular class.

(ii) It provides a framework from science course which is of real value to students.

(iii) The system is most successful when the teaching is in hands of one teacher because then he can preserve continuity in the teaching and keeps his expanding circle concentric.

(iv) It provides opportunity for revision of work already covered in a previous class and carrying out new work.

(v) It enables the teacher to cover a portion according to receptivity of learner.

(vi) Since the same topic is leamt over many years so its impressions are more lasting.

(vii) It does not allow teaching to become dull because every year a new interest can be given to the topic. Every year there arc new problems to solve and new difficulties to overcome.

The Demerits : For the success of this approach we require really capable teacher. If a teacher becomes over ambitious and exhausts all the possible interesting illustrations in the introductory year then the subject loses its power of freshness and appeal and nothing is left to create interest in the topic in subsequent years.

In case the topic is too short or too long then also the method is not found to be useful. A too long portion makes the topic dull and a two short portion fails to leave any permanent and lasting impression on the mind of the pupil.

Conclusion : It is a good method for being adopted for arranging the subject matter. It should be kept in mind by the organisers, while organising the subject-matter that no portion is too long or too short. It would also be much useful if the same teacher teaches the same class year after year so that he can reserve some illustrative examples for each year and thus can maintain the interest of the students in the topic.

Unit Method

It is one of the latest methods in the field of education. It involves pupils more actively in learning process.

Different authors define unit in a different way. Hanna, Hageman, Potter define it as, "a unit is a purposeful learning experience that is focussed on some socially significant understanding which will modify the behaviour of learner and adjust him to adjust to a life situation more effectively."

However, all the definitions of unit imply that it possesses the following characteristics:

(i) It is an organisation of activities around a purpose.

(ii) It has significant content.

(iii) It involves students in learning process.

(iv) It modifies the students behaviour to such an extent that he can cope with new problems and situations more competently.

Types of Units : Mainly the units may be classified as :

(i) Subject matter units.

(ii) Experience units.

(iii) Resource units.

The teaching of general science can be carried out in a better way and it is better understood and appreciated by the students if it is taught as units of immediate interest to the pupils. Such units may be :

(a) life centred,

(b) environment centred, and

(c) life and environment centred.

For this The Tara Devi Seminar[1] (1956) recommended the following:

Life-centred Units

1. The world that science has built.
2. The air we breathe.
3. The water we use.
4. The food we eat.
5. How man gets his food.
6. The clothes we wear.
7. The homes we live in.
8. The machines we use.
9. The power we work with.
10. Protection from disease.
11. Our biological resources.
12. Our mineral resources.
13. Means of transport.
14. Means of communicate with the world.
15. The universe we live in.
16. Story of life.
17. How to be yourself.

Environment-centred Units

1. The atmosphere.
2. Water, a vital need of life.
3. The earth surface.
4. Fire and heat.

1. Report of All-India Seminar on the Teaching of Science in Secondary Schools, held at Tara Devi (Simla Hills), 1956, Ministry of Education, New Delhi.

5. Effects on heating and cooling in air and water.
6. Study of light.
7. Civilization and the use of metals.
8. Work and energy (the occupations of man).
9. Problems of transport and communication.
10. Plants and animals in relation to life.
11. The study of the body-machine.
12. Understanding ourselves.
13. Science and philosophy of life.

Environment of Life-centred Units

1. The world that science has built.
2. Your body-machine and how it works.
3. Health to you.
4. Using biological resources for better living.
5. Using mineral resources for better living.
6. Energy and machines for the world of tomorrow.
7. Time, measurement and mass production.
8. The weather and what we can do about it.
9. Astronomy;
   (a) The solar system in which we live.
   (b) Billions of stars and other universes.
10. Science for our homes.

For teaching science the lessions are grouped round the various topics. For learning a unit entitled 'means of transport' we can group the lessons dealing with various means of transport such as bicycle, steam engine, internal combustion engine, electric motor, aeroplanes, ships etc. While dealing with these we can introduce many ideas e.g. while teaching about bicycle we can introduce the study of levers, use of levers for harnessing energy, gaining speed with the help of livers etc. Some new terms as speed, velocity, acceleration, retardation brake, friction, lubrication, mechanical advantage etc., may also be introduced. While dealing with electric motors we can tell the use of such motors in electric trims, generation and transmission of electricity. The terms volt, ohm, resistance, capacitance etc., can also be introduced.

Similarly for teaching of biology 'Farm', 'Garden', 'Pond' etc., can be used as a unit. From it we can introduce the student to the teaching of various kinds of soils, insects, water, weather etc.

Similar interesting lessons can be developed on 'Air', 'Water' etc. These can be used for teaching of hydrogen, nitrogen, water, carbon dioxide etc.

Essentials of a Good Unit

(i) It should deal with a sizeable topic.

(ii) It should emerge out of students past experiences and should lead to broader interests.

(iii) It should be of appropriate difficulty in terms of child's understanding, interest.

(iv) It should provide scope for using a variety of materials and activities like community resources, audiovisual materials etc.

(v) It should allow use of sufficient amount of books and other learning materials.

(vi) Units should be such as to draw materials from several fields so that childen may develop richer in sight into human relationships and processes.

(vii) It should be functional and should be in accordance with the maturity level of the learner.

The Merits : This method of teaching has the following advantages:

(i) It brings about a closer integration between various branches of science.

(ii) It makes subject matter more interesting and realistic.

(iii) It provides a better understanding of the environment and life.

(iv) It focusses attention on significant facts and avoids confusion.

(v) The unit because of its flexibility provides facility in adopting instructions to individual's differences.

(vi) It is quite useful to teaching general science in elementary classes.

The Demerits :

(i) This method cannot be used if the teacher is required to complete some prescribed course in a specified time.

(ii) There are only a few teachers who are so widely read that they can introduce material and illustration from various branches of science while keeping before their students one central topic.

Unit method or topic method is a varied slightly in America. In American schools the teacher announces one topic and the students are asked to say what they already know about it. Then the topic is discussed in a question and answer session and those questions which no member of the class could answer are noted down for investigation. From this list of questions, such questions as are considered as too difficult for a particular class are eliminated by the teacher and the remaining questions are arranged in a planned manner for answers. These questions are then dealt within the class according to the plan. The great thing about such a course is that boys feel that it is their course and not something thrust upon them by authority.

In some American schools the teacher announces a topic

and then hands over to the class a piece of mechanism, say electric bell, and asks them to discover everything about it. He advises them to consult books, to ask questions and then come prepared, for discussion with his, after a week.

Historical Method

Some teachers prefer to develop a subject by following the stages through which the subject has passed during its course of development from its early beginnings. This type of teaching has a fascination which appeals to pupils. Various science subjects such as Chemistry, Physics, Bacteriology etc., which have an interesting historical background can be taught successfully by such a technique. It is possible to develop a topic starting from its early history and the various stages through which it developed before attaining the modem shape.

Chemistrty, in particular, has a very interesting history and the works of Priestley, Lavoisier, Davy, Black and Dalton etc., can be given this type of treatment. The gradual development of atomic theory can be unfolded gradually by this method which will be quite interesting. Similarly, the teacher can use stories from the history of science (e.g. Archimedes and his bath, Newton and the apple etc.) to arouse interest of the students in the topic under consideration.

While discussing the subject of Bacteriology the historical treatment can include invention and development of the microscope.

Through such a treatment may not be possible for all the topics but an occasional resort to such a treatment has its own uses.

Discussion Method

This method is found quite suitable for those topics in science which cannot be easily explained by demonstration or other such techniques. The discussion may be about a certain specimen or model or chart.

In this method the topics for discussion is announced to the students well in advance. The teacher gives a brief introduction about the contents of the topic and then suggests to his students various reference books, text books and other books. Students are then required to go through the relevant pages of these books and come prepared from a discussion of the topic on a specified day. During actual discussion period teacher poses a few problems and thus provides the necessary motivation. The students are then asked to answer the questions one by one and whenever the teacher thinks fit advises some students not to go out of the scope of a particular question or topic under consideration. This check is essential otherwise immature students may go out of the scope of the topic.

Following points if kept in view will help make the discussion successful.

(i) The topics for discussion should be of common interest of students.

(ii) Teacher should establish a favourable atmosphere in the class before starting the discussion.

(iii) Teacher should see that every one participates in the discussion. The whole essence of discussion is "Thinking together."

(iv) The teacher should talk to the bare minimum and also should not allow any one student to dominate the whole discussion.

(v) It is for teacher to see that the discussion remains a discussion and it does not change into a debate.

(vi) Teacher should keep a check on answers of the students and should not allow a student to go beyond the scope of a topic under discussion.

(vii) Teacher has to maintain discipline and he should see that only one student speaks at a time.

Inductive-Deductive Method

It is a combination of two methods. To be able to understand this combination it is necessary to understand them separately.

Inductive Method

In this method one is led from concrete to abstract, particular to general and from complex to simple role. In this method we prove a universal law by showing that if it is true in a particular case it is also true in other similar cases.

This method has been found to be quite suitable for teaching of science because most of the principles of science or the conclusions are results of induction. This process of arriving at generalisation can be illustrated as under.

Illustration: Take a piece of blue litmus paper and dip it in a test tube containing hydrochloric acid, observe the change in colour. (It turns red.)

Take another piece of blue litmus paper and dip it in a test tube containing nitric acid. Observe the change in colour. (It turns red.)

Repeat the experiments with other acids in different test tubes (e.g. oxalic acid, acetic acid etc.). (In each case blue litmus turns red.)

From the above experiments we can make a generalisation that *acids turn blue litmus red.*

Following the same procedure the students may be asked to drop a piece of chalk, duster, books, pen, pencil etc., and observe him falling these on earth. From these observations it can then be easily generalised that *all substances are attracted by earth.*

The Merits :

(i) It helps understanding.

(ii) It is a scientific method.

(iii) It developes scientific attitude.

(iv) It is a logical method and develops critical thinking and habit of keen observations.

(v) It is a psychological method and provides ample scope for students activities.

(vi) It is based on actual observations, thinking and experimentation.

(vii) It keeps alive the students interest because they move from known to unknown.

(viii) It curbs the tendency to learn by rote and also reduces home work.

(ix) It develops self-confidence.

(x) It develops the habit of intelligent hard work.

The Demerits : The method suffers from the following limitations :

(i) It is limited in range and cannot be used in solving and understanding all the topics in science.

(ii) The generalization obtained from a few observations is not the complete study of the topic. To fix the topic in the mind of the learner a lot of supplementary work and practice is needed.

(iii) Inductive reasoning is not absolutely conclusive. The generalization has been done from the study of a few (three or four) cases. The process thus establishes certain degree of profitability which can be increased by increasing the number of valid cases.

(iv) This method needs a lot of time and energy and thus it is a time consuming and laborious method.

(v) This method is not found to be suitable in higher classes because some of the unnecessary details and explanations may make teaching dull and boring.

(vi) The use of this method should be restricted and confined to understanding the rules in the early stages.

(vii) This method may be considered complete and perfect only if the generalization arrived at by induction can be verified through deductive method.

Deductive Method

Deductive method is opposite of inductive method. In this method the learner proceeds from general to particular, from abstract to concrete. Thus in this method facts are deduced or analysed by the application of established formula or experimentation. In this case the formula is accepted by the learner as a duly established fact.

In this method teacher announces the topics of the day and he also gives the relevant formula/rule/law/principle etc. The law/formula is also explained to the students with the help of certain examples which are solved on the black board. From these students get the idea of use or application of the concerned law/principle/formula. Then the problems are given to the students who solve the problems following the same method as explained to them earlier by the teacher. Students also memorise the results for future application.

Following example illustrates the procedure :

Principle: Cooling is caused by evaporation.

Confirmation by Application : It can be confirmed by numerous application, such as, by wearing wet clothes, observing feeling after taking bath, by applying alcohol on your hand etc.

The Merits :

(i) It is short and time saving and so this method is liked by authors and teachers.

(ii) It is quite a suitable method for lower classes.

(iii) It glorifies memory because students are required to memorise a large number of laws, formulae etc.

(iv) For practice and revision of topic it is an adequate and advantageous method.

(v) It supplements inductive method and thus completes the process of inductive — deductive method.

(vi) It enhances speed and efficiency in solving problems.

The Demerits :

(i) It is not a scientific method because the approach of this method is confirmatory and not explanatory.

(ii) It encourages rote memory because pure deductive work requires some law; principle formula for every type of problem and it demands blind memorisation of large number of such laws/formulae etc.

(iii) Being an unscientific method it does not impart any training in scientific method.

(iv) It causes unnecessary and heavy burden on the brain which may sometimes result in brain fag.

(v) In this method memory becomes more important than understanding and intelligence which is educationally not sound.

(vi) It is an unpsychological method because the facts and principles are not found by the students themselves.

(vii) In this method students cannot become active learners.

(viii) It is not suitable for development of thinking, reasoning and discovery.

Conclusion : A careful consideration of merits and limitations of these two methods leads in to conclude that Inductive Method is the fore-runner of Deductive Method. For effective teaching of science, both inductive and deductive approaches should be used because no one is complete without the other. Induction leaves the learner at a point where he cannot stop and the after work has to be done and completed by deduction. Deduction is a process that is particularly suitable for final statement and induction is most suitable for exploration fields. Induction gives the lead and deduction follows. In science if we want to teach about *composition of water* then its composition is determined by a endiometer tube (inductive process) and confirmed by the process of electrolysis of water (deductive process).

Scientific Method

This method of teaching of science is based upon the process of finding out the results by attacking a problem in a number of definite steps. It is possible to train the students in scientific method. In this method student is involved in finding out the answer to a given scientific problem and thus actually it is a type of discovery method.

Fitzpa trick defines science as, "science is a cumulative and endless series of empirical observations which result in the formation of concepts and theories, with both concepts and theories being subject to modification in the light of further empirical observation. Science is both a body of knowledge and the process of acquiring and refining knowledge."

Considering this definition of science it becomes imperative that the students be exposed to the scientific way of finding out. Scientific method of teaching helps to develop the power of reasoning, application of scientific knowledge, critical thinking and positive attitude, in the learner.

This method proceeds in the following steps:

(i) Problem in identified.

(ii) Some hypotheses are framed and these are proposed for testing.

(iii) Experiments are then devised to test the proposed hypothesis.

(iv) Data is collected from observations and the collected data is then interpreted.

(v) Finally conclusions arc drawn to accept, reject or modify the proposed hypothesis.

Scientific method is therefore a well-sequenced and structured method for finding the results through experiments.

Role of Teacher : For the success of scientific method the role of teacher is very important. He should act as a coinvestigator along with students and must also find sufficient time and have patience to attend to students' problems. Under the proper guidance of the teacher the science laboratory should become the hub for implementations of this method.

The Merits : Scientific method has following advantages:

(i) Students learn science of their own and teacher works only as a guide.

(ii) It helps students to become real scientists as they learn to identify and formulate scientific problems.

(iii) It provides to students a training in techniques of information processing.

(iv) It develops a habit of logical thinking in the students as they are required to interpret data and observations.

(v) It helps to develop intellectual honesty in students.

(vi) It helps the students to learn to see relationships and patterns among things and variables.

(vii) It provides the students a training in the methods and skills of discovering new knowledge in science.

The Demerits : Some important limitations of the method are as under.

(i) It is a long, drawn out and time consuming method.

(ii) It can never become a full fledged method of learning science.

(iii) Due to lack of exposure to this method most of the science teachers fail to implement it successfully.

(iv) This method is suitable only for very bright and creative students.

Problem-solving Method

In this method of teaching science the students is required to solve a problem by an experimental design making use of his previous knowledge. Hence the method is almost similar to scientific method and involves almost those very steps for its implementation. Since the method is similar to scientific method so it has the same advantages and limitations as discussed for a scientific method.

Choice of the Method

In the previous pages a number of methods for teaching of science have been discussed. Some of them have been recommended for use, some have been disapproved and some have been recommended for use with caution. Out of the methods available a choice is not entirely left to the whims of the teacher but has to be made by the teacher in the light of facilities available and nature of work to be done. This does not mean that a teacher may select any one method and then cling to it lavishily throughout his service or even an entire academic session. This is a great mistake because each method has its own merits. Our preference for only one of the methods deprives us of the merits of other methods. A good teacher should therefore try to imbibe the good qualities of all methods instead of depending on any one methods. The teacher should keep himself on the right side of every method. The best method of a teacher is his own individualised and personalised method which is the result of his varied and long experience in teaching. Some of the points which a teacher should keep in mind are as under:

(i) Heuristic approach be used to start a lesson. Thus the lesson be introduced in a problematic way so that the students feel that they arc going to leam something really useful and worth learning.

(ii) He should choose a pupil-dominated method in preference to a teacher dominated method.

(iii) He should have a bright manner of presentation and should illustrate his lesson with experiments, pictures, charts, diagrams etc., specimens and models are preferred for illustration.

(iv) Teaching should be made a cooperative enterprise. Teacher should give maximum opportunity of participation to the students so that they feel that their active participation in quite important for the solution of problem and successful growth of the subject.

(v) Teacher should made all possible efforts to properly correlate the topic in hand with other subjects.

(vi) Teacher should avoid the use of difficult phrases, scientific expressions and lengthy definitions.

(vii) Though Heuristic approach dominates yetthe historical method of teaching be utilized at places and the lives and achievements of famous scientists be told to the students. These are a source of inspiration to the students.

(viii) Instructional method and plans must be flexible. In a lesson if, in addition to planned illustrations and experiments, students want some more experimental evidence then the teacher should make all possible efforts to satisfy the students.

(ix) After a constant use of some method teacher can break the monotony by using project method and laboratory method.

Thus, we conclude that no single method could be the best method and a good teacher will have to evolve his own individual method consisting of good points of all the methods. He will remain a true master of all of them and will never become a slave to any method.

Questions

1. Give various methods of teaching of physical sciences. Which is the best method in your opinion ? Give reasons.
2. What do you understand by demonstration method ? What points must be kept in mind for the success of a demonstration ?
3. "In the present circumstances the lecture-cum-

demonstration method is the only method that suits best for the teaching of physical sciences in our schools." Discuss.

4. Explain the merits, demerits and applicability of the Heurestic method for the teaching of physical sciences.

5. What is laboratory method ? Discuss its merits and demerits for teaching of physical sciences.

10

Planning Lessons

A careful lesson planning is the road to successful teaching. Lack of planning encourages fumbling and indecision, with accompanying discipline problems.

It is a best to organise the teaching syllabus around a few broad areas of experience of pupils. This will divide the course into a number of units.

A unit is a related learning segment which consists of a few lessons, along with an outline of its actual execution in the classroom. Thus a unit consists of the subject-matter as also the methodology to be used for its delivery to the students.

A unit as defined by Hoover, "The teaching unit is a group of related concepts from which a given set of instructional and educational experience is derived. Unit normally range for three to six weeks long."

Preston's definition is, "A unit is a large chunk or a block of related subject-matter as can be viewed by the learner."

Unit Planning

After dividing the whole syllabus into a number of units the teacher will compare the number of units and the time available and will then break up each unit in a number of lessons. As far as possible each lesson should be complete in itself.

Features of a Teaching Unit : A unit is a related learning segment made up of a few lessons along with an outline of its actual execution in the class-room. Thus a unit will consist of both the subject-matter and methodology of its delivery to students.

Hoover defines units as, "The caching unit is a group of related concepts from which a given set of instructional and educational experiences is derived. Unit normally range from three to six weeks long."

In view of Preston a unit is a large chunk or a block of related subject-matter as can be over viewed by the learner.

After having divided the prescribed syllabus into a number of teaching units the teacher will decide the time that could be allotted to each unit. After that he can break up each unit in a number of lessons and each lesson should be complete in itself. After this the teacher will enter in his diary the scheme of wort under the following headings :

Unit No.

Date	*Course Content*	*Demonstration*	*Equipment Material*	*Student's activities*	*Remarks References*

Advantages of Unit Planning : Some important advantages of unit planning are :

(i) It provides a basic course structure around which specific class activities can be organised.

(ii) It enables the teacher to integrate the basic course concepts and those related areas into various teaching experiences.

(iii) It provides an opportunity to the teacher to keep a balance between various dimensions of the prescribed course.

(iv) It enables the teacher to break away from traditional textbook teaching.

If the prescribed course has to be covered in a number of years it is unwise to distribute the course in units spread over a number of years.

Unit Planning Proforma for Physics

Grade Level.................................

Unit title.......................................

Behavioural objectives..............................

(i) ....

(ii) ....

(iii) ....

Sr.No.	*Major concepts from the content*	*Number of periods and lessons*	*Teaching method to be used*	*Teaching aids to be used*
1.				
2.				
3.				
4.				
5.				

Lesson Planning

Lesson plan in the actual plan of action and is key to effective teaching. A physics teacher must know in advance the subject-matter and the mode of its delivery in the class-room. Such an advance knowledge gives the physics teacher an idea of how to introduce the topic, how to develop various key concepts, how to bring about a correlation between various concepts of the daily life and how to conclude the lesson. For evaluation of students performance and for evaluation of his own performance the physics teacher must know the objectives of his lesson.

The lesson planning in a difficult task and it entails hard work. According to G.H. Green; lessons must be invariably planned in advance.

A proper planning of the lessons is key to effective teaching. The teacher must know in advance the subject-matter and mode of its delivery in the class-room. This gives the teacher an idea of how to develop the key concepts and how to correlate them to real life situations and how to conclude the lesson. Lesson planning is also essential because effective learning takes place only if the subject matter is presented in an integrated and correlated manner and is related to the pupil's environment. Though lesson planning requires a hard work but it is rewarding too. L.B. Stands conceives a lesson as 'plan of action implemented by the teacher in the class-room. According to G.H. Green, "The teacher who has planned his lesson wisely related to his topic and to his class will be in a position to enter the class-room without any anxiety, ready to embark with confidence upon a job he understands and prepared to carry it to a workmanable conclusion. He has foreseen the difficulties that are likely to arise, and prepared himself to deal with them. He knows the aims that his lesson is intended to fulfil, and he has marshalled his own resources for the purpose. And because he is free of anxiety, he will be able coolly to estimate the value of his work as the lesson proceeds, equally aware of failure and success and prepared to learn from both."

The Advantages

Some of the advantages of planning a lesson are as under :

(i) Lesson-planning makes the work regular, organised and more systematic.

(ii) It includes confidence in the teacher.

(iii) It makes teacher quite conscious of the aim which makes him conscious of attitudes he wants to develop in his students.

(iv) It saves a lot of time.

(v) It help in making correlation between the concepts with the pupils environment.

(vi) It estimates the teacher to ask striking questions.

(vii) It provides more freedom in teaching.

The Characteristics

Some important features of a good lesson plan are as under:

Objectives: All the congnitive objectives that are intended to be fulfilled should be listed in the lesson plan.

Content: The subject-matter that is intended to be covered should be limited to prescribed time. The matter must be interesting and it should be related to pupil's previous knowledge. It should also be related to daily life situations.

Method(s): The most appropriate method be chosen by the teacher. The method chosen should be suitable to the subject-matter to be taught. Suitable teaching aids must also be identified by the teacher. Teacher may also use supplementary aids to make his lesson more effective.

Evaluation : Teacher must evaluate his lesson to find the extent to which he has achieved the aim of his lesson. Evaluation can be done even by recapitulation of subject-matter through suitable questions.

Hearbartian Steps

Formal steps in lesson planning are :

1. Introduction (or Preparation),

2. Presentation,

3. Association (or Comparison),
4. Generalisation,
5. Application, and
6. Recaptulation.

Introduction : It pertains to preparing and motivating children to the lesson content by linking it to the previous knowledge of the student, by arousing curiosity of the children and by making an appeal to their senses. This prepares the child's mind to receive new knowledge. This step though so important must be brief. It may involve testing of previous knowledge of the child. Sometimes the curiosity of pupil can be aroused by some experiment, chart, model, story or even by some useful.

Presentation : It involves the stating of the object of lesson and exposure of students to new information. The actual lesson begins and both teacher and students participate. Teacher should make use of different teaching aids to make his lesson effective. Teacher should draw as much as is possible from the students making use of judicious questions. In science lesson it is desirable that a heuristic atmosphere prevails in the class.

Association : It is always desirable that new ideas or knowledge be associated to the daily life situations by citing suitable examples and by drawing comparisons with the related concepts. This step is all the more important when we are establishing principles or generalising definitions.

Generalisation : In science lessons generally the learning material leads to certain generalisation leading to establishment of certain formulates, principles or laws. An effort be made that the students draw the conclusions themselves. Teacher should guide the students only if their generalisation is either incomplete or irrelevant.

Application : In this step of lesson plan the knowledge gained is. applied to certain situations. This step is in confirmity with the general desire of the students to make use of generalisation in order to see for themselves if the generalisations are valid in certain situations or not? No lesson of science may be considered complete if such rules, principles, formulae etc., are not applied to life situations.

Recapitulation : In this last step of his lesson plan the teacher tries to ascertain whether his students have understood and grasped the subject-matter or not. This is used for assessing the effectiveness of the lesson by asking students questions on the contents of the lesson. Recaptulation can also be done by giving a short objective type test to the class or even by asking the students to label some unlabelled sketch.

One most important point to remember is that the six steps given above for lesson planning are formal Herbartian step and teacher should not try to follow these very rigidly. These are only guidelines and in many a lessons it is not possible to follow all these steps.

There is another way of lesson planning which is gaining currency these days. It is known as *Glover Plan*. This plan has four steps as follows :

> ***Questioning :*** Teacher must introduce and develop his lesson through related and sequential questions. Start the lesson by asking questions about previous knowledge of the Students. The questions should then lead to new knowledge under consideration.
>
> Lesson can also be introduced with the help of some teaching aid like a picture, chart or model etc. The introduction can also be made by describing a situation or by telling a short story.
>
> However, teacher should bear in mind that the introduction is brief and interesting.
>
> ***Discussion :*** For discussion the class be divided into smaller groups and insufh groups students be encouraged to express their ideas and opinions freely. This helps the students in removal of their difficulties.
>
> ***Investigation :*** The students are encouraged to do a project or investigation on the lesson topic either individually or in small groups by processing information or by laboratory work.

Expression : It concerns the strategy in which the student's and teacher's communication of ideas through observation and listening (passive expression) or through doing (active expression) or through performing arts (artistic expression) or by arranging learning situations (organisational expression).

In developing a lesson a teacher must keep in mind the following psychological principles :

Principle of Selection and Division : The teacher should wisely select and divide the learning material into smaller segments. It is also for the teacher to decide about the quantum of subject-matter to be covered by him and that which has to be illicited from the students.

Principle of Successive Clarity : It is for the teacher to see that the different learning segments of lesson are well-structured, sequenced and connected. Teacher must ensure, at each segment, that students have grasped the subject-matter given to them.

Principle of Integration : Teacher should conclude his lesson only after combining various learning segments to produce some generalisation.

Design for Writing a Lesson Plan

Lecture-cum-Demonstration Method

The style given below is generally followed for writing a lesson plan:

Class: Date:

Subject: Duration of period:

Topic:

Instructional Material ______________________________

____

General Objectives ______________________________

____

Specific Objectives____________________

Previous Knowledge

Questions

1.____________________?

2.____________________?

3.____________________?

Introduction

Question

1.____________________?

2.____________________?

*Announcement of Aim*____________________

____

Presentation

Matter	*Method*	*B.B. Summary*

*Generalisation*____________________

____

____

*Application*____________________

____

Reception

Question

1.____________________?

2.____________________?

3.____________________?

Home Task

SPECIMEN LESSON PLAN—1

Date.................... **Class:** IX

Subject: Physics Time: 40 minutes

Topic : Effect of Reduced Pressure on boiling point of a liquid (water) Average age of pupils.......

Instructional Material

(a) Black board, duster, chalk etc.

(b) Iron stand, round-bottomed flask, burner, wire gauze, tripod stand, trough, cork, piece of cloth etc.

Aims of the Lesson

(a) General Aims:

(i) To develop scientific attitude among the students.

(ii) To familiarize the pupils with the world around them and to make them understand the impact of science on their life.

(iii) To develop the power of critical thinking in the students.

(b) **Specific Aim;** To familiarize the students with the effect of reduced pressure on the boiling point of water.

Previous Knowledge (Assumed)

The students are familiar with the term boiling point of a liquid. They also know that the pressure of atmosphere decreases with the increase in height from sea leyel.

Introduction

The lesson will be introduced with the personal experience of the teacher in breathing and cooking food at high places. In addition the following questions will be asked :

1. What is the boiling point of water? (100°C).
2. Do you know that water can be boiled even below its boiling point? (No)

Announcement of the Aim

When the students fail to answer the second question, the problematic situation arises and the teacher will then say "Well, students today we will boil water even below its boiling point under reduced pressure."

Presentation

Matter	*Method*
1. After fitting up the apparatus for the experiment and showing it to the students.	What is this? (Round-bottomed flask).
2. The water in the flask is heated.	If something present above the water level in the flask? (air)
3. Water boils and steam starts coming out of it.	One of the student calling for help teacher will ask. What is the temperature of water now.
4. Burner is removed and mouth of the flask tightly closed by a cork.	What do you see rising above the neck of the flask? What is the effect of heat on air, present in the flask? [In the meantime figure will be drawn on blackboard]
5. The flask is fitted upside dowo on a tripod stand.	One of the students will be asked come near the demonstration table and see vapours above water level.
6. Cold water is poured by a wet handkerchief on the rounded end of the flask.	What happens on pouring water on rounded end of flask.
7. Condensation of water vapours takes place. The pressure of vapours is reduced in flask.	What is the effect of the condensation of water vapours? What happens due to reduction of pressure of vapour?
8. As soon as the pressure above water in the flask becomes equal to pressure at the temperature, water begins to boil, although temperature is much below the normal boiling point of water.	Why does water begin to boil even below its normal boiling point?

Generalisation

From this experiment we can generalise that under reduced pressure, the boiling point of liquid decreases.

Application

The teacher will acquaint the pupils with the application in cooking food properly on hills. On the top of mountains because of reduced pressure, boiling point of water decreases and water boils much below 100°C. Thus cooking of materials like pulses, meat and potatoes etc., cannot be properly carried out and takes more time.

To avoid this difficulty, pressure cooker has been invented in which the boiling point of water is increased by increasing pressure in the cooker.

Blackboard Summary

The teacher will write the statement. "The reduced pressure decreases the boiling point of water."

Recapitulation

Following questions will be asked :

1. What is the effect of reduced pressure of the boiling point of water ?

2. What is the effect of increased pressure on the boiling point of water?

3. Where do we apply the above principles ?

Home Assignment

Describes an experiment to show the effect of reduced pressure on boiling point of water. Give its applications in daily life.

They will also be asked to try this experiment at home by improvising a flask out of a fused electric bulb.

LESSON PLAN—2

Class: X
Date:

Subject: Chemistry
Duration of period : 40 minutes

Topic : Composition of Air

Instructional Materials

1. Chalk board,duster, coloured chalks.
2. Trough, jar, match box, phosphorus etc.
3. Candle, glass tumbler, household plate, baby feeder etc.

General Objectives

1. To develop scientific attitude amongst the pupil.
2. To develop level of observation and sense of enquiry amongst the pupil.
3. To develop reflective thinking in the pupils.

Specific Objective

To tell the students that air contains one part of oxygen and four parts of nitrogen by volume.

Previous Knowledge

It is presumed that students know that air contains oxygen and nitrogen. They also know that oxygen is a supporter of combustion and that a burning candle goes out in nitrogen.

Introduction

To introduce the lesson teacher will pick up a coin in his

fist and will ask the following questions while taking away the coin.

1. What is in my fist? (A coin)
2. When the coin has been taken away? . What is now in my hand? *(Air)*
3. It is possible for us to live without air? (No)
4. Name the gases present in air? '(oxygen, nitrogen and some CO2, inert gases etc.).
5. What is the proportion of oxygen and nitrogen in the air?

Announcement of Aim

On our receiving a proper reply to question , teachers will announce the aim "Today we will try to know about the proportion of oxygen and nitrogen in air."

Generalisation

From the above experiments we conclude that oxygen and nitrogen are present, in the ratio of 1 : 4 by volume, in air.

Recapitulation

Teacher will ask the following questions for recapitulation.

(i) Does phosphorus burn if exposed to air?

(ii) What is the ratio of oxygen and nitrogen (by volume) in air?

(iii) Which compound is formed when phosphorus burns in air?

Home Task

Students will be asked to perform a similar experiment using a candle instead of phosphorus.

LESSON NOTES—3

Sodium and its Chief Compounds

Aim : To teach the physical and chemical properties of the metal sodium, and the names and common uses of some of its important sails.

Previous knowledge : Students know the distinctive features of metals. They are also familiar with the names and know the common uses of washing soda, caustic soda and common salt."

1st Stage : Introduction.

Presentation

Matter	*Method*	*Black-board Summary*
1. Yellow phosphorus in air at 307K.	Showing phosphorus, teacher asks what is this? Does phosphorus burn in air ?	Yellow phosphorus is kept under water. It burns in air.
2. Yellow phosphorus is kept in water.	What is yellow phosphorus stored water?	
3. Yellow phosphorus burns in air.	What happens if a piece of yellow phosphorus is kept in air?	
4. Fitting up the apparatus for the experiment	What is this? What is this? What is this?	
5. Phosphorus piece is allowed to burn by touching it with hot iron rod.	What happens? Why does phosphorus burn? What is this cloud like substance?	
6. Water rises upto mark No. 1.	Why has water risen up in the bell jar?	
7. Phosphorus pentoxide is soluble in water.	What does it signify? Where has phosphorus pentoxide gone?	
8. No more oxygen is present in the bell-jar now.	Absence of oxygen in the bell-jar can be tested by taking in burning match stick inside the bell-jar.	Air contains one part of oxygen and four parts of nitrogen. It is soluble in water.

Following questions will be asked to test previous knowledge :

(i) Name the chief characteristics of metals.

(ii) Give some important properties that distinguish metals from non-metals.

(iii) Name an element which though lighter than water is yet a metal. Why do you suppose it to be a metal?

(iv) To what use do we put caustic soda, washing soda and common salt?

Teacher will then declare the aim: 'We shall learn more about the metal sodium and substances like caustic soda, washing soda, etc. today.'

2nd Stage : Some properties of sodium.

Teacher will put a freshly cut piece of sodium on a filter paper and pass it around the class to show its metallic lustre; a student will be asked to cut another piece and its soft waxy nature will be brought home. Similarly, its lightness and the effect of exposure to air will be shown and reasons for storing it under kerosene oil will be explained.

Blackboard: Sodium is a light, soft metal. When freshly cut it shows a metallic lustre. When exposed to air it soon gets tarnished. It floats on water and soon disappears, so it is kept under kerosene oil.

3rd Stage: Action of sodium on water.

Experiment: To show that hydrogen is given out when sodium react with water, and that an alkali is also formed which turns red litmus solution blue, will be shown. A glass tubing of slightly wide bore will be supported in a beaker containing red litmus solution. One or two small pieces of sodium will be dropped inside the tube. The gas coming out of the tube will be ignited with a match. The litmus solution inside the tube will be seen to have turned blue.

Blackboard: When a piece of sodium is thrown into water it swims around with a hissing sound, reacts with water, giving hydrogen and forming an alkali which turns red litmus blue.

4th Stage : Some common compounds of sodium and their uses.

Samples of common salt, caustic soda, washing soda, and sodium bicarbonate will be shown, and the class will be told that all of them are compounds of metal sodium. Students will be asked some of the uses of these salts and other uses will be told to them. Their chemical names will also be given to the students.

Blackboard:

(i) Common salt—sodium chloride is used for

(a) eating,

(b) curing hides and fish,

(c) preservative in achars and other things,

(d) in the making of washing soda and caustic soda, and preparation of hydrochloric acid.

(ii) Washing soda-sodium carbonate is used for

(a) washing,

(b) softening hard water, and

(c) making caustic soda.

(iii) Sodium bicarbonate is used in

(a) medicine, and

(b) baking powders.

(iv) Caustic soda-sodium hydroxide is used in making soap and paper.

5th Stage : Recapitulation.

(i) Why is sodium not stored under water or in an empty bottle?

(ii) Give some physical and chemical properties of sodium.

(iii) List the uses of common salt, soda and caustic soda.

Blackboard Summary: Main properties, uses etc., as above will form B.B. Summary.

Preparation and study of the chief properties of carbon dioxide gas in the Laboratory

Aim : To get pupils to fit up the apparatus for the preparation of carbon dioxide in the laboratory, prepare the gas and study its chief physical and chemical properties.

Previous knowledge: The preparation and properties of the gas have been demonstrated in demonstration period.

Procedure: The students will be asked the following questions:

(i) How was carbon dioxide prepared in the laboratory?

(ii) Was it heavier or lighter than air?

(iii) Was it soluble in water?

(iv) How can you collect the gas?

A sketch of the apparatus will be drawn on the blackboard and teacher will ask them to fit the apparatus accordingly.

The following precautions will also be emphasized:

(i) The apparatus should be tested to be air-tight.

(ii) The thistle funnel should dip in the liquid.

(iii) Water should be just enough to cover the pieces of marble. (These will be written on blackboard).

The boys will then be asked to fit up the apparatus. The teacher will go round giving individual help. While the boys are busy collecting the gas, he will put down on the blackboard a list of experiments to be performed and properties to be tested by the boys as given below:

(i) Colour and smell.

(ii) Action on litmus solution.

(iii) Heaviness.

(iv) Action on a burning taper.

(v) Action on lime water for a short-time and for a long-time.

He will ask them to record their work in the following tabular form:

Experiment	*Observation*	*Inference*
1	2	3

When the boys are busy performing the experiments to

study the properties of gas, the teacher will go round, give individual help and tick off portions of written work examined.

At the end of the period he will sign the note books and supervise the return of clear apparatus to the cup-boards.

Note: In the specimens of lesson notes given above the apparatus required has not been shown. Pupil teachers should always give in their notes the list of apparatus required. This list may be put below the aim under the heading "Apparatus".

LESSON NOTES—4

Atmospheric Pressure

Aim: To teach that air exerts pressure in all directions: The method of measuring this pressure; and the application of atmospheric pressure to daily life.

Previous knowledge: properties of matter; air a material body, air has weight.

1st Stage : Introduction

Following questions will be put so as to test previous knowledge:

(i) Name some important properties of matter.

(ii) Can you show experimentally that air has weight?

2nd Stage : Air exerts pressure in all directions.

Teacher will put a number of notebooks on the palm of the outstretched hand of a pupil and ask him what he feels. He will increase the number of notebooks and ask again what he feels. He will go on increasing the weight on the palm, and go as asking what the pupil feels. He will thus reduce that air exerts pressure due to weight.

The following experiments will be performed to show that air exerts pressure in all directions:

(i) Take a funnel to which a piece of thin rubber is tied. Whenever, the rubber is pressed inwards when air is sucked out of the funnel. This happens in whatever position the funnel be kept.

(ii) Take a jar full of water, covered with a piece of paper at its mouth. Invert the jar and see that the water does not fall when the jar is inverted.

(iii) Air is pumped out of an open bell jar mounted on the disc of an air-pump with sheet rubber tiedon the end of the belljar. The rubber is pressed inwards and bursts with a loud noise after sometime.

(iv) With Magdeburg hemispheres. (Anecdote of Guericke's experiment with hemispheres 18" radius being pulled apart by a team of 16 horses will be related and an illustration of it will be shown).

Blackboard Summary: Air exerts pressure in all directions due to its weight.

3rd Stage : Extent of air pressure exerted.

(i) The teacher will fit up a barometer and make the students observe that mercury falls by a few inches. The length of the column of mercury will be measured and with the help of suitable questions it will be deducted that a column of about 30" of mercury can be supported by the column of air.

(ii) The mercury in the tube will then be poured in a glass vessel weighed and put on a dial scale. The movement of the needle any indicates that it is due to the weight of the mercury. It will be shown that the weight is equal to about 7 Ib. (tube of 1/2" cross section area was taken).

Blackboard Summary: Air can support a column of mercury about 30" in height. Air exerts a pressure of about 14 lb. per square inch. A diagram of a barometer.

4th Stage : Application to daily life.

(i) Sucking water or soda through a straw tube.

(ii) Placing a hollow key to the lip when air is sucked out of it.

(iii) Rise of water in a syringe.

(iv) Water-pump.

(v) Eye-dropper, etc.

5th Stage : Recapitulation.

(i) How does an elephant drink water through its trunk?

(ii) Why do lizards not fall ?

(iii) Why do we not feel the considerable (50 tons) pressure of air?

Blackboard Summary

(i) Air exerts pressure due to weight.

(ii) Air exerts pressure in all directions.

(iii) Air can support a column of mercury 30" in height.

(iv) Air exerts a pressure of about 14 lb. per square inch.

Convection in Liquids

Aim : To teach pupils how liquids get heated and some applications of this process to daily life.

Previous knowledge: Pupils know how solids get heated.

1st Stage: Introduction.

Following questions will be asked to test the previous knowledge of the students.

(i) When one end of a poker is put in fire what happens to the other end?

(ii) How has heat travelled to the other end ?

(iii) Can heat travel in water in the same way ?

The teacher will perform an experiment (sketch A). He will fill a test tube with water and place a pebble coated over with wax at the bottom of it. He will place a tube over a burner so that the flame heats the lower part of the tube and not the pebble which is thus farthest from the flame. From the experiment he will deduce that water is bad conductor of heat.

He will then ask: 'How do we heat water in our homes?" 'Where do we put fire?'

Blackboard Summary: Water is a bad conductor of heat.

2nd Stage : The process of convection.

The teacher will heat some water in a flask and put a few crystals of potassium permanganate in the flask (sketch B). He will ask the students-to-observe the coloured water rising from the centre and going down the sides. He will explain this and with the help of suitable .questions deduce the process by which liquids get heated. This is known as convection .

Blackboard Summary: Definition of convection as deduce from the class (also sketch of the apparatus).

3rd Stage : Applications of convection

(i) Showing the experiment sketched in C in which coloured water from the lower flask can be seen rising up the straight tube to the top of the upper flask and colourless water from the upper flask coming down the bent tube. The heating of rooms by hot water pipes will be explained in this way.

(ii) Formation of currents will be explained with the help of the experiment shown in sketch D.

(iii Water will be boiled in a paper bag and it will be explained why the paper does not catch fire for sometime.

4th Stage : Recapituation.

(i) Describe the process by which liquids get heated.

(ii) Differentiate between convection and conduction?

(iii) Name some applications of convection to daily life.

Blackboard Summary

(i) Water is a bad conductor.

(ii) Convection is the process by which liquids become heated by the actual movement of their particles due to difference of density.

(iii) Uses of the process of convection in daily life:

(a) heating rooms by hot water pipes;

(b) formation of ocean currents.

A first Lesson on Magnetism

Aim: To teach the class the forms, properties and uses of a magnet.

Previous knowledge: Pupils are familiar with a horse-shoe magnet, and know its property of picking up iron objects.

1st Stage : Introduction

Showing a small horse-shoe magnet to the class and the following questions will be asked.

(i) What is this?

(ii) Do you know anything about it ?

(iii) What is its shape ?

(iv) What is it made of ?

(v) Have you seen a magnet of any other shape ?

2nd Stage : Magnet and its forms.

(a) Different forms of magnets will be shown and their names will be told;

(b) Brief history of the discovery of a loadstone will be narrated. (The anecdote of the shepherd and his crook). Explanation of the word 'magnet' will be given;

(c) Classification of magnets into natural and artificial.

3rd Stage : Properties

The following properties of magnets will be illustrated with the help of experiments:

(i) Attract iron filings.

(ii) When suspended freely always point north and south. (Explanation of word 'loadstone' will be given).

(iii) The force of attraction is greatest at the ends (idea of poles and their names will be given at this stage).

(iv) Like poles repel and unlike poles attract (primary law of magnetism). Repulsion is the sure test of magnetism.

4th Stage: Application of the properties of magnets.

(i) Separation of iron filings from other objects-brass, powdered glass, snuff, clay, wheat; removal of pieces of iron from eyes of workers; lifting scrap iron with the help of a magnetic crane, etc.

(ii) Compass to find directions.

Blackboard Summary

Forms of magnets and their kinds :

(i) Horse-shoe magnets.

(ii) Bar magnets.

(iii) Magnetic needles.

(iv) Loadstone. The first three are artificial, and the fourth natural.

Properties of magnets :

(i) Attract iron filings.

(ii) When suspended freely they point in a north and south direction.

(iii) The force of attraction is the greatest at the poles.

(iv) Like poles repel each other and unlike poles attract each other. This is called the primary law of magnetism.

(v) Repulsion is the sure test of magnetism.

Uses of magnets :

(i) In separating iron filings from other objects.

(ii) In finding directions.

Observation and Criticism

It has been found that the pupil teachers observe the Demonstration and Criticism lessons very subjectively, ignoring or overemphasising certain aspects. Broadly, following aspects of the lesson should be carefully observed and criticized.

1. Preparation on the part of the teacher.
2. Subject-matter. (Correct, well-planned and systematic)
3. Aims of the lesson. (Extent to which it has been realised)
4. Introduction of the lesson. (It should be stimulating, problematic and adequate)
5. Method of teaching. (Lecture-cum-demonstration method)
6. Practical demonstration. (Clear, striking, successful)
7. Audio-visual aids used. (Extent of such aids used properly)
8. Questioning. (Adequate, suitable, properly worded, well-distributed)
9. Recapitulation.
10. Blackboard work.
11. Application of the scientific principle taught in daily life.
12. Class discipline.
13. Students interest and involvement.
14. Teacher's personality and behaviour.
15. Overall assessment.

Evaluation of Lessons

According to one study, the lessons of pupil-teachers can be objectively evaluated on the following five-point rating scale:

		A B C D E
1.	Clarity of objectives	8 6 4 2 0
2.	Mastery of subject-matter	8 6 4 2 0
3.	Pupils involvement in the teaching process	8 6 4 2 0
4.	The activities or experiments demonstrated	8 6 4 2 0
5.	Presentation of the lesson	8 6 4 2 0
6.	The extent to which interest is created	8 6 4 2 0
7.	Attitude towards pupils	8 6 4 2 0
8.	The technique of evaluation used	4 3 2 1 0
9.	Correlation with actual life situations	4 3 2 1 0
10.	Class management	4 3 2 1 0
11.	Clarity of thought	4 3 2 1 0
12.	Consistancy and logical nature of thought	4 3 2 1 0
13.	Efficiency and adequacy of language	4 3 2 1 0
14.	Preparation for the lesson	4 3 2 1 0
15.	Blackboard work	4 3 2 1 0
16.	Neat and tidy work habit	4 3 2 1 0
17.	Use of teaching aids	4 3 2 1 0
18.	Home work and assignment	4 3 2 1 0
	Total	

Questions

1. What is meant by lesson planning ? What are the different approaches that can be adopted for planning lessons in physical sciences ?
2. Discuss any one approach of lesson planning that is generally adopted in our schools.
3. Prepare a lesson plan on any topic of physics, chemistry for class **X**,
4. What is the importance of lesson planning in teaching of physical sciences ?

11

Process of Enrichment

Content of chemistry is to be given to the students as it is the students who have to learn. Thus for chemistry learning the content should be as good as the method of teaching. It is with this view in mind that some content portion is assigned to the syllabus for teaching of chemistry. In the pages to follow we will take up certain concepts in chemistry.

Preparation of Gases

Oxygen : It is present in the air (atmosphere) in the free (native) form and it is about 20% of air by volume. Lavasior detected the presence of oxygen in atmosphere. Sheele obtained the gas in laboratory and studied its properties.

Preparation : In the laboratory oxygen gas is prepared by heating, a mixture of potassium chlorate (4 parts) and manganese dioxide (1 part), in a hard glass test tube fitted with a delivery tube. The other end of the delivery tube is placed under beehive shelf kept immersed in a through of water. Over the beehive shelf is placed an inverted gas cylinder filled with water. On beating test-tube gently the gas bubbles can be seen rising in the gas and the gas is collected by downward displacement of water. The chemical reaction taking place can be represented as under:

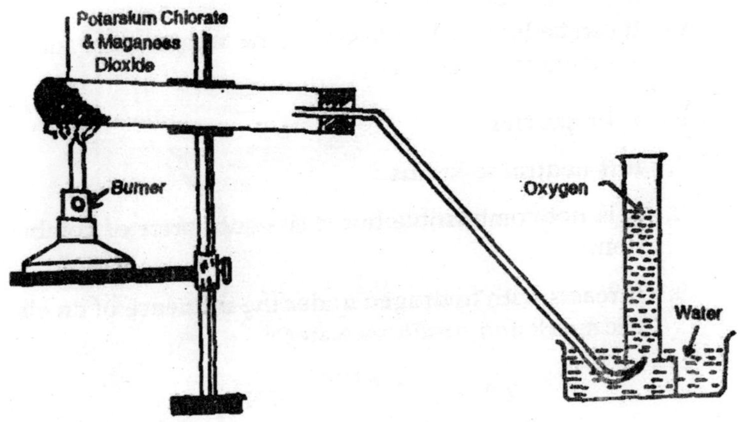

Fig. Preparation of Hydrogen gas in the Laboratory.

Precautions :

(i) Always use pure manganese dioxide.

(ii) Before removing the flame remove the delivery tube from the beehive shelter water as the water may rush into the test-tube resulting into its breakage.

(iii) The test-tube should be clamped in the stand in a slanting position to avoid breakage of the tube by the condensed vapour.

(iv) Test-tube should be heated gently and slowly.

(v) A glass lid should be placed on the mouth of the jar after filling it with the gas. It may be made air tight by applying a little glycerine or vaseline on its surface.

Properties of Oxygen Gas

Physical Properties :

(i) It is a colourless, tasteless and odourless gas.

(ii) It is slightly soluble in water. The dissolved gas is used by the animals living in water for respiration.

(iii) It is slightly heavier than air.

(iv) It can be liquified by lowering the temperature and increasing the pressure.

Chemical Properties :

1. It is neutral to litmus.
2. It is not combustible but it is a supporter of combustion.
3. It reacts with hydrogen under the influence of an electric spark and produces water.

$$2H_2 + O_2 \xrightarrow[\text{Sparks}]{\text{Electric}} 2HO_2$$

4. It reacts with metals its form their oxides.

2Mg	+	O_2	→	2MgO
4Na	+	O_2	→	$2Na_2O$
4Fe	+	$3O_2$	→	$2Fe_2O_3$

5. It oxidises ammonia to nitric oxide.

$$4NH_3 + 5O_2 \xrightarrow{\text{Pt.800}^{\circ}\text{C}} 4NO + 6H_2O$$

6. It can be converted to ozone (ozonised oxygen) by passing electric sparks at ordinary temperature and pressure.

$$3O_2 \xrightarrow[\text{Discharge}]{\text{Electric}} 2O_3$$

Uses :

1. It is used as an oxidising agent.
2. It is used in welding.
3. It is used in artificial respiration.
4. It is used in preparation of ozone.

Hydrogen Gas : It is the lightest element and also the lightest gas. It was discovered by Heavy Cavandish in 1663. The name hydrogen was given by Lavasior in 1783.

Preparation : It can be prepared from acids, alkalies, water etc.

In the laboratory hydrogen gas is prepared by the action of zinc with dilute HC1 or dil H_2SO_4. The chemical reactions taking place can be represented as :

$$Zn + H_2SO_2 \rightarrow ZnSO_4 + H_2\uparrow$$

$$Zn + 2HCl \rightarrow ZnCl_2 + H_2\uparrow$$

The gas is prepared in a Woulfs bottle. The apparatus is fitted as shown in Fig.

$$2\,KClO_3 \xrightarrow[\text{(catalyst)}]{Mno_2} 2KCl + 20_2\uparrow$$

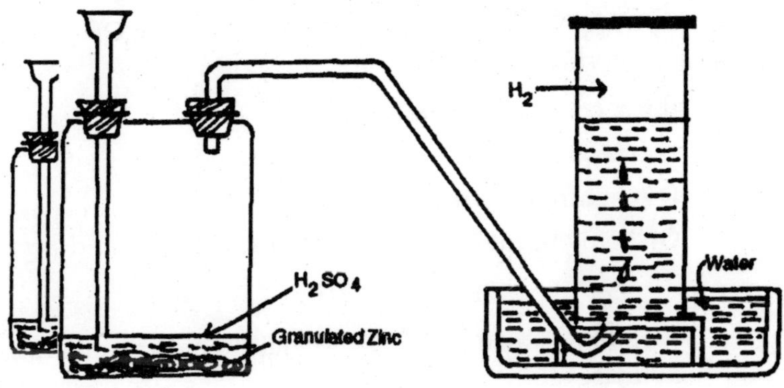

Fig. Preparing Oxygen gas in Laboratory.

A Woulfs bottle is taken and some pieces of granulated zinc are placed in it. Then a thistle funnel is fitted in one mouth and in the other mouth a delivery tube is fitted. Some water is added to cover the zinc pieces. Then conc. H_2SO_4 or HC1 is through the funnel. The hydrogen gas coming out of the Woulfs bottle through delivery tube is collected by downward displacement of water.

Precautions :

1. The apparatus should be made air tight.
2. The lower end of thistle funnel must be under water in the Woulfs bottle.
3. No flame be allowed near the apparatus.
4. Pour the cone. acid slowly in the Woulfs bottle.
5. Gas is always stored in inverted gas cylinder.

Properties :

Physical Properties

1. It is a colourless, odourless and tasteless gas.
2. It is lighter than air.
3. It is insoluble in water.
4. It can be liquified by decreasing the temperature and increasing the pressure.

Chemical Properties

1. It is a combustible gas.
2. It explodes in presence of air.
3. It is neutral to litmus.
4. On being burnt in oxygen, it forms water.

$$2H_2 + O_2 \rightarrow 2H_2O$$

5. It combines with halogens to yield the corresponding halides.

$$H_2 + cl_2 \rightarrow 2HC1$$

$$H_2 + Br_2 \rightarrow 2HBr$$

$$H_2 + I_2 \rightarrow 2HI$$

6. It is a strong reducing agent.

$$CuO + H_2 \rightarrow Cu + H_2O$$

$$Fe_2O_2 + 4H_2 \rightarrow 3Fe + 4H_2O$$

Uses :

1. It is used as a reducing agent.
2. It is used in preparation of ammonia, methyl alcohol, hydrochloric acid etc.
3. It is used in preparation of Vanaspati Ghee.
4. It is used in welding (Oxy-hydrogen flame).

CARBON-DIOXIDE GAS (CO_2)

CO_2 is produced during the respiratory by all living beings including vegetable kingdom. During the day in the presence of sunlight plants absorb carbon-dioxide and give out oxygen gas. In this way carbon cycle is formed to keep its balance in nature.

Preparation of Carbon-Dioxide : It can be prepared by the action of an acid on a carbonate or a bicarbonate.

In the laboratory carbon-dioxide is prepared by the action of marble or chalk ($CaCO_3$) with dilute HC1 or H_2SO_4.

$$CaCO_3 + 2HCl \rightarrow CaCl_2 + H_2O + CO\uparrow$$

Experiment : The apparatus is fitted as shown in Fig.

A Woulfs bottle is taken and some pieces of marble, chalk or shells are put in it. A little of water is added to cover the marble. A thistle funnel and a delivery tube bent at-right angles is fitted.

Acid is added through the thistle funnel. The reaction occurs. The gas is collected by upward displacement of air. The gas is not collected over water because the gas is highly soluble in water. The gas can be tested with the help of a burning splinter. It extinguishes a burning splinter or a match stick.

Precautions :

1. The apparatus should be air tight.
2. The lower end of the thistle funnel should remain dipped in the acid contained in the Woulfs bottle.

3. The marble pieces should be completely immersed in dilute hydrochloric acid.
4. Use dry cylinders for collecting the gas.

Physical Properties

1. It is a colourless gas.
2. It has a characteristic smell.
3. It is heavier than the air.
4. It is soluble in water.
5. It is acidic in nature.

Chemical Properties

1. It is neither combustible nor a supporter of combustion. Burning objects get extinguished in carbon-dioxide gas.
2. Some metals such as magnessium, sodium, potassium continue to burn in carbon dioxide gas while carbon is set free

$$2Mg + CO_2 \rightarrow 2MgO + C$$

$$4Na + CO_2 \rightarrow 2Na_2O + C$$

3. When carbon-dioxide dissolves in water, it forms an acidic solution which turns moist blue litmus paper red.
4. It reacts with alkalies to form carbonates

$$2NaOH + CO_2 \rightarrow Na_2CO_2 + H_2O$$

$$Ca0 + CO_2 \rightarrow CaCO_2$$

5. When CO, is passed through lime water i.e.,Ca(OH), it turns it milky

$$Ca(OH)_2 + CO_2 \rightarrow CaCO_2 + H_2O$$

If we continue passing CO_2 gas in lime-water in excess, it again turns colourless.

$$CaCO_3 + H_2O + CO_2 \rightarrow Ca(HCO_3)_2$$

6. On being passed over red hot coal, it is reduced to carbon monooxide.

$$CO_2 + C \rightarrow 2CO \uparrow$$

7. Carbon-dioxide gas is absorbed by green plants in the presence of chlorophyl,sunlight and water to form glucose, starch, sugar or cellulose. This process is called photosynthesis.

$$6CO_2 + 6H_2O \xrightarrow[\text{Sunlight}]{\text{Chlorophyl}} C_6H_{12}O_6 + CO_2 \uparrow$$

Uses :

1. Carbon-dioxide is used in preparing aerated water.
2. It is used in the manufacturing of solid carbon-dioxide called dry ice.
3. It is used in the manufacturing of baking soda and washing soda.
4. It is used to neutralize the effect of lime in sugar industry.

Acids, Bases And Salts : Important concepts (theories) of acids and bases are proposed by :

(i) Arrhenius (1887)

(ii) Bronsted-Lowry (1923)

(iii) Lewis (1923).

Arrhenius Concept

Arrhenius (1887) defined acid as a substance that will dissociate to yield a hydrogen ion while base in one that will dissociate to yield a hydroxyl ion in aqueous solution.

Thus

$$\underset{\text{Acid}}{HCl(aq)} \qquad H^+ (aq) + Cl^-(aq)$$

$$\underset{\text{Base}}{NaOH (aq)} \qquad Na^+ (aq) + OH^- (aq)$$

According to this concept HNO_3, HCl, H_2SO_4, CH_3COOH etc., are acids and NaOH, KOH, NH_4OH etc., are bases.

This definition is of limited application and is applicable in aqueous solution only. It does not cover those substances which fail to give H^+ or OH^- ions but behave as acids or bases.

Bronsted-Lowry Concept

According to this concept an add is a substance that can donate a proton and a base is a substance that can accept a proton e.g.

HCl (aq)	+	H_2O(I)	H_3O^+ (aq)	+	Cl (aq)
Acid		Base	Acid		Base
NH_4 + (aq)	+	H_2O(I)	H_3O^+(aq)	+	NH_2 (aq)
Acid		Base	Acid		Base
H_2O(I)	+	NH_3(aq)	NH_{4+}(aq)	+	OH^-(aq)
Acid		Base	Acid		Base
H_2O(I)	+	CO_3^{2-} (aq)	HCO_3^- (aq)	+	OH^-(aq)
Acid		Base	Acid		Base

It may be noted that an acid after losing a proton becomes base where as a base after accepting the electron becomes an acid.

A base formed by the loss of proton by an acid is called *conjugate base* of the acid. An acid formed by the gain of proton by a base is called *conjugate acid* of the base. Acid-base pairs such as H_2O/OH^-, NH_4^+/NH_3 etc., are called *conjugate acid-base pairs.*

Those substances which can act both as an acid and a base are called *amphoteric substances.*

It is important to note that:

(i) all Arrbenius acids are Bransted acids but all Arrhenius bases are not Bransted bases, and

(ii) Bransted-Lowery concept is not limited to molecules to act as acids and bases but ionic species may also be considered as acids or bases.

This concept serves well in protonic solvents like water, ammonia, acetic acid etc., but fails in case of some obvious acid-base reactions e.g., it can not explain how acidic oxides such as an hydrous carbon-dioxide, sulphur dioxide, sulphur trioxide etc., neutralize basic oxides like calcium oxide and barrium oxide even in the absence of solvent.

Lewis Concept

According to this concept an acid is a substance (molecule or ion) that can accept an electron pair to form a covalent bond and base is a substance that can supply an electron pair to form a covalent bond. Thus an add is electron pair acceptor and a base is an electron pair donor. An acid need not contain hydrogen.

Lewis acids are of several types :

(i) Compounds having a central atom with incomplete octet.

(ii) Compounds containing multiple bonds.

(iii) Simple cations.

(iv) Compounds in which the octet of the central atom can be expanded.

The acids and bases according to this concept are interrelated by the equation

$$HA + H_2O \rightarrow H_3O^+ + A^-$$

Acid Base Acid Base

Classification of Acids

The acids can be classified as :

(i) Hydra acids, and

(ii) Oxy-acids.

Hydra acids are those acids in which we find no oxygen e.g. HCl, HBr, HI etc. They contain only two elements i.e., hydrogen and some non-metal.

Oxy-acids always contain oxygen as one of the elements. They contain hydrogen, oxygen and a third element e.g. HNOy H^SO^, HgPO^ H^OO, etc.

Relative Strengths of Acids and Bases

The relative strength of an acid and a base depends upon their relative capacity to liberate H^+ and OH^- ions in aqueous solution. The higher the $[H^+]$ in aqueous solution, the greater is the strength of the acid. Similarly, greater the $[OH^-]$ is aqueous solution greater is the strength of base.

Alkali and Base : As already discussed all those substances which give OH in aqueous solution are called bases. Out of these *only those bases which are soluble in water are called alkalies.*

Salts

Salts are the compounds formed by the neutralisation reaction between an acid and an alkali.

NaOH	+	Hd	→	NaCl	+	H_2O
Alkali (base)		Acid		Salt		Water

NaCl is a neutral salt.

NaOH	+	H_2SO_4	→	$NaHSO_4$	+	H_2O
Base		Acid		Salt		Water

$NaHSO_4$ is an acidic salt because in it hydrogen of the acid has been partly replaced.

Concept of Oxidation and Reduction

Oxidation might be defined as a chemical reaction. Wherein oxygen is gained or hydrogen is lost.

Reduction may be defined as a chemical reaction wherein oxygen is lost or hydrogen is gained.

For example when hydrogen is passed over heated cupric

oxide (CuO) the following reaction occurs :

$$CuO(s)+H_2(g) \rightarrow Cu(s)+H_2O(g)$$

CuO loses oxygen and so is reduced to Cu. Hydrogen gains oxygen and is oxidised to H-0.

The hydrogen which is required to reduce CuO is called *reducing agent* and CuO which is required to oxidise H_2 is called *oxidising agent.*

Definition of oxidation and reduction in terms of electron loss or gain is more useful because all reactions do not involve oxygen and hydrogen. According to this concept,

Oxidation is a process which involves loss of one or more electrons by some atom or group of atoms. For example :

$$Cu \rightarrow Cu^{2+} + 2e^-$$
$$Zn \rightarrow Zn^{2+} + 2e^-$$
$$Ag \rightarrow Ag^+ + e^-$$
$$H \rightarrow H^+ + e^-.$$

The substance which loses electron is said to be oxidised and the one which gains electron is said to be reduced.

Reduction is a process which involves gain of one or more electrons by some atom or group of atoms. For example :

$$Cu^{2+} + 2e^- \rightarrow Cu$$
$$H^+ + e^- \rightarrow H$$
$$Ag^+ + e^- \rightarrow Ag.$$

Oxidation and Reduction : We have already studied the electronic concept of oxidation and reduction. If some substance loses electrons (i.e. undergoes oxidation) then the electrons lost by it must be accepted by some other substance. The substance that accepts electrons undergoes reduction. Hence, it is clear that oxidation and reduction occur simultaneously. For example in the reaction:

$$Zn + Cu^{2+} \rightarrow Zn^+ + Cu \quad \text{(redox reaction)}$$

Zn is oxidised to Zn^{2+} and Cu^{2+} is reduced to Cu. The reactions involving simultaneously oxidation and reduction are called *redox-reactions. A* redox reaction can be split into two *half reactions* are representing oxidation and the other representing reduction. For example, the above redox reaction may be represented as :

$Zn \rightarrow Zn^{2+} + 2e^{-}$ (oxidation half reaction)

$Cu^{2+} + 2e^{+} \rightarrow Cu$ (reduction half reaction)

In such reactions the substance that loses electrons is called *reducing agent* and the substance that accepts electrons is called *oxidising agent.*

In a redox reaction the total number of electrons lost by reducing agent is equal to the total number of electrons accepted by the oxidising agent.

Oxidation State : The system of oxidation states (or oxidation numbers) has been devised to give a guide to the extent of oxidation or reduction in a species the system is without direct chemical foundations, but is extremely useful being appropriate to hope ionic and oovakntly bonded species.

The oxidation state can be defined simply as the number of electrons which must be added to a positive ion to get a neutral atom or removed from a negative ion to get a neutral atom e.g. Fe^{2+} (aq) has oxidation state of +2 and Cl^{-} has oxidation state of -1.

For covalent species the oxidation state is found using the following rules :

(i) The oxidation state of all elements in uncombined state is taken as zero.

(ii) The algebraic sum of oxidation states of elements in a compound is always zero.

(iii) The algebraic sum of oxidation states of elements in an ion is equal to the charge on the ion.

(iv) The oxidation state of oxygen is -2 (except in oxygen gas and peroxides).

(v) The oxidation state of hydrogen is +1 (except when combined with group I and II metals as hybrids).

Atomic Structure

John Dalton (1808) proposed that matter is composed of small indivisible particles called atoms.

Particles in Atom

Atoms are composed *of protons, neutrons* and *electrons.* These are known as fundamental sub-atomic particles. The following table compares the properties of these particles :

Name of particle	*Mass*	*Charge*
Proton, p	I amu	+1
Neutron, n	I amu	0
Electron, e	negligible	-1

A neutral atom contains equal number of protons and electrons in it. This number of protons or electrons present in an atom is called its *atomic number (Z).*

The total number of neutrons and protons present in an atom gives the *mass number (A)* of the atom.

So

Atomic Number (Z) = Number of protons

= Number of electrons

and

Mass Number (A) = Number of protons + Number of Neutrons

= Number of Nucleus

Rutherfords' Atomic Model

According to this model atom consists of two parts :

(i) nucleus, and

(ii) extra-nuclear part.

(i) Nucleus : The protons and neutrons in each atom are tightly packed in a positively charged nucleus and the electrons move around the nucleus. Nucleus in a small positively charged part of atom and is situated at the centre and carried almost entire mass of atom. The diameter of nucleus is of the order of

10^{-12} -10^{-13} cm which is only about $\frac{1}{100,00}$ part of the diameter

of an atom. In chemical reactions nucleus remains unchanged.

(ii) Extra-nuclear space : This is the empty part of the atom. In this part electrons revolve at very high speed in fixed path called *orbits* or *shells.*

Drawbacks of Rutherford's Model : Following serious objections against the Rutherford's model were reported :

(i) When an electron revolves around the nucleus, it will radiate out energy, resulting in the loss of energy. This loss of energy will make the electron to move slowly and consequently it will be moving in a spiral path and ultimately falling inside the nucleus Fig. Thus, the atom remains unstable. Fortunately, the atom is stable.

(ii) If an electron loses energy continuously, the observed spectrum would be continuous and have broad bonds merging into one another. But most of the atoms give line spectra. Thus Rutherford's model could not explain the origin of spectral lines.

Bohr's Theory : In order to overcome the drawbacks of Rutherford's model and to account for the line spectra of hydrogen, Niel Bohr in 1913 put forward a theory called Bohr's theory. The main postulates of Bohr's theory are as follows :

(a) That within an atom an electron can move in certain specific orbits without radiating out energy. Such orbits were termed as stationary orbits. These orbits are numbered as 1,2,3,4 etc., or K, L, M, N, etc., starting from the nucleus.

(b) The mathematical condition for stationary orbits is that the angular momentum of the moving electron is an integral multiple *of* $h/2\pi$, where A is the Planck's constant.

$$mvr = n\frac{h}{2\pi}$$

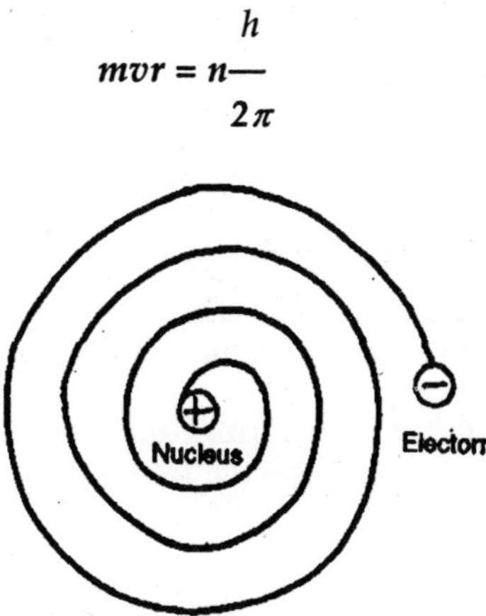

Fig. Gradual decrease in the radius of orbit.

where *mvr* denotes the angular momentum and n is called principal quantum number and is equal to 1, 2, 3 ...

(c) When an electron gets energy, it will go to higher energy orbits. Similarly, in the reverse process, the excited electron jumps down to lower energy level by emitting absorbed energy in the form of radiations'of suitable wavelength. The frequency of this radiations (v) is given by the difference in the energy between initial and final orbits.

$$E_1\text{-}E_2 = hv$$

Simple representation of sodium atom on Bohr's model.

A sodium atom consists of 11 electrons ($^{23}Na_{11}$) and they are arranged as 2, 8, 1. It may be represented as :

Electrons partly because of their very small size are impossible to locate at any particular time. It is however possible to locate a region or volume where the electron is most likely to be found. Thus region is called *Orbital*. Each orbital can hold a maximum of two electrons. Orbitals can be divided into *s-*, *p-*, *d-*, *f-* types. Each type of orbital has its own characteristic shape.

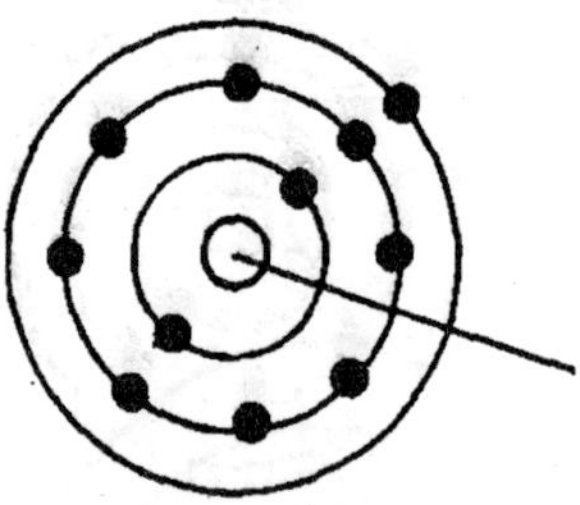

Fig. Simple representation of sodium atom.

Quantum Number: The term quantum number is used to identify the various energy levels that are available to an electron in an atom.

Type of Quantum Number : Four quantum numbers are necessary to characterise completely any particular electron in a particular orbit. They are as follows :

(a) *Principal quantum number:* This is designated as n and gives the number of principal shell in which the electron is revolving around the nucleus. It designates the average distance of the electron from the nucleus, (hence this quantum number represents the size of electron orbit.

(b) *Azimuthal or subsidiary or orbital quantum number :* This is designated as /. This determines the orbital angular momentum and the shape of the orbital, /can have value ranging from 0 to n -1, i.e.

$$l=0, 1, 2...(n-2), (n-1)$$

The orbital with l= 0 is called s-orbital, that with l= 1, *is* called p-orbital, that one with l= 2 is called rf oribtal and the one with 1=3 is called *f*-orbital.

(c) *Afagnetic quantum number:* This quantum number is designated as *m*. This quantum number determines the direction of the orbital relative to the magnetic field in which it is placed. m can have values from -*l* to + *l* through zero, i.e., m = + *l*; -*l*. 1 - 2....0. **-1,** -2,..-(*l*-1). -*l*.

In other words, the number of m values for a given values of *l* is 2*i* + 1 through zero.

(d) *Spin quantum number:* This is designated as *s*. The quantum number indicates the direction in which the electron is spinning clockwise or anticlockwise. There are only two possible values for this quantum number and for electrons these are +½ and -½ according to the direction of spin being clockwise and anticlockwise respectively.

Pauli's Exclusion Principle : This is the most important principle which cannot be derived from any fundamental concept. Pauli's exclusion principle states that no two electrons in a single atom can have all their quantum numbers identical. By this principle it means that if two electrons possess the same value of *n*, l and *m*, they must have different values of *s*.

Hand's Rule of Maximum Multiplicity : This rule has a spectro-scopic basis and is mainly concerned with the situation when two orbitals of a sub-group are incompletely filled. This rule can be stated as:

"When electrons enter a set of orbitals in a given shell, electrons will pair up, when all the available orbitals have one electron each."

Hund's rule is energetically possible.

Aufbau's Principle : The word Aufbau is a German expression which means build up or construction. This Aufbau principle is mainly concerned with the building up process in which extra electrons are being added to the various available orbitals so as to balance the nuclear charge. Broadly speaking, this principle states that every electron enters the lowest possible state available.

Isotopes : These are the atoms of the same element with same atomic number but different atomic mass (mass number) e.g. ${}_{6}^{12}C$ and ${}^{13}_{6}C$, ${}^{1}_{1}H$

Isobars : These are the atoms of different elements having different atomic numbers but same atomic mass (mass number) e.g. ${}^{210}_{32}Pb$ and ${}^{210}_{83}Bi$.

Isotones : These are the atoms having same number of neutrons but different mass numbers e.g. $^{30}_{14}Si$, $^{31}_{15}P$, $^{32}_{16}S$. All these have 16 neutrons in their nuclear.

Electronic Configuration of the First 20 Elements

Al. No.	*Element*	*Orbital Electronic Configuration*			
1.	Hydrogen	Is^2			
3.	Lithium	Is^2	$2s^1$		
4.	Beryllium	is^2	$2s^1$		
5.	Boron	Is^2	$2s^2 2px^1$		
6.	Carbon	Is^2	$2s^2 2px^1 2py^1$		
7.	Nitrogen	Is^2	$2s^2 2px^1 2py^1 2pz^1$		
8.	Oxygen	$1s^1$	$2s^2 2px^2 2py^1 2pz^1$		
9.	Flourine	Is^2	$2s^2 2px^2 2py^2 2pz^1$		
10.	Neon	ls^2	$2s^2 2px^2 2py^2 2pz^2$		
11.	Sodiumla[2]	Is^2	$2s^2 2px^2 2py^2 2pz^2$	$3s^1$	
12.	Magnesium	IS^2	$2s^2 2px^2 2py^2 2pz^2$	$3s^2$	
13.	Aluminium	Is^2	$2s^2 2px^2 2py^2 2pz^2$	$3s^2 3px^1$	
14.	Silicon	Is^2	$2s^2 2px^2 2py^2 2pz^2$	$3s^2 3px^1 3py^1$	
15.	Phosphorous	$1s^2$	$2s^2 2px^z 2py^2 2pz^2$	$3s^2 3px^1 3py^1 3pz^1$	
16.	Sulphur	ls^2	$2s^2 2px^2 2py^2 2pz^2$	$3s^2 3px^2 3py^1 3pz^1$	
17.	Chlorine	$1s^2$	$2s^2 2px^2 2py^2 2pz^2$	$3s^2 3px^2 3py^2 3pz^1$	
18.	Argan	$1s^2$	$2s^2 2px^1 2py^2 2pz^2$	$3s^2 3px^2 3py^2 3pz^2$	
19.	Polonium	ls^2	$2s^2 2px^2 2py^2 2pz^2$	$3s^2 3px^2 3py^2 3pz^2$	$4s^1$
20.	Calcium	$1s^1$	$2s^2 2px^2 2py^2 2pz^2$	$3s^2 3px^2 3py^2 3pz^2$	$4s^2$

Wave Nature of Particles

Light can act as a particle as well as a wave under different conditions. In 1905, Albert Einstein suggested that light is propagated in space in small bundles or packages of energy called photons and the energy of each photon is given by the *Plank's relation:*

$$E = hv = h \frac{c}{\lambda} 1 \qquad ...(1)$$

where E = energy of photon,

v = frequency of radiation
λ = wavelength of radiation
h = Plank's constant

It is clear from the above that light has particle like nature and that each particle possesses wave characteristics, having a wavelength given by Eq. 1.

Phenomenon like *interference* and *diffraction* cannot be explained by considering light as having a particle character, they are best explained by considering wave motion of light.

Dual Nature of Particle in Motion

In 1924, the French Physicist Louis de-Broglie proposed his postulate that matter in motion is not only corpuscular (particle-like) in nature but that each particle possesses wave characteristics, having a wavelength (λ) given by the equation.

$$\lambda = \frac{h}{mv} \quad ...(2)$$

where m = mass of the particle
v = velocity of the particle
h = Plank's constant

He further suggested that the motion of bodies produces waves which are different from mechanical waves (e.g., sound waves) and electromagnetic radiations. These waves are known as *matter waves.* Such waves are produced by the motion of all bodies including those not electrically charged. These waves have very short wavelengths as compared to mechanical and electromagnetic radiations.

From de Broglie's equation (Eq. 2) it is clear that the wavelength associated with a moving object or electron is inversely proportional to the momentum of the particle.

Greater the mass of moving particle, shorter the wavelength of the matter associated with it. Therefore, the particles with smaller masses have significant wavelengths.

It is a well-known fact that diffraction of light & a phenomenon associated with its wave character. If a particle exhibits diffraction it can be safely concluded that it is associated with waves or has a wave-character C.P. Davison and L.H. Germer showed that a beam of electrons is diffracted by a nickel crystal at exactly the angle that would be predicted by Bragg's law on the basis of assumption that the beam of electrons has a wave-length given by the de-Broglie equation (Eq. 2). For this work, they shared the Nobel prize in physics for 1937.

Wave Motion

The wave motion is a sort of disturbance, which travels through the medium on account of repeated periodic vibrations of the particle about their mean position the disturbance being handed on from one particle to adjoining particle.

Types of Wave Motion : Wave motion is of two types :

1. Longitudinal wave motion.
2. Transverse wave motion.

Longitudinal Wave Motion : Wave motion is said to be longitudinal, when the particles of the medium through which the disturbance travels vibrate about their mean positions in the same direction, along which disturbance/wave is propagated.

Sound waves travel through air in the form of longitudinal waves.

Transverse Wave Motion : Wave motion is said to be transverse, when the particles of the medium through which the disturbance travels, vibrate about their mean position in a direction perpendicular to the direction of propagation of the wave.

Vibrations in a stretched string of a sonometer are transverse vibrations. In fact all electromagnetic waves (including light waves) are transverse in nature.

The transverse waves move in a medium in the form of crests and troughs.

Some Definitions Compression : It is the region of the medium in which particles come closer i.e., particles are at distances less man their normal distance.

There is a temporary decrease in volume and consequent increase in density of the medium in this region.

Refraction : It is the region of the medium in which particles get farther apart than what they normally are. "Here is a temporary increase in volume and a consequent decrease in density of the medium in the region.

Crest **:** It is a portion of the medium which is raised above the normal position of rest of the particles of the medium, as transverse waves pass through it.

Portion ABC in Fig. represents a crest, B is the centre of the crest.

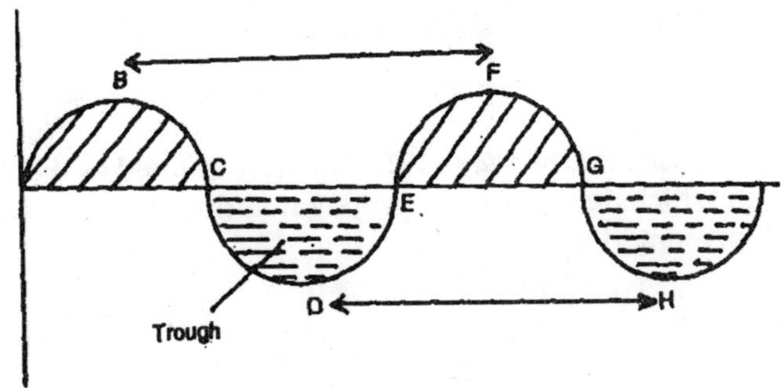

Fig.

Trough **:** It is the portion of the medium which is depressed below the normal position of rest of the particles of the medium as a transverse wave passes through it. Portion CDE in Fig. represents a trough. D is the centre of trough.

Wave Length λ **:** It is the distance travelled by the wave during the time any one particle of the medium completes one vibration about its mean position. It is represented by λ.

It is measured by the distance between the centres of two consecutive crests or troughs BF = DH = λ.

Frequency **:** It is the number of vibration extended by the particle in one second. It is also equal to the number of complete wavelength traversed by the wave in one second. It is represented by *n*.

Time Period **:** Time period of vibration of a particle is the time taken by the particle to complete one vibration about its mean position. It is also equal to the time taken by the wave to travel a distance equal to one wavelength. It is represented by T.

Relation between Frequency and Time Period :

$$T = \frac{I}{n}$$

$$\text{or } n \times T = l.$$

Relation between Velocity, Frequency and Wavelength :

Wave Velocity = frequency x wave-length

$$v = n \times \lambda$$

Phase Velocity or Wave Velocity : It is defined as the velocity with which disturbance is propagated through the medium. It is represented by *v*.

$$\mathbf{v = n\lambda}$$

$$\text{or} \quad v = \frac{2\pi n\lambda}{2\pi}$$

$$\text{or} \quad v = \frac{\omega.\lambda}{2\pi} = \qquad (\omega = \text{angular velocity})$$

$$\text{or} \quad v = \frac{\omega}{\beta} \qquad (\beta =s \frac{2\pi}{\lambda} \text{ phase constant })$$

$$\text{thus velocity} = \frac{\text{Angular velocity}}{\text{Phase constant}}$$

Characteristics of Wave Motion :

1. It is the disturbance which travels through the me-

dium. Particles of the medium do not leave their positions.

2. Particles of medium vibrate in a simple harmonical motion about their mean position.
3. There is a continuous phase difference amongst the successive particles of medium i.e. particle 2 starts vibrating a little later than particle 1 and so on.
4. The velocity of particles during their vibration is different at different positions. It is maximum at means position and zero at extreme positions.
5. The velocity of motion/disturbance through the medium is constant.
6. Energy is propagated alongwith the disturbance, without any net transport of the medium.
7. For propagation of wave motion, a material medium is essential. The medium must possess the properties of elasticity and inertia and frictional force amongst the particles of medium must be minimum.
8. Waves can undergo reflection, refraction, diffraction, dispersion. Moreover two waves can interfere with each other on superposition.

Laws of Motion

A body is said to be in *motion* when it is constantly changing its position with respect to other objects.

A minute study of motion was carried out by English Physicist Sir Issac Newton. On the basis of his studies, in 1687, he established three law of motion which are generally known as *Newton's Laws of Motion.*

Newton's Laws of Motion : First Law of Motion : An object at rest or in uniform motion in a straight line it will continue to remain in state of rest or in uniform motion in a straight line unless some external force is applied to change its position of rest or of uniform motion in a straight line. This law is also referred to as *'law of inertia'*.

Second Law of Motion : The rate of change of momentum of a body is proportional to the external force applied on it and it takes place in the direction of the applied force.

Momentum is defined as the product of mass and velocity.

Momentum = mass x velocity

Rate of change of momentum is given by the following equation.

$$\text{Rate of change of momentum} = \frac{mass\ (v-u)}{t}$$

(Where v = final velocity
u = initial velocity
t = time for which force is applied

$$\text{Since} \quad \frac{v-u}{t} == \text{acceleration}$$

Therefore, Rate of change of momentum = mass x acceleration.

In accordance with second law of motion rate of change of momentum is directly proportional to applied force

thus $F \alpha m \times a$.

It means that to impart acceleration to a heavier body larger force shall have to be applied as compared to the force required to impart the same acceleration to a lighter body.

Third Law of Motion : "Every action has an equal and opposite reaction."

Following examples from our daily life help us to understand these laws of motion.

First Law of Motion: When we are travelling by bus and the driver suddenly applies brakes we will be thrown forward. This can be explained by the *law of inertia*.

Similarly, our observation that a bullet shot at a glass pane passes through it and leaves a small hole in it can also be explained by the *law of inertia*.

Second Law of Motion : For causing more destruction such as to destroy large buildings, we fire large bombs having more mass.

We also observe that blacksmith makes use of a hammer that is quite heavy and drops it from certain height in order to increase the momentum when it falls on the envil.

Third Law of Motion: The rocket in fire works rises up with high speed because the explosions are occurring downwards. This principle is also utilised in Jet aeroplanes which can travel in space without atmosphere.

When a gun is fired the person is pushed back because of the momentum of the bullet.

Theory of Relativity

The theory of relativity was first formulated by Einstein at the beginning of the 20th century. The work of Lorentz might be regarded as having paved the way for it.

The term *relativity* is applied to Einsteins theory because the primary quantities in mechanics and astronomy such as space, time and mass are shown by him to be relative. None of them is absolute which is in direct contradictions with the fundamental ideas of Newtonian mechanics, where these quantities are considered as absolute.

Einsteins theory rejects this absolute nature of fundamental quantities space, time and mass by denying their independence from the position or motion of bodies or observer.

It must be made clear that Einstein's theory does not break off completely from every thing contained in Newtonian theory.

Newtonian Principle of Relativity

It may be stated as, "Absolute motion is the translation of a body from one absolute place to another absolute place can never be detected, for translatory motion can be perceived only in the form of motion relative to other material bodies."

For obvious reasons Newton did away with distinction

between a state of rest and that of rectilinear motion and thus "all systems which move uniformly in a straight line, relatively to one another, are equivalent with regard to all mechanical laws". This was known much before Newton and was first formulated by Galileo from common experience.

From the experiments conducted in a stationery state and those by an observer in a train with a uniform rectilinear motion we could not distinguish between the state of rest and of uniform rectilinear motion. From such experiments we find that all iniitial frames are equivalent in describing the laws of motion, or the laws that govern motion have the same form for all inertia I observers. This is known as *principle of relative motion* or *Newton's relativity principle.*

Special Theory of Relativity

The velocity of light is considered to be absolute. Michelson and Morley were the first to attempt the detection of any change in the speed of light due to the motion of earth relative to a hypothetical medium *ether.*

The failure of Michelson Moriey experiment gave a severe jolt to the hypothesis of ether as a fixed frame of reference. On the basis of this Albert Einstein eliminated the concept of absolute motion with respect to a fixed frame of reference. According to him all motion is relative and has to be measured relative to a certain frame of reference, which may itself be moving. The results of Michelson Morley experiment led Einstein to develop his special theory of relativity which deals with the physical laws as determined in two frames of reference moving with constant velocity relative to each other.

There are two fundamental postulates used in the special theory of Relativity. They are :

(i) The laws of physical phenomenon are same in all frames of reference moving at constant velocity relative to each other, and

(ii) velocity of light is constant and same for all observers and is independent of the velocity of the source of light relative to the observer.

The most important and remarkable consequence of the transformation equation is the fact that $t \neq t'$. This means that the clocks in the two systems run at different rates. Let an observer in an aeroplane travel with a velocity along the positive direction of the X-axis is s'. Another observer at rest in system *s* finds that the journey takes a time (as measured according to his own time watch. To find time t' of the same journey for observer on the plane, taking the relation, $t' = a\ t - \frac{vx}{c^2}$ Putting $x = vt$

Since it is the distance travelled by the plane for the observer at rest in time t :

Hence, there are two proper times one for the observer at rest and other for the observer in motion in plane. The time of journey is greater for the first than for the second, which means that the movement of plane appears slower for the observer at rest, than the observer in the plane.

Sources of Energy

Energy is defined as the capacity to do work. It can be measured by its capacity to do work or by the actual work performed by the energy used.

Some forms of energy we generally come across are as under:

(i) Mechanical energy.

(ii) Heat energy.

(iii) Chemical energy.

(iv) Electrical energy.

(v) Light energy.

(vi) Magnetic energy.

(vii) Sound energy.

(viii) Atomic energy or nuclear energy.

Important source of energy are :

(i) Food

(ii) Fuels

(iii) Wind

(iv) Water

(v) Sun

(vi) Atomic energy.

Food : The food we eat provides us energy to maintain our body and to do work. Food taken by us undergoes various chemical changes and during these changes produces a lot of *chemical energy* as also *heat energy.* In addition to these various other kinds of energy also produced. Various types of energies produced are used for performing many type of works e.g., mechanical energy is used up for producing motion.

Fuel: A fuel is a substance which can produce a large amount of heat energy when burnt.

Wood is used as a fuel. In steam engine heat energy produced by burning *coal* is used to generate steam which is used to run the engine. Steam can be used to run various types of machines.

Fossil fuels are available in abundance in the bottom of the earth. Fossil fuels are nothing but patrified vegetable and animal remains burned under earth for quite long e.g. coke coal and petroleum. In modern times petroleum products are used as fuels to produce heat energy which is used to run various types of machines.

Biogas is the latest and cheapest source of energy. For producing bio-gas animal dung and other waste is collected in a big pit and allowed to be petrified. The pit is covered in a proper manner and the gases produced are carried out using pipes to households and used as fuel gas.

In big cities bio-gas is being produced from city wastes.

Wind Energy : Wind with high velocity is an important source of energy. Wind blowing with high velocity is used to run big Can like blades and the rotation of these blades is used for running mills. In the last century wind energy has been used to a very large extent in Holland. In India also efforts are under way to make maximum use of wind energy.

Water Energy : Running water is another important source of energy. In modern times big drawns are constructed for storing water which is then allowed to fall through big pipes to run turbines to produce electricity. This is called Hydro-electricity which is distributed over long distances and is used in various industries.

Solar Energy : Sun is the primary source of energy. The energy from sun gets converted into various forms which are more useful e.g., in the form of electricity with the help of 'solar cells'. It is then used for various purposes 'solar cells' are fitted in satellites and they produce sufficient electricity to send messages from these satellites.

These days solar cooker have also been developed which convert the solar energy to heat energy which is then used for cooking.

Atomic Energy or Nuclear Energy : It is the most modern and the big source of energy. Atomic energy can be obtained either by the process of *fusion* or by the process of *fission* of the nucleus. In fusion two small nuclei combine to form a bigger nuclei with release of enormous amount of energy where as in fission a nucleus breaks up evolving a large amount of energy.

To get energy by *fusion* a device is used to fuse two nuclei and it sets in a chain reaction releasing a large amount of energy. The chain reaction can be controlled by using *Atomic Reactors.* To control radioactivity thick wall of lead metal and concrete are constructed. The large amount of energy produced can be used by converting it into heat energy. This energy can be used to run turbines and produce electricity.

Fission energy can be produced by fission of a nucleus of a heavy metal such as $U^{2''}$. It is broken up by a high speed neutron into nuclei of barium and krepton together with three extra neutrons. These extra neutrons further breaks another nucleus of IP^{5} in the same way as above. In this way a chain reaction is set up evolving a large amount of energy. One gram of U2" can produce energy approximately equal to that obtained by burning 20,000 tons of coal.

Radioactivity

Soon after the discovery of X-rays in 1895, Henri Becquerel discovered that photographic plates (wrapped in black paper) which has been placed near uranium salts were fogged or blackened. He demonstrated that the fogging was caused by radiations emanating from the uranium salts. This spontaneous radiations by an element is called *radioactivity*. The elements which show this behaviour are known as *radioactive element e-g.* uranium, polonium, radium etc. At present we know of about 40 natural and a large number of artificial radioactive elements.

Radiations from Radioactive Substances : Radioactive emission consists of three different types of particles/ rays as demonstrated by Rutherford in 1902. These are known as α-rays, β-rays and Y-rays.

Alpha (α-) rays are composed of positively charged particles, *Beta (β-) rays* are composed of negatively charged particles and *gamma (γ-) rays* are neutral. Characteristic properties of these three types of rays are as under:

Characteristics of α Radiation :

1. They consist of positively charged particles which are four times as heavy as an atom of hydrogen i.e., they are He^{2+} particles.
2. They move with a velocity $\frac{1}{}$— th of the velocity of light rays. 10 The energy range 10 in 4-9 MCV.
3. They can penetrate only a thin layer of mica or aluminium.
4. They ionise the air through which they pass.
5. They cause luminiscence in ZnS screen and also affect the photographic plate.

Characteristics of β-radiations :

1. They consist of negatively charged particles known is B-particles which are merely electrons with same e/m value.
2. They move with a velocity that ranges between 33% of 99% of velocity of light.
3. They can penetrate through more thickness of aluminium foil as compared to a-rays (0.2 cm thickness).
4. Their ionising power is small.
5. Their effect on photographic plate is more in comparison to α-rays.
6. They have very little effect on ZnS plate.
7. They are more dangerous biologically as compared to α-rays.

Characteristics of γ -radiations

1. They are electrically neutral particles and actually short wavelength (10 pm) electromagnetic radiations similar to light.
2. They move with the same velocity as light (3×10^{10} cm/sec.).
3. Their penetrating power is maximum (100 cm).
4. They possess least ionising power.
5. Their effect on photographic plate is least.
6. They have practically no effect on ZnS plate.
7. Biologically they are more dangerous as compared to α-rays and Y-rays.

Types of Radioactivity

Radioactivity is known to be of two types :

(i) Natural Radioactivity, and

(ii) Artificial or Induced Radioactivity.

Natural Radioactivity: Naturally occurring elements e.g. uranium, polonium, radium etc., keep on emitting α-, β- and γ-radiations from their nuclei and changing to some other elements. This spontaneous change of naturally occurring elements to some other elements by emission of some nuclear particles is called natural radioactivity.

In natural radioactivity only a single nucleus is involved in its changes. Only heavier elements undergo natural radioactive changes.

***Artificial or Induced Radioactivity** : A process by which an element is converted into a new radioactive isotope of a known element by artificial means is called artificial or induced radioactivity.* In this phenomenon an unstable isotope is first produced which decays to a stable isotopes by emission of a position.

The artificial production of radio elements was first achieved by Curie and Joliot in 1934 during the bombardment of boron, magnesium and aluminium with a-particles.

$${}_5B^{10} + {}_2He^4 \text{ ------------> } {}_7N^{13} + {}_0N^1$$

$$\downarrow 10 \text{ min}$$

$${}_6C^{13} + {}_1e^0$$

$${}_{12}Mg^{24} + {}_2He^4 \text{ ------------> } {}_{14}Si^{27} + {}_0N^1$$

$$\downarrow 7 \text{ min}$$

$${}_{13}Al^{27} + {}_1e^0$$

$${}_{13}Al^{27} + {}_2He^4 \text{ ------------> } {}_{15}P^{30} + {}_0N^1$$

$$\downarrow 3 \text{ min}$$

$${}_{14}Si^{30} + {}_1e^0$$

Artificial Nuclear Transmutation

The first artificial transmutation was achieved by Rutherford in 1915. He bambarded ${}_7N^{14}$ with α-particles. The α-particles were emitted by ${}_{84}PO^{214}$.

The nuclear reaction can be written as :

$$^{14}_{7}N + ^{4}_{2}He \longrightarrow ^{17}_{8}O + ^{1}_{1}H$$

Difficulties in Transmutation : The reaction was very slow. This was attributed to the repulsion between the positively charged α-particles and the target nucleus which is also positively charged.

To overcome this repulsion, the bombarding particles were given very high energy with the help of various types of particle accelerators.

The particle accelerators used are :

(i) Linear accelerators.

(ii) Cyclotron.

(iii) Synchroton.

To produce new elements by transmutation the nuclei of some elements are bombarded with α-particles or some other particles. When positively charged particles are used for bombardment the reaction was found to be slow due to repulsion between the positively charged particle used for bombardment and the target nucleus. To overcome this repulsion the positively charged particles are given high energies before using them for bombarding atomic nuclei to produce new elements.

To bring about transmutation α-particles ($^{4}_{2}$ He), protons ($^{1}_{1}$H), deutrons ($^{2}_{1}$D) and neutrons ($^{1}_{0}$n) etc., are used. Some heavier nuclei have also been used to bring about artificial transmutation.

Neutrons are more useful as a bombarding particle because of their neutral nature. Since they do not carry any positive charge so they are not repelled by the nucleus. This makes them more useful.

Valves and Transistors

The Diode : It is the simplest radio tube which was introduced by Sir Fleming in 1904.

The diode is based upon the phenomenon *of thermionic emission* and *Edison effect* i.e. when a material is suitably heated, electrons are ejected. These are attracted to a plate maintained at a positive potential in the vicinity of the material, and as electric current is generated.

A *diode valve* consists of a highly evacuated glass bulb containing two elements. *Cathode* which is usually a fine wire of tungsten. It may be directly or indirectly heated type. The filament is coated with a thin layer of barium or strontium or caesium oxide. It has to be heated to about 800°C for obtaining a large supply of electrons. *Plate* which is generally a hollow metallic cylinder of nickel, molybdenum or iron. It surrounds the filament completely. The plate serves as the collector of electrons.

The bulb is mounted on our *insulated base* provided with base pins to which terminals of the electrodes are connected. The tube can be fitted in a socket with the help of *base pins.*

Diode can be used as a *rectifier.* A rectifier is a device used for converting alternating current/voltage into direct current or voltage. The diode valve can be used as a rectifier in two ways viz., as a *half wave rectifier* and a *full wave rectifier.*

Half-wave rectifier involves a lot of wastage of energy and hence is not in much use.

The Triode : It is essentially a modification over the diode value. Dr. Lee De Forest in 1907, introduced a (bird element called *control grid* to make the diode more useful for a variety of purposes. Triode valve is also based upon the phenomenon of thermionic emission and Edison effect. It consists of highly evacuated glass tube containing three elements *Cathode, Control grid* and *Plate.*

The *grid* is generally placed closer to the filament than to the plate.

The glass bulb is mounted on an *insulating base* provided with *brass pins* to which the terminal of three elements are connected. The tube can be Fitted in a *socket* with the help of the base pins.

A triode can be used as an *amplifier* as also as an *Oscillator.* An *amplifier* is a device which is used for increasing the amplitude of variation of an A,C. signal. Amplifiers can be classified as voltage amplifiers and power amplifiers. An *oscillator* is a generator of an alternating current, usually of high frequency and constant amplitude. An oscillator may be taken as a device which converts d.c., energy drawn from battery into a.c. energy of high frequency.

Junction Transistor : A transistor is a semiconductor device obtained by growing either a very thin layer of N-type crystal between two much thicker P-type layers or thin layer of P-type crystal between two much thicker N-type layers. The first type is called P-N-P transistor and second type is called N-P-N transistor.

Transistors can be used as amplifier and also as oscillator.

12

The Curriculum

To be dissatisfied with the existing curriculum is natural in a keen and up-to-date teacher of any subject, particularly if, like chemistry, that subject is itself undergoing change. Such dissatisfaction provides the impulse for reform of science curriculum within school and leads, usually gradually, to changes in both content and teaching strategy. During 1950*s considerable amounts of money were made available in several countries for large scale reforms. Large scale curriculum development stated in the united states in 1950's and were taken up in Britain in the 1960's. During 1960's curriculum reforms were initiated in many countries all over the world. It would not be an exaggeration to say that the changes in school chemistry that have occurred on a world-wide scale during the 1960's and 1970's have greatly exceeded those of the previous fifty years.

Gist of Lessons

Curriculum is a gist of lessons and topics which are expected to be covered in a specified period of time in any class. However, this traditional concept of curriculum has undergone a change in modern times. Now curriculum refers to the totality of experiences that a child receives through various class-room activities as also from activities in library, laboratory, work shop, assembly hall, play fields etc. Thus according to modern concept curriculum includes the whole life of the school. TTius those activities which were previously referred to as co-curricular or extra-curricular activities have now become curricular activities.

According to this concept the curriculum can be considered to include the subject-matter, various co-curricular activities etc.

Curriculum is derived from Latin word "currere" meaning "to run." Thus curriculum in the medium to realise the goals and objectives of teaching a particular course of study.

Science Curriculum

Before venturing to form a curriculum in science for being taught in our schools we have to take into consideration the kind of school population and other requirements. We shall also have to keep in mind the aim of teaching science in our schools. It is our endeavour to include in the science curriculum various natural phenomenon, physical laws and some simple applications of science that we come across in our eveiy day life. Moreover since knowledge of science in the basis of various vocational courses (e.g., medicines and engineering etc.) so the currimculum in science must also include such topics as are required for success in such a vocational course.

For formation of curriculum in science we can easily classify the school population in two classes as under :

(i) Those students who complete their education at the primary or middle stage, and

(ii) Those who continue in high/higher secondary schools.

Only a small fraction of the students who continue their education in high/higher secondary school offer for science courses.

The curriculum in science should be different for the above two classes of school population. For those students who are not likely to continue with education after middle stage we should offer a general science course that may be of use to them as a part of sound liberal education. For those students who are likely to continue with science subjects at high/higher secondary stage we should offer a course that provides specialised knowledge of one or more branches of science.

If we look at the existing science curriculum we find it to be defective as it is a hotch-potch mixture of various branches of science. It appears that it has no definite goals to achieve and so if defeats the very purpose of teaching science. It burdens the students mind with dead information and does not provide him any encouragement for taking up creative and useful activities.

The Secondary Education Commission (1953) refers to the criticism of the existing curriculum as under :

(i) It is narrowly conceived curriculum..

(ii) It is theoretical and bookish.

(iii) It is overcrowded.

(iv) It does not provide rich and significant subject-matter.

(v) In it there is inadequate provision for practical work.

(vi) It fails to develop a balanced personality.

(vii) It fails to cater to the various needs and capacities of adolescents.

(viii) It is an examination dominated curriculum.

The Kothari Commission (1966) also considered it and according to it the dissatisfaction with science curriculum in our schools may be due to the following two factors :

(i) The tremendous explosion in knowledge, in various branches of science, that has occurred in recent years. This explosion in knowledge has led to reformulation of some of the basic concepts in physical sciences, biological sciences and social sciences. This advancement in knowledge of science has intended the already existing gulf between the school and the university in major academic disciplines.

(ii) There is a rethinking in the duration of education that is imparted in ordinary schools. There is a unanimity in the views of educationist all of whom now favour the increase in the period of general education thereby postponing the entry into specialised courses of study. This has necessitated the introduction of some more significant topics in an already over packed school curriculum. For this we have to discard some topics from the existing curriculum.

Principles of Curriculum Formation

There are certain basic principles of curriculum planning which should form the basis for the formation of a good science curriculum. These are:

1. The principle of child centredness: The curriculum should be based on the present needs and circumstances of the child.
2. Curriculum should provide a fulness of experience for children.
3. The curriculum should be dynamic and not static.
4. It should be related to every day life.
5. It must take into account the economic aspect of life of the people to whom an educational institution belongs.
6. The curriculum should be realistic and rationalistic.
7. While forming the curriculum a balance be struck between the education of nature and education of man.
8. It should lay emphasis on learning to live rather than on living to learn.
9. In curriculum such activities must be included, which help in preserving and transmitting the traditions knowledge and standards of conduct on which our civilisation depends.
10. It should be elastic and flexible.
11. It should be well-integrated.

12. It should provide both for uniformity and variety.
13. It should be able to serve the needs of community.

As far as science curriculum is concerned it should be elastic and variable, child-centred, community-centred, activity-centred. It should be such as to be use for adjustment in life and helps to integrate the activities of die child with his environment. It should be helpful to conserve and transmit the traditions, culture and civilisation. It must help in arousing the creative faculties of the children.

Approaches to Curriculum Planning

There are a number of approaches to curriculum planning in science. The extremes of such approaches are given in Table.

Actually no single way of curriculum planning exclusively based on one approach can fulfil the curricular needs of pupils. It is always better to combine different approaches to plan an effective curriculum in science.

The Extreme of Curriculum Formation

One extreme	*Other extreme*
Integrated	Disciplinary
Child-centred	Teacher-centred
Flexible	Structured
Process-based	Content-based
Conceptual	Factual

Curriculum Styles

Curriculum can be classified as :

(i) Instrumental curriculum.

(ii) Interactive curriculum.

(iii) Individualistic curriculum.

Instrumental Curriculum

In this type of curriculum more emphasis is placed on the utility value or vocational value of science. It makes learning an intense competition among students.

The basic approach in such a curriculum is disciplinary and emphasises the acquisition of knowledge or, information. The role of teacher is that of a dominant teacher in such a curriculum.

Interactive Curriculum

This type of curriculum is society oriented and lays more emphasis on the social development of child. In this type of curriculum class-room instructions becomes an interactive or a cooperative process. The approach is interdisciplinary and the curriculum is loosely structured and consists of learning packages.

Individualistic Curriculum

In this type of curriculum more emphasis is placed on the personal development of the individual and it is based on interdisciplinary approach. It helps to develop creativity in the individual. This type of curriculum is based on self-calculation by the student.

Various Curricula Projects

In this section an attempt will be made to describe some of the chemistry curricula that have been developed over last thirty years or so. An attempt will also be made to give reasons for their introduction as also the way in which they were introduced.

The three early projects in chemistry were the following:

1. Chemical Bond Approach (C.B.A.) in United States.
2. Chemical Education Material Study (CHEM study) in United States.
3. Nuffield O-level chemistry in United Kingdom.

These projects influenced the mechanism for science curriculum reform in many countries through out 1960's and beyond.

Though there are a number of significant differences between the three projects cited above but they all arose at a time when a shortage of qualified scientific personnel was felt worid-wide. Keeping in view, the short comings of the existing curricula all these projects emphasised the following:

(i) Updating chemistry in the light of modem knowledge of the subject.

(ii) Giving the students a good understanding of the subject.

To achieve these ends the new curricula placed particular emphasis on such concepts as *periodicity* and *the mole.* They also incorporated some major chemical ideas underlying the *structure of materials, chemical bonding, kinetics* and *energetics.* These are sometimes referred to as "concept-based" which indicates the attention given to the principles of chemistry in their development. To make aware the students about the importance of chemistry topics like plastics, synthetic fibres, elastomers, detergents, drugs and insecticides were also included.

These curricula also emphasised the role ofpracticals (laboratory work) in chemistry which was seen as having a dual role. Firstly, to illustrate and 'make real' the chemistry being taught and secondly, to encourage scientific mode of thinking.

These projects were adopted by schools because of participation of leading scientists like Glenn Seaborg (nobel prize winner) in United States and Sir Ronald Nybolm in United Kingdom.

Regional Projects

In 1960's, in addition to national projects for curriculum development a number of projects were started to serve a laige regional area consisting of several countries. One such project was file *Unesco Pilot Project for Chemistry Teaching in Asia.* This project was aimed at bringing together chemical educators from various Asian countries in touch with one another and with their counterparts at other places in the world for the purpose of providing the necessary training in curriculum development

The well-equipped laboratory at Bangkok in Thailand served as a regional meeting and working centre. The 'study groups' located in each Asian country provided information and consultancy services on innovations in chemistry teaching. The project lasted from 1964 to 1970.

Another regional project was the one which came to be known as the *school science project in East African Countries* of Kenya, Uganda and the United Republic of Tanzania. On the initiative of science teachers of these countries a British organisation then known as the Centre for Curriculum Renewal and Educational Development Overseas (CREDO) helped and G. Van Praagh ran courses for chemistry teachers. At a conference held in Nairobi in 1968, representatives from Uganda, Kenya and United Republic of Tanzania agreed to work together to produce new, 4-year courses in biology, chemistry and physics. These courses were intended to be up-to-date and relevant to the needs of the countries concerned. They were to be so designed as to stress understanding and for this purpose a substantial laboratory based component is to be incorporated in them. For curriculum preparation the ideas found in Nuffeld Chemistry Project were extensively used. Drafts were prepared and tried in some schools and on the basis of feed-back they were revised. United Republic of Tanzania withdrew from the scheme in 1970. In Kenya and Uganda now a decision has taken to fuse the traditional and newer courses into a single programme of study.

The project, helped to raise the standard of awareness of and interest in, modem chemistry curricula in East Africa. It also helped to the publication of easily read background readers such as *Salt in East Africa—Fermentation and Distillation.* CREDO played the role of coordinator.

The decision to choose between 'traditional' and *new' curricula was left to schools. They may be considered as a good decision keeping in view the difficulties involved in preparing all teachers adequately and in a short-time, for large-scale science curriculm reform.

National Projects

Modern Chemistry Project in Malaysia is one such project. It not only concerns with development of modern curriculum but also concerns to help teachers to use it effectively, to improve the provision of laboratories and equipment and to produce a more appropriate form of examination for students who complete the course.

Another example is the nationally based chemistry project of Cuba. The new curriculum for schools in Cuba was developed with the assistance of specialists from USSR and the GDR. The new curricula is based upon two cycles, the first in grades 8 and 9 (two lessons per week) and the second in grades 10 to 12 (three lessons per week). In the first type, students study the principal types of inorganic compounds, their properties and general behaviour. They are also introduced to some fundamental chemical concepts and phenomenon. It includes teaching of the periodic law, electronic structure of atom and introduction to organic chemistry. The second cycle contains theory of electrolytic dissociation, energetics, chemical kinetics and chemical equilibria and organic compounds. The selection of content clearly illustrates the importance of Cuba's developing chemical industry.

Advanced Projects

Important advanced courses include those developed in Thailand and in India.

Thailand Project : New advanced chemistry course which is now in use in all secondary schools in Thailand is built around the chemical themes illustrated in the Figure.

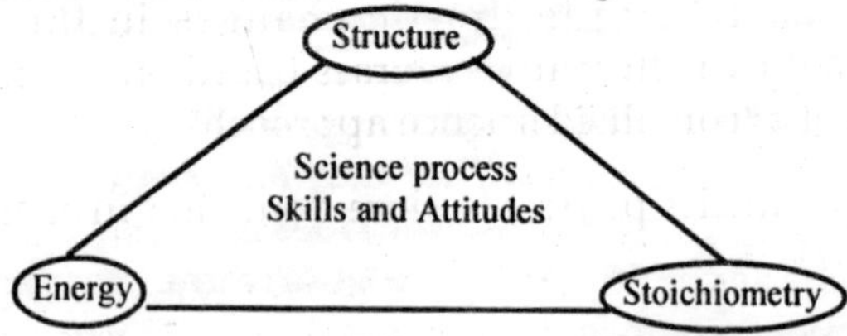

Fig. Theme for chemistry curricula, grades 11 and 12 flluilxnd).

There were many difficulties in implementation of the new curriculum. However, inspite various difficulties including those of finances the programme has been implemented across the whole of the Thailand. It has been well-received and no need has been felt to make much revision in the course.

Indian Project. National Council of Educational Research and Training (NCERT) has developed a model senior-secondary level curriculum which has been adopted either as such or with slight modifications by a large number of states in India.

In a major change concerning traditional chemistry courses in India, in the new curriculum chemistry is presented as a unified subject. There is no traditional classification as physical, inorganic or organic chemistry. Some basic chemical concepts are developed in the beginning and these are later on applied during the study of elements and their compounds. An effort has also been made to relate macroscopic behaviour to microscopic behaviour. Two separate text books have been developed for classes XI and XII. Though some traditional open-ended and environmental investigations have been retained in the laboratory part of the course but the course is basically designed to develop; skills, scientific attitudes and future training for research. Keeping in mind the interests of students who are likely to join vocational and professional courses an effort has been made to blend facts and theory by putting emphasis on the applications of the principles rather than their derivation. Equal emphasis has been given to chemical principles and descriptive chemistry.

Chemistry course at secondary level has also been revised. A review committee set up by the Ministry of Education to reduce work load, made drastic changes in the course recommending two alternative courses based on 'disciplinary approach' and a 'combined science approach'.

In some countries physics is more dominant in curriculum than chemistry.

In many countries, curriculum innovation in l°70's became increasingly involved with chemistry, not so much as a single subject, but as a part of a larger whole, chemistry now forms a part of courses in:

(i) physical science,

(ii) general science, and

(iii) integrated science.

Physical Science course adopted in some countries combines physics and chemistry courses together with omission of some subject matter.

General Science course combines the courses of physics, chemistry and biology. This type of course was based on the idea that general science should form an essential part of general education of all young people but unfortunately general science to meet the ideals.

Component of Integrated Science

Some difficulty arises in the terminology in using 'General Science', 'science' and 'combined science' as all these have similar meaning. It may be clearly understood the 'integrated science' is in no way possesses a higher degree of integrtion than that possessed by 'science' or 'general science'.

Integrated science is generally more closely integrated usually with an element of social and environmental sciences. Most of the applications and social implications of science (e.g. Fertilisers, motor cars etc.) involve more than one science. Integrated science is widely associated with the movement to teach science for the majority. Making use of integrating theme 'Investigating the Earth' was an ambitions effort which exerted a considerable influence on the junior secondary curriculum in the United States. It includes structure, properties of matter and chemistry of the oceans, soils, minerals and atmosphere. This curriculum inspired many texts. Many countries are now adopting some form of integrated science, particularly in the early years of secondary school.

We can conclude the discussion by observing that despite disappointment with outcomes of some earlier projects, the 1980s brought a renewed commitment to science curriculum reform. In comparison to the earlier reforms the recent science curriculum initiatives identify the teacher or the teacher and learner as the focus of the reform so that curriculum improvement becomes essentially a matter of teacher development. Some curriculum initiatives have tried to accommodate 'metacognition' by fostering students' knowledge and awareness of, and thereby control over, their own learning.

The changed social and political context of 1980's has also had a marked effect upon school science education. Now we have courses which arc concerned with science e.g., technology and society (STS) and the Chemical Education for the Public Understanding of Science Project (CEPUP).

However, one trend has been remarkedly constant, that towards laboratory work. Actually speaking, the school chemistry curriculum, in many countries, is now essentially laboratory based.

Curriculum in Physics

A study conducted by Unesco in China about teaching of physics brings out the following facts about the teaching of physics in schools in China.

Purpose and Content : The purpose of physics teaching in secondary schools is to enable students to grasp systematically the basic knowledge of physics needed for further study of modern science and technology and to understand its applications. In addition it should help them to acquire experiment skills, develop the ability to think and use mathematics to solve physical problems, cultivate a diaelectrical materialistic view point and make them aware of the need to study hard and to struggle for modernisation, along socialist lines, of industry, agriculture, national defence and science and technology in China.

In that country the junior school physics includes topics like measurement, motion and force, density, pressure, buoyancy, simple machines, work, energy, elementary optics, heat, states of matter, static electricity, current electricity etc.

In senior secondary physics the topics included are: force,

equilibrium of bodies, rectilinear motion, the interaction of bodies, collinear motion, universal gravitation, mechanical energy, vibrations and waves, molecular motion theory, heat and work, properties of gases, liquids and solids, electromagnetic induction, a.c., atoms and atomic nuclei, the reflection and refraction of light etc.

In India NCERTwas established in 1961. This body has developed new national science curriculum programmes which have been implemented. However, some other agencies that have helped in the science curriculum improvement programme involviug physics are as under :

1. Unesco Planning Mission,
2. Indian Education Commission,
3. Ishwar Bhai Patel Committee, and
4. New Policy on Education.

Unesco Planning Mission

Important recommendations made by this mission can be summarised as follows:

(i) Learning of physics be made compulsory.

(ii) More time be devoted to impart elementary knowledge of modern areas of physics like atomic physics, nuclear physics, social state physics, electronics etc.

(iii) More emphasis be put on the practical applications of physics.

(iv) Learning activities be built into the teaching of physics.

(v) The teaching of physics should start as a part of general science from class VI.

(vi) Physics be taught as a separate subject from class XI.

Indian Education Commission

The recommendations made by Indian Education Commission (1964-66) about the physics education in schools can be summarised as follows;

(i) Physics education should form a part of environmental education in primary classes.

(ii) Physics be taught as a separate school subject in middle classes. In these classes more emphasis be laid on acquisition of knowledge, logical thinking etc.

(iii) In secondary classes provision be made for teaching of physics as a compulsory subject. In these classes the subject should cover wider areas with deep penetration in the subject-matter.

(iv) Physics be allowed as an elective subject at senior secondary stage and be allowed to only those students who are interested to offer it as an elective subject.

Ishwar Bhai Patel Committee

Following in the summary of important recommendation made by this committee regarding the teaching of physics in our schools.

(i) Physics be taught in primary classes (I to V) as a part of environmental studies and approximately 20% of school time be spent on teaching of environmental studies.

(ii) In middle classes (VI to VIII) physics be taught as a part of integrated science. About 4-5 hours per week be allotted to the science teaching at this stage.

(iii) In secondary classes (IX and X) physics be taught as a part of general science course. Such a general science course may have two options i.e., course I and course II and student be free to choose one option. 4-5 hours per week be given to teaching of this course in schools option I (course I) be allowed only to such students who intend to continue to study physics after class X. In these classes some practicals in physics be also included in syllabus.

(iv) In senior secondary classes (XI and XII) physics be taught as a separate elective subject.

New Policy on Education (NPE)

New policy on education announced in 1986 is a bold

experiment. It is for the first time in India that education has been taken as a tool for human resource development. In this new policy more emphasis has been placed on sound science education as becomes quite clear by some of the quotes we come across while going through this document. Some lines from it are reproduced to illustrate the point,

— Science education will be strengthened so as to develop in the child well-defined abilities and values such as the spirit of enquiry, the courage to question and an aesthetic sensibility.

— Science education programmes will be designed to enable the child to acquire problem solving and decision making skills and to discover the relationship of science with health agriculture and other aspects of life. Every effort will be made to extend science education to the vast numbers who have remained outside the pale of formal education.

In view of the above the following suggestions are given:

(i) In physics curriculum more emphasis be put on scientific method and an attempt be made to develop scientific attitude and scientific temper in the students.

(ii) Upto secondary level integrated and interdisciplinary approach be encouraged.

(iii) Science foundation courses be taken up through open university system.

(iv) At senior secondary stage physics be taught as a separate elective subject.

Emphasising the use of multi-media educational technology for imparting science education the NPE document says.

— Modern communication technologies have the potential to bypass several stages and sequences in the process of development encountered in earlier decades. Both the constraints of time and distance at once become manageable. In order to avoid structural dualism, modern educational technology must reach out to most distant areas and the most deprived sections of beneficiaries simultaneously with the areas of comparative affluence and ready availability.

— The media have a profound influence onthc minds of children as well as adults; some of the tend to encourage consumerism, violence etc., and have deleterional effects.....An active movement will be started to promote production of children's film of high quality and usefulness.

— Institutions will be encouraged to generate resources using their capacities to provide services to the community and industry. They will be equipped with update learning resources, library facilities and computer facilities.

Maximum use will be made of available infrastructures.

Physics Education and NPE

NCERT undertook the revision of science text-books in order to make them adhere to the various recommendations of NPE. The Revised National Curriculum (1987) in its framework provides for science education in the form of instructional package upto middle school level. The content and activities included in the book are so arranged that they inculcate knowledge, skills and attitudes on the basis of specific objectives. The book states its philosophy in the following lines. "This book (the physics textbook) is not about facts. Rather, it is to show you how we discover facts in the light of that exhilarating experience, we begin to make our lives manageable and fulfilling. We must organise our activities so that it is with understanding of the natural world."

At another point NCERT says about physics textbooks, "This book (the physics textbook) is to provoke you to pose questions by showing how scientists before you asked those questions that led to great discoveries. It is to lead you to determine ways how to answer their questions and varify their correctness."

In light of the NPE document physics is to be taught as a part of integrated science course upto class X and it be studied as a separate subject in classes XI and XII. NCERT framed the syllabus for classes IX and X where physics forms a part of nature study. For classes XI and XII the syllabus has been prepared in consultation with univeisity professors. The main features of this syllabus in physics can be summarised as under;

(i) An attempt has been made to give a syllabus that involves students actively in the study of physics.

(ii) Enough provision has been made to allow for supplementary activities, demonstrations and learning outside the class-room.

(iii) There is an attempt to keep a link between the work done in theory class and experiments performed in physics laboratory. In this way an attempt has been made to bring out the fact that physics is an experimental science.

(iv) There is an attempt to correlate the physics curriculum with laboratory work.

In the laboratory manual various experiments have been classified as :

(i) 'D' : These are only to be demonstrated by the teacher. However, if possible such experiments may be done collectively by the class and then a discussion be arranged.

(ii) 'E' : The experiments so designated are meant for students to be done by them individually in the laboratory. These experiments are to be recorded by them in their practical note books.

This practical note-book duly signed by the teacher has to be presented by every student at the time of annual practical examination.

(iii) 'SE' : The experiment so designated arc such as can be completed in 20-30 minutes by the students. The main aim of these experiments is to develop in students manipulative and manual skills.

(iv) 'A' : These are activities that are to be take up out of class-room and such activities are to be pursued by individual student at home.

Critical Study of Syllabus

The syllabus in physics that is currently in use has been prepared by NCERT and is known as *New Pattern Physics Syllabus.* This syllabus is open to the following criticism.

(i) Ordinary student finds a wide gap in the physics education when he moves from class X to class XI.

(ii) It adopts narrative style and it is responsible for the loss of 'technical' touch in the physics textbooks.

(iii) The number of exercises and problems to be solved, as given in the books, is so large that solving them needs a lot of time and energy which kills the joy of learning physics.

(iv) The textbooks of physics for classes XI and XII are voluminous. Actually a physics textbook should be snappy and illustrative.

(v) Most of the diagrams given in NCERT text-books are not illustrated properly. Many of them have no labelling and some of them have not even been captioned.

Curriculum in General Science Content

Keeping in view that the major aim of teaching science is to acquaint the students with himself and his environment (i.e., things around him), it is desirable if the student is imparted a working knowledge of almost all the main branches of science. To achieve this the general science course should include topics from the following branches of science:

(i) Physics,

(ii) Chemistry,

(iii) Botany,

(iv) Zoology,

(v) Geography,

(vi) Physiology,

(vii) Astronomy,

(viii) Geology, and

(ix) Home Science (for girls).

For selecting different topics, from various branches of science, for inclusion in general science curriculum the following points be given due consideration.

(i) Content should be selected in terms of broad concepts and principles of science.

(ii) Content should be related to the different age-groups and daily life.

(iii) It should be able to serve the needs of community.

(iv) It should be very closely associated with the environment.

(v) It should be such as could be dealt within the available time under existing conditions of staff, equipment etc.

Arrangement of Material

In case of general science curriculum the best arrangement is the one based on 'topics' or 'units' because such an arrangement provides a natural method of learning. In such an arrangement the 'units'should be such as are of immediate interest to the student and are related to the local environment and community. 'Topics'should arise out of environment and experiences of the pupil and the study material should be arranged around these topics in such a fashion that it brings about a closer integration between various branches of science. It should also bring about a greater correlation with life situations and every day experiences of the child.

The general science course for elementary schools can be organised around the following main units:

(i) Living things,

(ii) Earth and universe, and

(iii) Matter and Energy.

Alternatively it can be organised around the following main units:

(i) Our surroundings.
(ii) Nature of things.
(iii) Energy and work.
(iv) Life.
(v) Human machine.

The curriculum must include some experiments for the children in addition to subject-matter. It should also indicate various related activities for different topics. Following example illustrates it :

Content	Demonstration	Experiment	Activities
Unit			
Our surroundings			
(i) The earth, rocks and soil, different kinds of rocks and minerals	(i) Three classes of rocks (ii) Identification of minerals (iii) Making artificial rocks	(i) Study of some rocks (ii) Making a model of volcano	Visit to hilly and arid areas and collecting rocks and minerals

All-India Seminar on Science Teaching has suggested the following for bringing about a closer cooperation between various branches of science. The units be :

(i) Environment centred,
(ii) Life centred,
(iii) Environment and life centred.

Units based on Environment Based Topics :

Unit I	The atmosphere
Unit II	Water, Elixir of life
Unit III	The earth
Unit IV	Heat
Unit V	Light
Unit VI	Metals and non-metals

Unit VII	Work and energy
Unit VIII	Means of transport and communication
Unit IX	Plant and animal life
Unit X	The study of the Body Machine.

Unit based on Life-centred Topics :

Unit I	Importance of science in our life
Unit II	The air
Unit III	The water
Unit IV	The food
Unit V	The clothes
Unit VI	Tie homes
Unit VII	The machines
Unit VIII	Power and Energy
Unit IX	Protection from disease
Unit X	Biological resources
Unit XI	Mineral resources
Unit XII	Means of transport
Unit XIII	Means of communication
Unit XIV	Our universe
Unit XV	Story of life.

Units based on Environment and Life-centred Topics :

Unit I	Importance of science
Unit II	Human body, the machine and its working
Unit III	Our health
Unit IV	Our biological resources and their use for better living

Unit V	Our mineral resources and their use for better living
Unit VI	Energy and machines
Unit VTI	Time, measurement and mass production
Unit VIII	The weather
Unit IX	The solar system, stars and other universes
Unit X	Science in daily life
	(a) Heating our homes
	(b) Lighting our homes
	(c) Electronics in our homes
	(d) Sound in homes.

Curriculum in Science for Different Stages

Primary Stage : The students at primary stage are in the age group 5-10 and so they are quite immature. Thus they be given only a formal education in science. At this stage it is desirable to develop the subject-matter under the following heads:

(i) Living things

(ii) Universe •

(iii) Matter and Energy.

The curriculum must provide for some students activity in addition to the subject-matter. Of the estimated 100 hours allotted to teaching of science in a class about 20 hours be spent on excussions and visits, about 50 hours on projects and other activities and the remaining 30 hours be given to class from teaching.

Kothari Commission (1966) recommended as under :

(i) In lower primary classes, the focus should be on the child's environment—social, physical and biological.

(ii) In classes I and II accent should be on :

(a) cleanliness,

(b) formation of healthy habits,

(c) development of lower of observation.

(iii) In addition to emphasising the above qualities in classes lll and IV the information be provided about:

(a) Personal hygiene,

(b) Sanitation,

(c) Plants and animals in surroundings of the child,

(d) Air,

(e) Water,

(f) Weather,

(g) Earth,

(h) Simple Machines,

(i) Care of body, and

(j) Heavenly Bodies.

(iv) To provide direct and valuable experiences of natural phenomenon, it is recommended that school gardening be encouraged.

Middle Stage : At this stage it is desirable to place more emphasis to the acquisition of knowledge and the ability to think logically. It should also be the aim at this stage that a student is encouraged to draw conclusion and take decisions. It would be desirable if science at this stage is taught as physics, chemistry and biology etc. At this stage this disciplinary approach will be more effective.

Keeping in view the above recommendations of Kothari Commission *(1966)* science is taught as Physics, Chemistry and Biology in our schools.

However, now NCERT has framed a syllabus for integrated

science course from classes VI, VII and VIII and the outlines of this newly framed curriculum arc given below:

Integrated Science Curriculum

Objectives :

1. To put emphasis on the relevance of science to daily life.
2. To develop scientific attitudes.
3. To create an environment that is conducive to more reliance on the use of principles and practices of science.
4. To familiarise the students with different natural phenomena.
5. To emphasise the experimental nature of science.
6. To emphasise the unity of methods of various disciplines of science.

Nature of the Course : In this we have tried to integrate science with the environment of the child rather than making an artificial integration of various disciplines of science. The students with the background of general science at primary level, would, find this course as a continuation of their earlier knowledge. They will also be mentally prepared to offer science courses at secondary level. NCERT have developed Composite Integrated Science Kit alongwith text-books for classes VI, VII and VIII.

High School Stage : The recommendations of Kothari Commission (1966) are as under:

(i) In classes IX and X it would be desirable to introduce newer concepts of Physics, Chemistry and Biology. Moreover, the experimental approach to learning of science be emphasised at this stage.

(ii) It was also recommended that provisions be made for advanced courses in science subjects for talented students in some selected secondary schools. Such schools be provided with necessary facilities of staff and laboratories.

(iii) As far as possible science teaching in rural areas be linked to agriculture and in urban areas to technology.

The content of specialized science courses in Physics, Chemistry and Biology should be such as to useful for further vocational studies in the respective fields. An effort be made to present the subject-matter as a synthetic whole and not merely as collection of few principles and facts. Various examples and illustrations be given from daily life of students and from their local environment. For this purpose the subject-matter be arranged around broad based units.

National Policy on Education as given by Government of India states as under:

"With a view to the growth of the national economy, science education and research should receive high priority. Science and mathematics should form an integral part of general education till the end of school stage."

With the above policy statements in view new Integrated Science Curriculum were prepared by NCERT. Outlines of these are given below:

New Integrated Science Curriculum of N.C.E.R.T.

Class VI

1. Measurement,
2. Materials around us,
3. Separation of substances,
4. Changes around us,
5. Motion, force and pressure,
6. Simple machines,
7. The universe,
8. The living world,
9. Study of structures and functions in plants and animals,
10. Food and health,

11. Man's dependence on plants and animals and the balance of nature,
12. Environment,
13. Water, and
14. Energy.

Class VII

1. Motion, mass and friction,
2. Pressure and buoyancy,
3. Heat,
4. Light,
5. Sound,
6. Current Electricity,
7. Static Electricity,
8. Magnetism,
9. Nature and composition of substances,
10. Air,
11. Water,
12. Acids, bases and salts,
13. Preservation of self,
14. Population Explosion, and
15. Pollution.

Class VIII

1. Light,
2. Electricity,
3. Electrical energy,

4. Electrical magnetism,
5. Structure of atom,
6. Nuclear energy,
7. Carbon,
8. Our living world,
9. Cell and tissue,
10. Reproduction,
11. Growth and development,
12. Heredity and variation,
13. Organic evolution,
14. Materials,
15. Agricultural practices and implements,
16. Our crops,
17. Improvement of crop production,
18. Some useful plants and animals,
19. Animal husbandry,
20. Conservation of natural resources, and
21. Science for human welfare.

Questions

1. What do you mean by the term 'Curriculum'? How does it differ from term 'syllabus'? Discuss it with particular reference to science education.
2. Define curriculum? Discuss in brief various principles of curriculum construction.
3. Discuss recent trends in curriculum construction.
4. Give in brief the recommendations of Kothari

Commission regarding science curriculum at different stages of school education.

5. Discuss the role of CHEM and chemical bond approach in modernising physical science curriculum.

6. Write short notes on the following :

    (i) CHEM Efforts for curriculum improvement.

    (ii) Organisation of science curriculum of high school classes.

    (iii) Principles of curriculum construction.

13

Process of Evaluation

It has long been felt that for a successful curriculum development the assessment of students must be sensitive to the aims and objectives of curriculum. Judiciously employed assessment results can be used to evaluate curricula, particularly to determine difficulties. Evaluation is a new term in the field of education that has been introduced to replace the terms like testing or examination etc.

Evaluation has a wider meaning as compared to testing or examination. Concept of testing is very much limited in terms of objectives, scope, methodology etc., where as evaluation has a very wide meaning as it includes to access all educational outcomes and outputs which have been brought about by teaching-learning process. Recent trends in learning and evaluation link them to behavioural objectives specified for a course of study in chemistry. Actually a total change in behaviour of the learner related with all the three domains (conative, cognitive and affective) is expected by learning experiences provided to him.

In this chapter an attempt will be made to study the specific procedures for evaluating the effectiveness of chemistry teaching-learning.

Movement of Examination Reform

The sense of discontentment with the prevailing system of examination in India can be easily traced back to British days. A report submitted by Zakir Hussain Committee in 1938 recommended for longer duration test so as to cover the whole of the curriculum. The examination be given in such a form that would make marking objective and independent of individual judgement.

The examination committee of the Central Advisory Board of Education gave its report on, "Post-War Examination Developments in India" in 1944 and recommended as under "....every attempt should be made to devise and standardise objective-type tests for use in this country so that they may supplement and ultimately replace the old type of examinations."

These recommendations were never implemented and they remained on paper only.

After attaining independence in 1947, proper attention was given to examination reforms. Radhakiishnan Commission (The First Education Commission) on university education (1949) reported as under to bring to the fore the weaknesses essay-type examination prevailing in our universities.

"An unsound examination system Continues to dominate instructions to the detriment of a quickly expanding system of education. In our visits to universities we heard from teachers and students alike, the tale of how examinations have become the aim and end of education, how all instructions is subordinated to them, how they kill initiative in the teacher and the student, how capricious, invalid, unreliable and inadequate they are and how they tend to corrupt the moral standards of university life".

"....we are convinced that if we are to suggest one single reform in university education, it should be that of examination."

The Secondary Education Commission (1953) also

recommended a reform in system of examinations. In this report we find, "In order to reduce the element of subjectivity of essay-type tests, objective tests of attainment should be widely introduced side by side. Moreover, the nature of the tests and type of questions should be thoroughly changed. They should be such as to discourage cramming and encourage intelligent understanding."

Another commission commonly known as Kothari Commission (1966) made the following remarks in its report, about reforms in examinantion system.

"....but the task is a stupendous one, and it will take considerable time for new measures to make their impact on objectives, learning experiences and evaluation procedures in schools education."

The commission made many recommendations for lower primary, middle and other examinations.

Examination reforms have also been advocated with National Policy on Education (1968). It states, "A major goal of examination reform should be to improve the reliability and validity of examinations and to make evaluation a continuous process aimed at helping the student to improve his level of achievement rather than at 'certifying' the quality of his performance at a given moment of time."

Significance of Education

In words of Kothari Commission (1966) "Evaluation is a continuous process, it forms an integral part of the total system of education, and is intimately related to educational objectives. It exercises a great influence on the pupil's study habits and teachers methods of instruction and thus help not only to measure educational achievement but also to improve it the techniques of evaluation are means of collecting evidences about the students development in desirable directions."

Evaluation, thus may work as a connecting bridge between the objectives of teaching science and the ways and means of attaining these objectives in the form of learning experiences, learning methods and learning environment.

A students' learning is evaluated in terms of the extent of achievement and then behavioural objectives specified for a course of study in chemistry. Behavioural objectives are specific, observable and measurable aim and serve as a guide for learning and are desired for the eventual achievement of a general objective.

Relationship among Objectives, Learning Experiences and Evaluation

The learning experiences for any topic in a subject are designed keeping in view the study of that topic, These learning experiences are likely to bring about behavioural changes in the learner as specified through different objectives. Evaluation of students' performance is generally done in terms of marks or grades competitively. Sometimes students may be compared with some absolute performance standard instead of making comparison with other students of a given group. Thus, there are two kinds of evaluation:

1. Criterion-referenced evaluation, and
2. Norm-referenced evaluation.

Criterion-Referenced Evaluation

It assesses the students performance in term of a specified performance standard or criterion without any mention of the performance levels of the other students of the group. This evaluation method is related to mastery and developmental tests.

Norm Referenced Evaluation

It assessed the students performance relative to other students of the group. Students are awarded marks and relative ranks in this method of evaluation.

Purpose of Evaluation

Evaluation fulfills the following purposes:

(i) It assesses the extent of learning by students and gives them the feed-back about their performance.

(ii) It gives feed-back to the teacher about the learning gaps of the students. It also provides the teacher a feed-back about the quality of his class-room instructions.

(iii) It provides the student an opportunity to show his worth.

(iv) It serves as a screening tool for selecting students for special purposes.

Our evaluation has another goal besides assisting the teacher in assessing and modifying her teaching procedures. This goal of *self-evalualion* is not solely for the students. As teacher and students actively engage in all levels of a study such as initial planning, organising and carrying out activities they can be guided in developing ability to evaluate themselves. Knowing the general and specific goals can aid the pupil in checking himself all along the way. This makes the learner an active participant in class-room activities. It also places some of the responsibility on him for learning and assessing what and how much he has learned. Self-guided evaluation stimulates healthy and realistic achievement goals, A logical first step self-evaluations is setting up of realistic goals. These goals for chemistry in elementary schools are:

(i) *Functional understandings* such as concepts, principles, generalisations, and the facts needed.

(ii) *Problem Solving Skills* such as defining problems, proposing hypothesis and techniques necessary for the solution of the problems, observational techniques, discussion and interpretations skills.

(iii) *Scientific attitudes,* interests and appreciation such as open mindedness and humanity.

The easiest area to evaluate is functional understanding because a rich variety of tests are well-known and are widely used in elementary schools. Before we proceed to actual discussion of these tests let us consider the criterion of a good examination and pre-requisites of a physical test.

Criteria of a Good Examination

Though a variety of tests are available to test the functional understanding of the child but for true assessment of such aspects of growth as the elements of reflective thinking, scientific attitudes, resourcefulness, creativeness of such other objectives or interests we require more precise and accurate instruments of evaluation. According to most of the psychologists and educationalists the following are essential criteria of satisfactory evaluation.

1. *Validity* : Any good test should measure what it claims to measure.

2. *Reliability:* A good test is one that is reliable i.e., it gives same rating to a candidate even if he is examined by different examines and even at different times.

3. *Objectivity : A* test can be considered objective if the scoring of the test is not affected in any way by the examiner's personal judgment. Thus, the opinion, bias or judgment of the examiner can have no influence on the results of an objective test.

4. *Comprehensiveness:* By comprehensiveness of a test we mean that it covers the whole or nearly the whole course content and the questions are uniformly distributed to cover the course content.

5. *Practicability* : A test is called practicable if it can be easily administered and is acceptable to average examiner. While preparing such a test, the time and cost of administration must be taken into consideration. The test should be usable and should serve a definite need in the situation in which it is used.

6. *Interpretiability* ; A test can be considered as interpretable if its scores can be used and interpreted in terms of a common base having natural or accepted meaning.

7. *Easy to Administer:* A good test should be easy to administer so definite provision be made for collection and preparation of test material. It should **give** simple, clear and precise instructions.

Pre-requisites of a Good Test

There are certain pre-requisites for preparing a good test. These are as under:

Aspects	*Description*
Aims	Acquisition of knowledge of various concepts and skills.
	Development of scientific attitude and interest.
	Development of laboratory skills.
	Highlighting the application of chemistry in every day life and technology.
	Development of skills of information processing, observation, enquiry and design-acquisition of problem-solving abilities.
Objectives	
(a) Knowledge:	**Recall and recognition of factual information such as:**
	(i) Definitions of various terms.
	(ii) Statement of laws, principles, rules, conventions etc.
	(iii) Description of construction and working of devices and instruments.
	(iv) Description of events, processes and phenomenon.
	(v) Recognising the parts of devices, instruments, appliances and apparatus.
	(vi) Identifying known physical phenomenon, events and occurrences.
(b) Comprehension:	Understanding facts, laws etc.
	(i) Comparing and contrasting various phenomenon.
	(ii) Locating errors, limitations and defects.
	(iii) Illustrating scientific phenomenon.
	(iv) Reasoning events on the basis of scientific principles and laws.

Aspects	*Description*
(c) Applications :	Using knowledge in various situations. (i) Solving numerical problems. (it) Making use of various scientific laws in various situations and events. (iii) Relating various scientific variables-using psycho-motor skills.
(d) Skills:	(i) Laying out an experimental set-up. (ii) Drawing diagrams, graphs, histograms, flow charts etc. (iii) Reading various measuring instruments.
(e) Analysis :	Breaking up information into parts to reach conclusions: (i) Interpretation of observations. (ii) Drawing inferences from observations. (iii) Generalising conclusions.
(f) Synthesis:	Combining parts of information to grasp a concept. (i) Designing an experiment. (ii) Improvising and experiment, apparatus or device. (iii) Improving the accuracy of an instrument.

Designing as Test

A good test should be constructed in accordance with a definite design or plan. The steps in designing a test are as under:

(i) Allocation of marks for the different cognitive levels to be tested.

(ii) Allocation of marks for different chapters or units.

(iii) Blue print for the question paper.

(iv) Allocation of marks to various types of questions.

Allocation of Marks for Abilities to be Tested

Ability	*Symbol*	*Marks*
Knowledge	K	45
Comprehension	C	26
Application	A	17
Skills	S	6
Analysis and Synthesis	An/Sn	6
	Total	100

After the blue-print is ready the actual question paper is set. Some of the commonly used tests in chemistry are fill-ins, true-false, multiple-choice, short-answer or essay-type etc.

Now we shall take up the discussion of some of these tests.

Evaluation of Functional Skills

Concepts, Generalisation and Principles : The need of written tests becomes increasingly important as children progresses through the elementary school grades. This is so because of the following reasons:

(i) In upper grades pressures for more "objective evaluation" in chemistry are greater as children are exposed to greater emphasis upon "subject matter grades."

(ii) As children's use of language increases, there can reasonably be greater emphasis upon meaningful written and verbal concept development.

(iii) As the child builds a background of chemistry concepts, facts, understandings and inter-relationships, a greater need is presented for accurately assessing the child's knowledge.

(iv) With larger classes, as is generally the rule for the intermediate and upper grades, teachers require evaluation techniques that are fast, accurate, and easy to apply, score and interpret.

One of the types of written testing devices is the short-answer tests. One major disadvantage is the superficiality and isolation of factual materials asked for rather than a breath and depth of understanding. They do however offer the teacher,

(i) Opportunities for including wide ranges of items to be tested.

(ii) An ease of writing questions because of the shortness of each.

(iii) A minimum of time and effort is needed for scoring because of the shortness of answers expected.

(iv) Opportunities for involvement of pupils in the self-evaluation because of the ease of scoring and following up incorporate responses.

Basically there are two types of short answer testing devices recall and recognition examinations.

Recall Tests

As the term implies, recall questions ask the student to bring back to mind information that the student was exposed to in the past. Psychologists have indicated that the people usually associate items to be recalled with other items and information and rarely, if ever, completely isolate them. The. way in which individuals associate isolated items is still much of a mystery. Even tests of isolation such as the ink blot design used in *Rorschach test,* evoke widely divergent responses because of unique back grounds and associations of individuals. Recall with children thus becomes a problem of framing questions in such a way as to stimulate the remembrance of the situation in which the intended information occurred. One of the ways in which this can be accomplished on recall tests is formulation of a question so that only one word or a few words is needed to answer the query. This simple question and answer procedure might look like this.

What is the approximate percentage of oxygen in air at sea level?

Another way of accomplishing recall of information in a chemistry content study is by supplying statements with blanks to be filled in.

For example : **Two by-products of the process of photosynthesis are———and—————.**

Recognition Tests

True and False tests are probably the most commonly used recognition tests in use today. The basic idea involved is illustrated below.

Carbon dioxide is a product of photosynthesis.

True	False

Such tests encourage guessing and it greatly reduces the validity and reliability of the Tests. Because it is very difficult to frame questions that are neither too obvious nor too ambiguous, this type of examination should be used very sparingly. Whenever, possible other types of recognition tests such as multiple choice test should be given.

Multiple-choice Items

There are generally two parts of a multiple-choice test-item, viz,, stem and plausible answers. The stem of the test-item contains the statement of the questioner problem. There are some important styles of writing the stem of a multiple-choice questions. These are:

1. Stating the stem in the form of a question.
2. Writing the stem as an incomplete statement.
3. Writing the stem as a problem to be solved.

The plausible answers are the options available to the student from which he has to choose the correct answer. These are generally written according to following guidelines:

1. Write the answers in such a way that to a student who has not read the topic thoroughly each answer seems to be plausible.
2. Include common misconceptions which an average student holds about a particular learning segment.

3. Options which are true on their own but defy the statement of the problem given in the stem of the test item.
4. Do not provide clues for the right answers.

Cognitive Levels and Multiple-choice Items

Generally at the school level, the multiple choice questions in chemistry are related to three cognitive levels, viz., knowledge, comprehension and application.

Limitation of Objective Type Tests : Some of the limitations of objective type tests are :

(i) They fail to test the ability to organise material.

(ii) They cannot test how well a thought is expressed.

(iii) They encourage guess work.

(iv) They are difficult to design.

Matching Tests

Besides the true and false and the multiple choice tests, there is a third type of recognition test, *the matching test.*

In this type of test items two mismatched columns are given, one working as problem statement and the other working as options. The questions and answers given in two columns are required to be matched or compared by the students. By giving the pupil two columns of items and asking him to match the related items, the teacher can quickly and easily see if his student recognises the relationships that exist between the items. There is less of a stress upon sheer memory or recall of fragmentary information because the materials are presented to the student for his correlation.

Because matching tests are focused mainly to measuring subject matter, it is not always indicative of the pupils ability to perceive the deeper meaning or real understanding of the relationship between the items used on the tests. Stress upon mere verbalization and memory of isolated bit of information should be avoided. Teachers will find it necessary to use all types of testing instruments so as to get a broad picture of the formulation of his children's chemistry concepts.

Short Answer Tests

With all the drawbacks of the short answer tests, there is a wide use for these tests in chemical education in schools. They are becoming quite popular these days. As the name suggests such questions expect brief, to the point, limited short answers. Generally the length of answers is specified. They offer the teacher an ease of construction and scoring not possible with other types of tests. The tests offer a greater degree of objectivity than other evaluating techniques and the results of tests can be helpful to the teacher for evaluating and reporting children's progress in chemistry education to their parents. With the teacher's guidance, the simplicity of tests can be useful for self-evaluative examinations for the children. Children can also be involved in writing examinations of this type as well as in scoring them. Teachers can be assured that the objective tests being discussed warrant the expenditure of time and effort required to construct them in correct way. Correctly made, administered and interpreted, the short answer test offers many advantages to the teacher; however, they should never be used as sole testing device. They should only be used in conjunction with other types of oral and written tests as well as teacher observation.

Advantages of Short Answer Questions

Some of the important advantages of this type of questions are:

(i) They are easy to design.

(ii) Scoring is less subjective and easy.

(iii) The question paper becomes comprehensive i.e., it covers the entire syllabus. The students lose the chance of spotting questions or topics.

Short Answer and Structured Questions

Perhaps the most interesting development over the past twenty years or so is that of the structured questions of the following type:

5.0 cm^3 of 2.0 m aqueous solution of Y chloride (where Y is a metal) was placed in each of eight similar test tubes. Different volumes of 2.0 m aqueous solution of silver nitrate were then added to the solution in each of the test tubes. The resulting mixtures were shaken and allowed to settle. The heights of the precipitates obtained in each test-tube were plotted against volumes of the silver nitrate solution added. The graph obtained is shown in Fig.

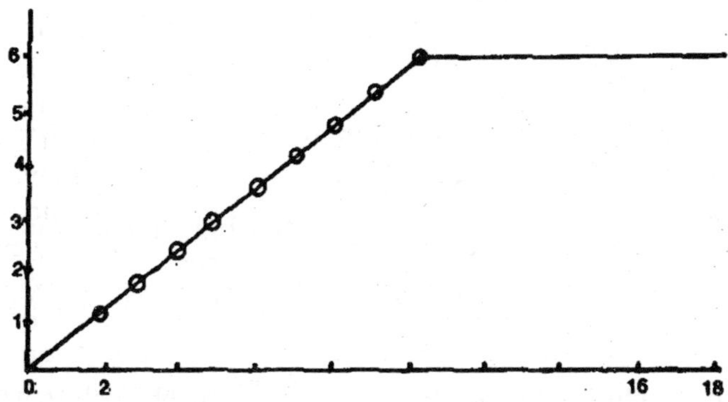

Volume of silver nitrate solution added

(a) (i) Name the precipitate formed.

(ii) What is the initial colour of the precipitate[7]

(b) How many moles of Y chloride is present in 5 cm^3 of 2.0 m solution of Y chloride?

(c) What is the volume of silver nitrate solution that will be just sufficient to react completely with 5.0 cm^5 of Y chloride solution?

(d) Calculate the number of moles of silver nitrate that will react with one mole of Y chloride.

(e) If the volume of aqueous solution of Y chloride used in slightly more than 5.0 cm^3, the maximum height of the precipitate obtained will be different. Sketch the graph you would expect to obtain on Fig.

(f) 14.0 cm^3 of silver nitrate solution is mixed with 5.0 cm^3 of Y chloride solution. The precipitate formed in filtered.

   (i) What will be observed if the precipitate obtained is exposed to sun light for a few hours?

   (ii) Metal Y is above copper in the electro-chemical series, describe what will be observed when a piece of copper foil is placed in the filtrate.

Certificate of Education

This involves the art of questioning, questioning so structured and phrased as to stimulate a response from most of the students and thus lead them to the understanding of the whole.

A structured question is essentially one in which the student is asked to study information given in the stem, usually complex and generally unfamiliar, and is then asked to respond *to* it through a series of questions, each requiring a short answer.

Though the use of such structured questions is on increase but training in their construction is not so readily available. Teacher can use the following guidelines for constructing such questions guidelines given below also summarise the form of this type of assessment.

Guidelines for Framing Structured Questions

1. The stem should provide information and act as a focus for the set of questions which follow it.

2. The questions following the stem should relate to the stem. These questions should be in a sequence according to one or more of the following principles :
   (a) a teaching sequence through which the information normally would be studied;
   (b) a logical sequence of operations such as steps of a calculation;
   (c) increasing difficulty a hierarchy of skills.
3. In formulation of questions due thought be given to expected responses. For a precise answer the question too should be precise.
4. Marks allotted to each questions be indicated against each.
5. Enough space be provided, between questions, for expected answers.
6. Normally five or six questions are framed from a stem.
7. Discretion be allowed to examiners for marking answers to such questions.
8. Generally choice is not allowed.
9. A set of question may have either a linear structure or a branched structure. The branched type is more common in chemistry. In this type the questions do not depend on one another although they all relate to common stem.
10. Like objective tests, structured questions can be used for formative evaluation and diagnosis.

Essay Tests

The essay-type examinations are in used in India since long and these have been greatly appreciated due to the freedom of response allowed. Essay tests aid in evaluating chemistry understanding in the intermediate and upper grade of elementary school. Like all testing devices, essays present many serious disadvantages. At the same time they present many possibilities for gathering informations. This type of test directs attentions to and places emphasis on a larger segment of the subject or on an integrated total unit. It provides the student a chance to create a new approach to a problem as it requires the student to express his views in writing. He is required to produce something and not merely to guess or recognise the answer. These tests can measure verbal fluency, skill of expression, organisation of thoughts and the attitude of examinees towards problems and subject considered in the class, however it lacks most of the qualities of a good measuring instrument.

Obvious advantages and disadvantages of essay test

1. Shows how well the student is able to organise and present ideas, but scoring is very subjective due to a tack of set answers.
2. Varying degrees of conectness since there is not justa right or wrong answer, but scoring requires excessive time.
3. Tests ability to analyze problems using pertinent information and to arrive at generalisation or conclusions, but scoring in influenced by spelling, handwriting, sentence structure and other extraneous items.
4. Gets to deeper meanings and inter-relationships rather than isolated bits of factual materials, but questions usually are ambiguous or too obvious.

Limitations of Essay Type Tests : These tests have low validity, low reliability and are less comprehensive. Discussing about the weaknesses of this type of tests Ross remarks, "The essay overrates the importance of knowing how to say a thing and under-rates the importance of having something to say".

This type of tests are not reliable because there is no agreement between teachers about the marks to be assigned and studies have shown that even the same teachers do not agree with themselves. Sandifbard, in his book on educational psychology refers to a study, "In one department of the University of Toronto, the same subject was set for an essay in different years. The essay which had secured 80 marks in one year, was exactly copied by the students in another year and scored 39 marks."

Ashburn who carried out a study at University of West Virginia concluded that, "the passing of failing of about 40% depends not on what they know or do not know, but on who reads the papers and that the passing or failing of about 10% depends on when the papers are read."

Another general complaint of students about essay type tests is that the questions 'did not suit them'. Certainly nine or ten questions generally set in this type of question paper cannot cover the whole syllabus. Hence this types of test is less comprehensive.

If an effort to offset the disadvantages the teacher must carefully consider the construction of each essay question. The teacher should word the question in such a fashion that the pupil will be limited to certain degree to the concepts being tested.

To minimise the shortcomings of excessive subjectivity teacher should prepare a scoring guide before hand. Each question be scored separately and a list of important ideas that are expected should be made.

Assessment of Practical Works

Assessment of practical work is the most difficult operational problem in assessment. The reason for it may that curriculum design is and teachers are not clear in their mind about the objectives to be achieved. In part the major aim of practicals was the mastery of manipulative skill, presently there are many other aims. In one study twenty-one aims have been given out.

For assessment of practical work there are three alternatives before us:

(i) The assessment be done by external examiners.

(ii) Internal assessment system may be followed.

(iii) Practical work may not be assessed at all.

Presently most of the practical assessment work is done by external examiners. However, this form of assessment of practical work has the following disadvantages :

(i) A large number of students have to be examined simultaneously.

(ii) A large number of apparatus, equipnient etc., are required for this type of assessment.

(iii) Reliability of single practical examination is suspect.

However, inspite of its various shortcomings this system of practical examination is in use because it is thought that any practical examination is better than none.

On a limited scale internal assessment of practicals has been undertaken. This type of assessment is based on the belief that assessment of practical work of students by their own teacher on several occasions during the course of study shall be more reliable than one single examination by external examiners. Source of the advantages of internal assessment of practical work are :

(i) The reliability increases because of increase in frequency of examinations.

(ii) In this system the range of attributes of student is extended and it includes those which are displayed during work as well as at the end of it.

(iii) In this type of assessment range of experiments and types of work can be extended.

However, the dual role of teacher in such type of assessment may sometimes result in adversely affecting the relationship between the teacher and the taught.

As a safeguard to such a system of assessment are may take recourse to moderating the scores by source external moderator.

But this is a lengthy and cumbersome process. Some other statistical methods such as moderation on the basis of some written examination can also be undertaken.

However, it can be easily seen that internal assessment of practical work involves both teachers and administrators in a good deal of work and it demands a high level of competence and professional integrity.

Assessment of Project Works

'In project work, pupils are expected *to* assume some level of personal responsibility for their work and to organise their time for constructive study.'

Types of Project

Three important types of project are :

Report Type : In this type of project students collect information from books, journals and other sources and then prepare a report in the form of a project report.

Discovery Type : In this type of project the students use the results of their own experimentation, observation etc., to answer a specific question of a specific hypothesis. These findings are then summarised as a project report.

Combination Type : In this type the theoretical and experimental aspects of a topic are combined and thus is actually a combination of report type and discovery type of project.

The objective of project work is to develop the skills of planning design, investigation and interpretation.

The assessment of project work becomes difficult because of such tall claims for projects as an educational activity, moreover most of the chemistry projects are of cooperative nature and so in such cases it would be difficult to differentiate between the performances and attributes of members of a group is self-evident.

This clearly brings about the problems in assessment of projects. However to have same type of project work and same type of its assessment is considered better to the rejection of all project work in chemical education just because it cannot be properly assessed.

Thus projects should allow the exercise and develop-ment of skills of planning, investigation and interpretation. The very fact that so much is claimed for projects as an educational activity makes their assessment difficult. In addition there are problems of assessing work which is done by groups of students rather than by individuals.

Despite the above stated problems, some experience is now available of the formal and public assessment of projects at school level.

Handy and Johnstone summarise the form of assessment of these projects as follows :

A dissertation marked mainly on the basis of five point scales. An oral discussion of the dissertation (with an external examiner) carried out in the presence of the class teacher, partly to reassure the candidate and partly to supply information not readily available to the examiner.

A discussion between the examiner and the class teacher to arrive at an agreed mark.

Handy and Jonstone demonstrate an acceptable validity and reliability for this assessment scheme.

Following points be considered for proper evaluation of laboratory work, project work etc.:

(i) Instead of holding one practical examination at the end of the session it is desirable to introduce a system of continuous assessment by regular evaluation of day to day practical activities of the students.

(ii) For evaluation of laboratory practical work from all possible angles the teacher may have a comprehensive checklist and he should tick mark various aspects while observing the work of a child. It would help him to make a very objective assessment.

(iii) *Viva-voce be* conducted so thoroughly that the examiner can properly test the student's knowledge and understanding of practical aspects, his ability to apply his knowledge in practical situations, his interest and attitude towards practical application of scientific facts and principles.

(iv) Students practical note-book be given due consideration in evaluating his practical work.

(v) The projects undertaken by a student during the session should also be given due place while assessing a student's practical work.

(vi) Weightage be also given for sessional work done by the student. It includes improvisation of aid material and equipment.

Designing a Test

A good physics test should be constructed in accordance with a definite design or plan. The steps in designing a physics test are as under :

(i) Allocation of marks for the different cognitive levels to be tested.

(ii) Allocation of marks for different chapters or units.

(iii) Blue print for the question paper.

(iv) Allocation of marks to various types of questions.

Allocation of Marks for Abilities to be Tested

Ability	*Symbol*	*Marks*
Knowledge	K	45
Comprehension	C	26
Application	A	17
Skills	S	6
Analysis and synthesis	An/Sn	6
	Total	100

Allocation of Marks to the Types of Questions

Question type	*Symbol*	*No. of questions*	*Marks*
Short Answers	S A	17	44
Structured	ST	4	56
	Total	21	100

Similarly, allocation of marks for content areas is also made. For example in case of physics the content area wise split up of the marks is illustrated in Table

Allocation of Marks by Content Area

Content Area	*Marks*
Mechanics	38
Sound	11
Heat	12
Light	15
Electricity	24
Total	100

Finally, on the basis of these allocations a blue-print of the question paper is prepared. The blue-print on the basis of the allocation of marks in the above three tables is as follows :

Blue-print for Question Paper for the Test

Content Area	*Abilities*										
	K		C		A		S		An/Sn	Total
	SA	ST	SA	ST	SA	ST	SA	ST	ST	
Mechanics	3	14	3	6	3	3	-	3	3	38
Sound	5	-	3	-	3	-	-	-	-	11
Heat	6	-	3	-	3	-	-	-	-	12
Light	3	5	-	5	-	2	-	-	-	15
Electricity	3	6	3	3	3	-	3	3	2	24
Total	20	25	12	14	12	5	3	6	5	100

After the blue-print is ready the actual question paper is set. Some of the commonly used tests in physics are fill-ins, true-false, multiple-choice, short-answer or essay type etc.

Now we shall take up the discussion of some of these tests.

Basically there are two types of short answer testing devices recall and recognition examinations.

Recall Tests

As the term implies, recall questions ask the student to bring back to mind information that the student was exposed to in the past. Psychologists have indicated that the people usually associate items to be recalled with other items and information and rarely, if ever, completely isolate them. The way in which individuals associate isolated items is still much of a mystery. Even tests of isolation such as the inkblot design used in *Rorschah test*, evoke widely divergent responses because of unique backgrounds and associations of individuals. Recall with children thus becomes a problem of framing questions in such a way as to stimulate the remembrance of the situation in which the intended information occurred. One of the ways in which this can be accomplished on recall tests is formulation of a question so that only one word or a few words is needed to answer the query. This simple question and answer procedure might look like this.

1. What is the approximate percentage of oxygen in air at sea level?
2. Name two organs of human body etc.

Another way of accomplishing recall of information in a physics content study is by supplying statements with blanks to be filled in.

For example

1. The part of the plane that develops thrust that pulls the plane forward is the____.

True	False

Recognition Tests

True and False tests are probably the most commonly used recognition tests in use today. The basic idea involved is illustrated below :

1. Freely suspended magnets always points towards North-South.

2. Like charges repel each other.

Such tests encourage guessing and it greatly reduces the validity and reliability of the Tests. Because it is very difficult to frame questions that are neither too obvious nor too ambiguous, this type of examination should be used very sparingly. Whenever possible other types of recognition tests such as multiple-choice test should be given.

Multiple-choice Tests

In this type of test, several alternatives are presented to the pupil from which he must select the one that makes the statement most correct. Such test items can reduce the subjectivity in marking and inter-examiner variability in marking. These tests are the most popular these days and are most useful because in this way guessing is minimised and intelligent thinking is encouraged. Some examples of this type of tests are :

1. An aeroplane flies 1000 km west and then 1000 km north. Then it flies back to the startingplace by the shortest route. Its speed is 400 kin/hour throughout. What is the average velocity over the entire trip?

(a) 0

(b) 100 km/hr

(c) 200km/hr

(d) 400km/hr

2. A car with a vertical wind shield moves along in a rain

storm at speed of 40 km/hour. The rain drops fall vertically with a terminal speed of 200 in/sec. The angle at which the rain drops strike the wind shield is :

(a) 18^{-1} (5/9)

(b) $\tan^{-1}$ (9/5)

(c) $\tan^{-1}$ (3/2)

(d) $\tan^{-1}$ (2/3)

3. A car travels due east on a level road for 3 km. It then turns due north at an intersection and travels 4 km before stopping. Find the resultant displacement of car.

(a) 1km

(b) 1km

(c) 5km

(c) 7km

4. A car covers the first half of the distance between two places at a speed of 40 km/hour and the second half at 60 kin/hour. Then the average speed of the car is :

(a) 100 km/hour

(b) 55 km/hour

(c) 50 km/hour

(d) 48 km/hour

5. A conveyor belt is moving horizontally at a speed of 4 m/sec. A box of mass 20 kg is gently laid on it. It takes 0.1 second for the box to come to rest on the belt. The distance moved by the box on the conveyor belt is:

(a) 0

(b) 0.2

(c) 0.4

(d) 0.8

Reasoning power can play a big part in answering this type of questions and so called educated guesses should be encouraged. Actually these educated guesses usually are formulated from vague relationships that are seen or sensed. Very often the person cannot explain his reason for selection of correct choices in this type of questions, he just knows. Because there are so many aspects of learning and teaching that are «till mysteries to us, teacher should not stand in the way of children learning. Intuition plays an important part in learning as well as in the scientific way of working.

Guidelines for Constructing Multiple Choice Items

While constructing multiple choice test items following instructions be followed :

1. A test-item should have a single concept to be tested.
2. A test-item should be such that it can be used to discriminate a group of students as low, medium and high achievers.
3. The statement of test-item should be very clear and unambiguous.
4. Be sure that of the plausible answers only one answer is correct.

Parts of Multiple-choice Item

There are generally two parts of a multiple-choice test-item, viz., stem and plausible answers. The stem of the test-item contains the statement of the question or problem. There are some important styles of writing the stem of a multiple-choice questions. These are :

1. Stating the stem in the form of a question.
2. Writing the stem as in incomplete statement.
3. Writing the stem as a problem to be solved.

The plausible answers are the options available to the student from which he has to choose the correct answer. These are generally written according to following guidelines:

1. Write the answers in such a way that to a student who has not read the topic thoroughly each answer seems to be plausible.
2. Include common misconceptions which an average student holds about a particular learning segment.
3. Options which are true on their own but defy the statement of the problem given in the stem of the test item.
4. Do not provide clues for the right answers.

Cognitive Levels

Generally at the school level, the multiple-choice questions in science are related to three cognitive levels, viz., knowledge, comprehension and application. Given below are a few examples of each kind of test-items.

(a) *Knowledge Level Test-item:* We have generally noticed that the passengers in a moving bus fall forward when brakes are suddenly applied to it because of:

(i) slippery seats

(ii) inertia of rest

(iii) interia of motion

(iv) passengers being caught unawares.

(b) *Comprehension Level Test-item:* Choose the one in which no work is done.

(i) A car is moving up hill.

(ii) A coolie is lifting the load up.

(iii) An arrow is shot from a bow.

(iv) A stone tied to a rop is whirled in a circle.

(c) *Application Level Test-item:* A car gets displaced by 4 m due east and then it gets displaced by 3 m due north. The vector substraction of these two displacements is:

(i) 5 m in W-N direction.

(ii) 5 m in S-E direction.

(iii) 5 m N-E direction.

(iv) 1 m in N-E direction.

The Limitations : Some of the limitations of objective type tests are :

(i) They fail to test the ability to organise material.

(ii) They cannot test how well a thought is expressed.

(iii) They encourage guess work.

(iv) They are difficult to design.

Matching Tests

Besides the true and false and the multiple-choice tests, there is a third type of recognition test, *the matching test.*

In this type of test items two mismatched columns are given, one working as problem statement and the other working as options. The questions and answers given in two columns are required to be matched or compared by the students. By giving the pupil two columns of items and' asking him to match the related items, the teacher can quickly and easily see if his student recognises the relationships that exist between the items. There is less of a stress upon sheer memory or recall of fragmentary information because the materials are presented to the student for his correlation. Here are two columns of words, draw a line between the word on the right and the correct one on the left to show me proper relationship.

Q.1.1. A unit used in expressing the relative intensity level of sound	(a) d' Arsonval principle
2. The principle employed in permanent moving magnet coil types of electric meters.	(b) motion down inclined plane-energy equation.
3. Insulating material used to separate the conducting plates of an electric capacitor.	(c) dielectric
4. $\frac{1}{2} mv^2 = mgh \sin \theta$	(d) decibel

Q.2.1. Torque x angle of rotation.	(a) Torricelli's theorem
2. Weight of liquid displaced.	(b) work done by couple.
3. $V=\sqrt{2gh}$	(c) upthrust
4. Force per unit length	(d) surface tension.
Q.3.1. $\frac{1}{2}$ stress x strain	(a) temperature rise
2. $\frac{\text{Potential energy}}{\text{Heat capacity}}$	(a) energy per unit volume.
3. $\frac{1}{2}$ tension x extension	(c) Young's modulus
4. $\frac{\text{Tensile stree}}{\text{Tensile strain}}$	(d) strain entery
Q.4.1. $\frac{F}{\text{A x Velocity gradient}}$	(a) Stake's law
2. $F = 6\pi\alpha\eta v$	(b) depolarizer
3. Unit of energy and work.	(c) joule
4. An agent for removing accumulated hydrogen gas , from the positive electrode of a voltaic cell.	(d) coefficient of viscosity.

Because matching tests are focussed mainly to measuring subject matter, it is not always indicative of the pupils ability to perceive the deeper meaning or real understanding of the relationship between the items used on the tests. Stress upon mere verbalization and memory of isolated bits of information should be avoided. Teachers will find it necessary to use all types of testing instruments so as to get a broad picture of the formulation of his children's physics concepts.

Short Answers

With all the drawbacks of the short answer tests, there is a wide use for these tests in science education for elementary schools. They are becoming quite popular these days. As the name suggests such questions expect brief, to the point, limited short answers. Generally the length of answers is specified. They offer the teacher an ease of construction and scoring not possible with other types of tests. The tests offer a greater degree of objectivity than other evaluating techniques and the results of tests can be helpful to the teacher for evaluating and reporting children's progress in science education to their parents. With the teacher's guidance, the simplicity of tests can be useful for self-evaluative examinations for the children. Children can also be involved in writing examinations of this type as well as in scoring them. Teachers can be assured that the objective tests being discussed warrant the expenditure of time and effort required to construct them in correct way. Correctly made, administered and interpreted, the short answer test offers many advantages to the teacher; however, they should never be used as sole testing device. They should only be used in conjunction with other types of oral and written tests as well as teacher observation.

The Advantages : Some of the important advantages of this type of questions are :

(i) They are easy to design.

(ii) Scoring is less subjective and easy.

(iii) The question paper becomes comprehensive i.e., it covers the entire syllabus. The students lose the chance of spotting questions or topics.

Instruments for Evaluating Scientific Attitudes

One of the most important ways of judging the effectiveness of science teaching is to evaluate the growth of individual children. This is especially due in the areas of scientific attitudes, appreciations and interests. The most suitable techniques for obtaining this information are teacher observation and anecdotal records, tape recording, rating scales, checklists, interviews, children's work products, essay tests and situation testing.

Observation and Record Keeping

Following forms have been found as useful aid by the teacher as it helps them in making their observations more accurate, systemic and time saving and also provides them with a permanent record of behaviour. These cared can be used for recording anecdotes of children's scientific or unscientific behaviour. As these records accumulate, the teacher can begin to see the direction of growth in behaviour and attitude. It is unsatisfactory to merely say that a child has improved in scientific thinking. We must have some records to substantiate our claims.

Tape Recordings

Use of tape recorder during science discussion period can be made for accessing the attitudes and interests of each student. Such tapes of discussions can be analysed by the teacher at his leisure. In many ways the tape recorded sessions have some important advantages over the written records of teachers observations. By use of tape records greater objectivity is possible. These tape recordings can also be used for self-evaluation by students. It is expected that such tapes be used for physics teaching and learning.

Checklists and Rating Scales

It is a faster but perhaps less comprehensive way of assessing growth in scientific attitudes and appreciations. A sheet is prepared by the teacher and she can use it for his own evaluation also and for modifying his teaching method.

Interviews

Personal interviews of individual or small groups of children enable the teacher to probe into their scientific attitudes and thinking. Interviews may last only a few minutes and the answers given by students are important primarily for the ways in which children attempt to answer and not the amount of factual material verbalised. A special session be organised for evaluation of skills in which practical situations are presented for assessing children's scientific thinking and attitude with greater elaboration.

Children's Work Products

Children's work in all aspects of the elementary curriculum

provide us with much evidence about their scientific thinking and attitudes. Children's writings, particularly in the intermediate and upper grades, provide enough information about their concepts of the world and their thinking processes. Creative writing allows freedom for the child to explore scientifically and to speculate. Projects and reports provide the format for students to present examples of their thinking.

Evaluation of Situation

The teacher can set up situations in which the student is required to find the answer to a practical problem. The student should be unable to supply the answer from memory because ideally he would never have encountered the particular situations. This procedure is quite helpful in the assessment of problem solving skills.

Questions

1. What is evaluation? Differentiate it with the term examination and testing.
2. What do you understand by evaluation in physical sciences? Discuss.
3. Discuss the criteria of a good test taking examples from physics/ chemistry.
4. Give a model scheme of evaluation for secondary classes in the subject of physical sciences.
5. Develop six objective type test items on any lesson in physical sciences.
6. Differentiate between achievement test and diagnostic test.
7. Write short notes on :
   (i) Merits and demerits of objective type tests.
   (ii) Criterion of a good test.
   (iii) Defects of present day examination system.

14

The Laboratories

No course in science cannot be considered as complete without including some practical work in it. The practical work is to be carried out by individual in a physical science laboratory. Most of the achievements of modern science are due to the application of the experimental method. At school stage practical work is even more important because of the fact that we 'learn by doing' scientific principles and applications are thus rendered more meaningful. It is a well-known fact that an object handled impresses itself more firmly on the mind than an object merely seen from a distance or in an illustrations. Centuries of purely deductive work did not produce the some utilitarian results as a few decades of experimental work. Practical class-room experiments help in broadening pupil's experience and develop initiative, resourcefulness and cooperation. Because of the reasons discussed above practical work forms a prominent feature in any science course.

Organisation of Practical Works

Out of the various teaching methods discussed earlier the *Assignment method* is the only method that continues theory and practice in a harmonious manner and can be easily practiced in our schools. The *Heuristic method is* preeminently a *laboratory method*. However, from this it should not be concluded that practical work in laboratory is impossible if the teacher makes use of any other teaching method. Thus irrespective of the method adopted by the teacher for teaching of physical science in the class, practical work in laboratory must be attempted. The following guidelines will help the physical science teacher to make his practical work effective.

Guidelines for Teachers

For smooth working in the laboratory teacher should give due consideration to the following points :

(i) If teacher follows the demonstration method to teach theory, he should remember the most important principle that practical work should go hand in hand with the theoretical work. Thus, if a class is doing theoretical work in physics it should also do practical work in physics during the practical periods.

(ii) An attempt be made to arrange the practical work in such a way that each student is able to do his practical individually. Thus, for practical work individual working be preferred in comparison to working in groups.

(iii) In case of a large class, it is convenient to divide the class in a suitable number of smaller groups, for practical work. A practical group in no case should have more than 20 students. The limit on practical group is essential otherwise teacher will not be able to devote individual attention to the students.

(iv) To save time on delivering a lecture about do's and don'ts in laboratory, card system is used. This card which contains certain amount of guidance printed on it is given to each pupil. In some laboratories where card system exists each student is given a card containing instructions about the experiment that he has to perform. This card also contains the details of the apparatus required. Student can complete his practical work according to instructions given in the card.

(v) The apparatus provided should be good so that students get an accurate result particularly in those experiments in which the student is likely to compare the numerical value of his result with some standard. However, every science teacher should guard against 'Cooking' of results by his pupil. If this bad habit of cooking is not checked in the beginning it persists through out the students' career.

(vi) A true and faithful record of each and every experiment be kept by pupils. The record should be complete in all respects.

(vii) To check the habit of 'cooking' teacher should see that students enterall their observations directly in their practical notebook.The teacher should insist that the pupils do not go to the balance room without Hist entering the data in their note books.

(viii) Students should not be allowed to erase any figures. To change any wrong entry the same be crossed and correct figure entered only with the permission of the teacher.

(ix) Students should not be allowed to calculate results or write data on scrap papers.

(x) In practical note book the right hand page be reserved for record while the left hand page be left for diagram and calculations. This practice be allowed for Assignment method.

For any other method the laboratory work be done on left hand page of practical note book and procedure etc., on right hand page of practical note book.

(xi) Teacher should see that students complete their practical notebook in all respects and get it signed before they are allowed to leave the laboratory. Incomplete practical note books be kept in the laboratory and students be asked to complete it in their spare time.

(xii) Teacher should thoroughly check and critically examine the account written by students.

(xiii) Whenever a student is required to make use of a piece of apparatus for the first time it is the duty of the teacher to explain to his students the working of the apparatus. He should also explains reasons for necessary care and accuracy.

(xiv) Teacher should see that students find no difficulty to get apparatus and chemicals needed by them. In the absence of provision for laboratory assistants in our schools it is for the teacher that be arranges the apparatus in such a way that things frequently needed by students are easily accessible to them. Teacher should also emphasise proper and economical use of apparatus and chemicals.

(xv) While working with larger groups and with limited apparatus teacher can act as under:

(a) He may use assignment method.

(b) He may allow students to work in groups.

(c) He may devise alternate simple experiments and work with improvised apparatus.

(d) He may allow use of home made apparatus.

(xvi) Whenever, the teacher is required to draw up suitable laboratory directions or instructions for practical work by pupils, be should keep the following points in mind:

(a) Beginner be given detailed directions.

(b) He should not tell the students what is actually going to happen.

(c) The man aim of the experiment should be made clear.

(xvii) During a practical class teacher should observe all children from his desk otherwise chances of accidents are there. Even when teacher has to move from his desk his power of control over the class should be such that students continue their work satisfactorily.

Physical Science Laboratories

Combined Lecture Room-cum-Laboratory : Laboratory is a spacious room where in a group of students carry out their practicals. The work of designing and building a physical science room (Laboratory and lecture room) is that of the architect but science master should collaborate with the architect in planning forwhat is best from the educational point of view. The plan of a combined lecture room and laboratory for use in schools upto matriculation standard, devised by Dr. R.H. Whitehouse, formerly principal of the Central Training College, Lahore, has been adopted as the official standard plan by Punjab Education Department.

This plan combines laboratory and class-room for science teaching. The suggested size of the room is 45" x 25' and it is meant for a class of 40 students which is sub-divided in two groups of 20 each for practical work.

The size of the room is most economical. Though the length of the room is 45' but it should not be considered as disadvantageous because the teacher is expected to address a class of 40 students who will be occupying only about half the room.

For constructing such a room walls are to be of 1' 16" thick keeping Indian conditions in view, use of distemper be preferred to white wash for the walls. A perfectly smooth floor is preferable to one exhibiting any roughness. Such a floor is easier to clean of the two doors, one is used for lecture room and the other is reserved for laboratory part. To provide side lighting three large windows (6' x 8') are provided. One of these is provided near practical benches and two near seating accommodation. Doors as also windows should open outwards. The inner window sills may be used as shelves for carrying out experiments. To avoid flies wire gauze screens be provided to the windows. If necessary, in such a case, the windows be constructed with an upper and a lower half. The lower half is fixed so that the inner sills of windows could still be used as shelves.

Furnishings and Fittings

In the area meant for lecture room a wall blackboard 10' x 4' is provided. About 3' away from this blackboard is the teachers table which is about 6' long and 2.5 feet high. Such a table can be conveniently used both as a writing table as also a demonstration table and causes no disturbance or in convenience to the students in watching the demonstration or observing the blackboard.

For seating dual table and chairs are most economical. Thus by providing twenty tables and forty chairs sufficient seating arrangement could be made. Dual tables should be of the size 3.5' x 1.5' x 2'. They may be provided with shelf. The top of these tables should be flat and plain having grooves for pen/ pencils. The chairs are 1.5' high in the seat, which in case of an iron chair, may be covered with a small mat. The area necessary fora dual table and two chairs is a square of 3.5'. Passages of 1.5' are sufficient for single file and 2.5' to 3.5' at the sides.

A sink is provided for use of the teacher. The size of the sink generally used is 18" x 12" x 6".

The advantages of table and chair system are as under:

(i) They are quite economical.

(ii) They provide quite natural seats.

(iii) They allow enough space for easy passage of the students.

(iv) They can be easily moved while cleaning the room.

(v) They can be used for other purposes such as accommodating guests at various school functions.

In the laboratory part of the room are provided six laboratory tables which are made of wood and are perfectly plain. A blackboard is also provided on this side of the room. The laboratory tables are of the size 6' x 3.5' and are provided with a shelf on the working side just below the top. Four students can work on each table. The whole of each table except top should be stained dark. The top should be treated with wax ironed with a hot flat iron in order to fill the pores of the wood and to prevent the easy penetration of the liquids. The space between the tables and walls varies between 3' and 4' and passage way at the end of the tables is 2' wide. At school level the laboratory tables are not provided with any sink. Some of the reasons for not providing the sinks are as follows:

Economy : A large economy is observed because much plumbing and a network of drains is avoided. Cost of sinks is also saved. For most of the experiments at school level a trough can serve the purpose.

Usefulness : The table is quite useful for both physics and chemistry. In absence of sinks more space is available for use as working spice. Such a table can also be used for other purposes.

Appearance and Cleanliness : The floor of the room is not broken for providing drains etc. It gives a better look.

Tidiness : The tables if provided with sink would make the room untidy because such tables invariably allow splashing of water which is likely to interfere with experiments and is likely to create problems.

As shown in the plan there are only three sinks, one for the teacher and two for the students. Of the two sinks for students one is placed in the window recess and the other in recess in the wall. Each of the sinks is provided with a drawing board having grooves arranged to drip over the sinks. It is used for placing beakers, flasks, etc., for drying.

For placing balances, recess in walls may be used. They may be about a foot wide at a height of about 3', 3". Such recess has the following advantages over wooden or stone shelf:

(i) It is very economical because only very small masonary is needed.

(ii) It is more substantial as compared to a bracket shelf.

(iii) It does not project into the room and so space economy can be made.

For providing ample accommodation for balances a length of 7' to 7.5' is sufficient.

In the plan provision has also been make for the storage of science apparatus, equipments etc. For this purpose there is a provision of eight almirahs (each with 7' x 5' dimensions). Each almirah is provided with shelves 1.5' deep, of this 1' is recessed in the wall and only 6" projects out. These almirahs provided sufficient space for the storage of not only the apparatus, equipment etc., but can also serve the purpose of storage of science library.

Reagent shelves can be very conveniently placed on either side of the recesses for balances space can also be found, for placing notice boards for assignments of work, results of tests, etc., on the wall between the windows or just inside the doors.

The Advantages : The combined lecture room-cum-laboratory discussed in previous pages has the following advantages:

(i) It is very economical.

(ii) It is compact and provides enough space for seating, working, storage etc.

(iii) It can be furnished easily and with meager resources.

(iv) It provides enough and comfortable seating space for the students.

(v) In this room science atmosphere prevails.

(vi) It provides an opportunity for better control. For a better control followings points be kept in view by a teacher:

(a) Every student has his assigned place which is indicated by his name written on a card placed in a brass card holder fixed on the leg of the table.

(b) The four boys working on any table be allotted number 1,2,3,4 and number 1 of each table be asked to collect four sets of articles required for each table. Number 2 be asked to remove the dirty apparatus, after the period, to drain board and number 3 will remove clean apparatus. Number 4 will wipe down the table with a duster.

(c) Class monitors be named for cleaning dirty apparatus after school hours or during recess period.

(d) Students be made responsible for the correct alignment of their tables. For this black and white lines be pointed on the floor.

Physics Laboratory

Physics is essentially a practical oriented subject and laboratory work forms an important part of physics education. For proper understanding of the subject, physics be taught using a large number of demonstration experiments. For carrying out demonstration experiments and for the performance ofpracticals by the students, a physics laboratory is a must for every school offering physics as a subject. Like any other science subject a physics laboratory is justified on the following grounds:

(i) In a physics laboratory the required apparatus and other equipment etc can be safely stored.

(ii) As in other science subjects so also in case of physics, laboratories are helpful in creating and promoting scientific attitudes in the pupils.

(iii) Laboratory provides a proper and longenial place for performing experiments and is helpful in developing a sense of cooperation among the students.

The Importance : The importance of physics laboratory as detailed in a NCERT report of 1988, is based on an accepted theory of physics learning, lists the following process of science that can be carried out in a physics laboratory.

(i) Experiments to make observations.

(ii) Stating empirical laws based on the generalisation of observations made during experimentation.

(iii) To test the empirical laws by further experiments and observations.

(iv) To make modifications/alterations in the empirical laws of required.

(v) To test the modified laws by further experimentation.

(vi) Making generalisations and thus stating the accepted laws.

Another alternative method as under has also been suggested to arrive at a theory or law.

(i) Mathematical derivation.

(ii) Confirmation of derived law by experiments.

(iii) Generalisations leading to a law.

Thus it becomes quite clear that physics laboratory is essential for all schools.

Setting of Physics Laboratory

In the previous section we have discussed the importance of a physics laboratory. The physics laboratory should help in the realization of the relevant objectives. A physics laboratory should be well-planned and adequately equipped. If a new laboratory is to be constructed it should be a joint venture of the teacher and architect. Two types of plans for the establishment of laboratories are:

(i) Lecture room-cum-laboratory

(ii) All Purpose Science Room.

In the following pages we will take up the discussion of lecture-room-cum laboratory which is quite common for high schools and a separate section shall be devoted to physics laboratory in senior secondary schools.

Laboratory Planning

In a senior secondary school the arrangements are made to provide education in chemistry as elective subjects in addition to teaching of general science. In senior secondary school a provision has to be made for a chemistry laboratory. The laboratory in senior secondary school is almost the same as in colleges. Each laboratory is provided with a preparation-cum-store room attached to it. The size of the laboratory will depend on the number of students likely to work in it at a time. About 30 sq. feet. If space be provided for each student. The structural details are generally provided by the architects but the following points be kept in mind :

Planning : It would be better if chemistry teacher is consulted and for this there should be frequent conferences between the chemistry teacher and the architect. Various points be thoroughly discussed. Some of the points of consideration are as under:

(i) Laboratories and class-rooms should not be mixed on the same corridor.

(ii) Laboratories be situated, as far as possible, away from crafts room, music room, play fields, main gate etc.

(iii) The consideration be given to proximity of stores, preparation room, balance room, green houses etc.

Following points be given due consideration while planning individual laboratories:

(i) Each student is easily accessible to the teacher.

(ii) There is minimum of movement.

(iii) Each student has a cupboard, bottles, heating point and a sink near him.

(iv) Teacher can easily watch each student.

(v) Blackboard is visible to each student.

(vi) Each student can easily see the demonstration.

(vii) There is enough space (4.5) between two laboratory tables.

(viii) Master switches be provided to control electricity, gas, water etc., in each laboratory.

Lighting : Proper lighting arrangements be made for laboratory tables and class-rooms. Special attention be given to the lighting of demonstration table and blackboard. It would be preferred if a provision could be made for electrical lights over tables through pulleys so that their height may be varied from 2 to 8 ft. Two way switches be provided for controlling the main lighting from doors and preparation rooms. Dark blinds or curtain must be provided for each laboratory.

Ventilation : If possible each laboratory should be surrounded by a 6' verandah on all sides to keep away the direct heat of the sun. Ventilators be provided as usual. In case of chemistry laboratory ceiling should be high and exhaust fans must be provided.

Water Supply : Provision of water supply must be made in every laboratory. Water supply is most essential item and for this purpose proper arrangement of water laps and sinks is a must in every laboratory. In case of non-availability of adequate water supply from municipal/local sources alternate arrangements have to be made. For making alternate arrangements suggestion given below be considered.

A water storage tank having a capacity of 1000 to 5000 litres be constructed with concrete and cement or a readymade tank of synthetic material be purchased and such a tank be then placed at the roof of the room. Water be then lifted using electric pump for filling this tank. The water supply is then provided from this storage tank to the laboratories. A tentative scheme for storage and supply of water is shown in Fig.

Sinks : Provision of sinks in each laboratory is one of the essential requirements. For a laboratory of ordinary size generally four sinks of 15" x 12" x 8" or 20" x 15" x 10" are sufficient. These sinks be fitted on side walls. These sinks are in addition to the one provided with the demonstration table.

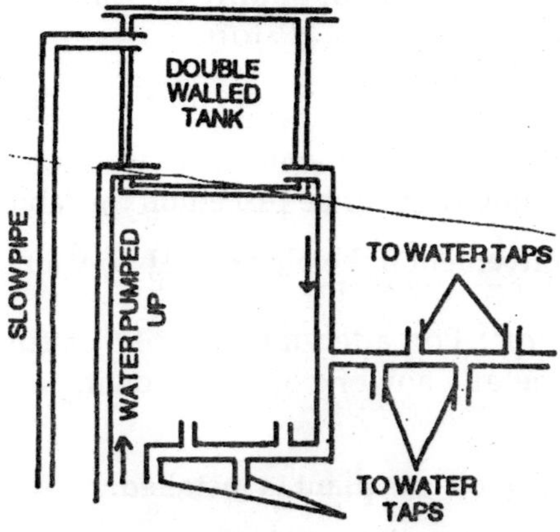

Fig. Showing Water-supply arrangement

Waste water from these sinks is carried to the drains with the helps of the lead pipes fitted with the sinks. In laboratories kitchen type sinks are preferred to wash basi type.

Waste Disposal

In laboratories two types of wastes (i.e. liquid and solid) are often encountered. Arrangements have to be made for disposal of these wastes. For disposal of liquid wastes use of lead pipes or earthenware pipes is considered most suitable. However, care be taken to avoid the flow of solids like pieces of filter paper, cork, broken glass pieces etc., through these pipes, otherwise these pipes get chocked. For disposal of such solid wastes metal boxes or wooden boxes be provided. Such boxes be placed in the corners of the laboratory and students be asked to put all solid wastes in these boxes. Such waste boxes can even be placed under the sinks as shown in next page in Fig.

Pipe Lines : Installation of water pipes and gas pipes is another important aspect for furnishing a science laboratory. While installing pipes some of the points that be given due consideration are given below:

(i) Not more than 4 or 5 half inches pipes be led from any

(i) Pipe for purpose of supply of water or drainage of water.

(ii) In case of physics laboratory all efforts be made to avoid iron pipes.

(iii) Pipes should never be placed on the laboratory tables.

(iv) It is convenient if the pipe fittings are not underground.

Gas Supply : For adequate supply of fuel gas to the laboratory generally any one of the following arrangements is made:

(i) Kerosene oil-gas plant is installed.

(ii) Coal-gas plant is installed.

(iii) Petrol-gas plant is installed.

(iv) Gobar-gas plant is installed.

The petrol gas plant is preferred as such a plant is economical and such plants are available in various capacities. A moderate capacity plant can feed 10-20 gas taps. Petrol gas plants are readily available and such plants are also manufactured at Ambala (Haryana). These plants can be easily operated.

For housing a petrol gas plant we need only a small room. The gas can be distributed to the practical tables using a 2" main gas pipe with further distributeries of 1/2" pipe. Each practical table is provided with gas taps and these taps should be of the rigid nozzle type and be fitted towards the back of the table. The gas tables be fitted in such a way that the point upwards and are at an angle of 45° from each other. If double benches are provided then taps should be fitted along the centre line of each bench. In most of the laboratories iron pipes are used but it would be preferable, in case of physics laboratory, if we use brass pipes. For controlling the supply of gas in addition to main control valve provision be made to control the supply of gas to each group of tables. These controls should be easily accessible to teacher and should not be easily accessible to students.

Laboratory Tables : The provision of laboratory tables is a must for each laboratory. The tops of laboratory tables be preferably made of teak wood. However, other hard wood such as *sheesham* or *deodar* can also be used for making tops of laboratory tables. These tops are generally 1" thick. Other parts of the table i.e., legs, drawers etc., may be made of any other type of locally available wood. Plywood or hardboard can also be used for drawers. In chemistry laboratory such drawers arc provided with the laboratory tables.

In addition to these provisions for boards be made in the laboratories. For this either wall blackboards be provided or movable wooden blackboards with stands can be used.

The organisation of laboratories in secondary schools was also discussed at a seminar (All-India) on the teaching of science in secondary schools. This seminar was held at Tara Devi (Simla) and it made some recommendations. Its recommendations are given below :

Layout :

(a) Provision be made for one laboratory for chemistry in every higher secondary school.

(b) A floor space of 30 sq ft per student be provided in each laboratory.

(c) Adjacent store room be provided with each laboratory.

(d) A part of store room may be earmarked for use as a preparation room.

(e) In science wing, some suitable place for work benches with tools, be provided.

(i) A minimum of two class-rooms provided with galleried seats be provided in each school.

Equipment for Chemistry Laboratory : The equipment for chemistry laboratory as recommended at the Tara Devi (Simla) Seminar is as under :

(i) Almirahs (wooden and steel).

(ii) Wallboard or blackboard.

(iii) Demonstration table (8' x 4') with cupboards, water and gas points.

(iv) Working tables with cupboards, shelves, water and gas points.

(v) Balance room should be attached to the laboratory.

(vi) Sinks on each working table or at least two large sinks at the corners of the laboratory.

(vii) A cupboard.

(viii) A wooden box half filled with sand for use as waste material box.

(ix) Acid proof drainage system.

(x) Shelves for reagent bottles on each working table and wall shelves for storage of reagent bottles.

Instructions to Pupils

When a group comes to laboratory for practical work it should be given a guidance for the experiment to be performed. Such guidance can be given by :

(i) Laboratory instructions,

(ii) Laboratory manuals, or

(iii) Instruction cards.

Laboratory Instructions : Laboratory instructions should be given in a clear and simple language. It should give a precise but systematic method of performing the experiment. Special emphasis be given on how the record is to be kept and number of observations to be taken. Calculations be clearly explained and precautions to be observed be specifically emphasised.

(a) It should contain full and complete directions about the experiment. Such directions should clearly give the procedure to be followed and the precautions to be observed.

(b) It should give the method of recording of observations. Tables if needed for recording observations be clearly given.

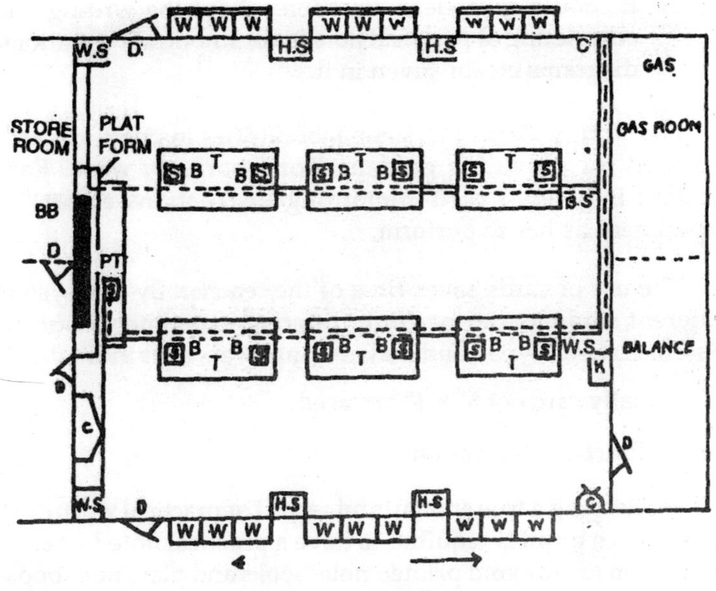

<———Verandah

NUMBER OF SEATS : 24

D:Door
BB: Black Board
P.T.: Platform
W.S.: Wall Sink
D.T.: Demonstration Table
S : Sink
B: Burners
T: Table
H.S. Hanging Wall Shelves
OS.: Water Supply Pipes
C: Cup Boards
C. Cup Boards
F.C.: Fume Chamber
K: Kipps (Apparatus Gas Stand)

Fig. A Chemistry Laboratory.

Laboratory Manuals : **Any good laboratory manual should contain the following:**

(c) It should give clear directions about the writing and completing of practical note book. Important equations, diagrams etc. be given in it.

Instruction Cards : In some laboratories instruction cards are used for providing guidance for laboratory work. Each student is given a card containing instructions about the experiment he has to perform.

The use of cards saves time of the teacher. By this system different students can perform different experiments but the system is stereo-typed and makes no allowance for individuals.

Usually cards of 6" x 4" arc used.

Pupils Practical Notebooks

For keeping a true and faithful record of practical work done by him each pupil is required to have a practical note-book. An effort be made to avoid printed note-books and plain note-books be encouraged. By using plain note-books teacher can make his students to follow any suitable method of keeping record of the experiment.

As a general practice description is given on the right hand page and observations are recorded on the left hand page. In case assignment method is used then the left hand page is reserved for preparatory work and laboratory record is kept on right hand page which contains description as also be observations.

The record of the method should be brief and in the first person singular. A three column system be used for keeping a record of experiments about the properties of gases etc. The three column be headed *Experiment, Observation* and *Inference.*

The precautions that have been observed while performing the experiment be recorded at the end in the first person singular (past tense).

All records in practical note-book be made with lead-pencil. The diagrams should be simple and will labelled.

Common Accidents and their Remedies

Burns : Burns by Dry Heat (i.e., by flame, hot objects etc.). For slight burns apply *Burnol* and *Sarson oil.*

In case blisters caused by burns apply *Burnol* at once and rush to dispensary.

Caution : *Heat burns should never be washed.*

Acid Burns : Wash with water and then with a saturated solution of sodium bicarbonate and finally with water. Even after this if burning persists, wipe the skin dry with cotton wool and apply *Sarson oil* and *Burnol.*

Caution : In case of conc. sulphuric acid, wipe it from the skin before giving the above treatment.

Alkali Burns : Wash with water and then with 1% acetic acid and finally with water. Dry the skin and apply *Burnol.*

Cuts : In case of a minor cut allow it to bleed for a few seconds and remove the glass piece if any. Apply a little methylated spirit or *Dettol* on the skin and cover with a piece of leucoplast.

For serious cuts call the Doctor at once. In the meanwhile try to stop bleeding by applying pressure above the cut. The pressure should not be continued for more than five minutes.

Note : Minor bleeding can be stopped easily be applying concentrated ferric chloride solution or alum.

Eye Accidents

Acid in Eye : At once wash the eye with water a number of times. Then wash it with 1% sodium carbonate solution by means of an eyeglass.

Alkali in Eye : *At* once wash with water and then with 1% boric acid solution by means of an eye-glass.

Foreign Particles in Eye : Do not rob the eye. Wash it by sprinkly water into the eye. Open the eye and remove the particle by means of a clean handkerchief or cotton wool. Again wash freely with water.

Poisons

If a solid or liquid goes to the mouth, but is not swallowed, spit it at once and repeatedly rinse with water. If the mouth is scalded, apply olive oil or *ghee.*

Acids : Dilute by drinking much water or preferably milk of magnesia.

Caustic Alkalines : Dilute by drinking water and then drink a glass of lemon or orange juice.

Arsenic or Mercury Compounds : Immediately given one table spoon full of salt or zinc sulphate is a tumbler of warm water.

Inhalation of Gases

Pungent gases like chlorine, sulphur dioxide, bromine vapours etc. when inhaled in large quantities often choke the throat and cause suffocation. In such a case remove the victim to the open air and loosen the clothing at the neck. The patient should inhale dilute vapours of ammonia or gargle with sodium bicarbonate solution.

Fire

Burning clothing : It clothes have caught fire then lay the victim on the floor and wrap a fire-proof blanket tightly around him. The fire in the burning clothes will thus be extinguished. *Never throw water on the person* as it will cause serious boils on his body.

Burning Reagents : In case of fire on the working table at once turn out the gas taps and remove all things which are likely to ignite. Following methods be used to extinguish the fire :

(i) If any liquid in a beaker of flask has caught fire, cover the mouth of the vessel with a clean clamp cloth or duster.

(ii) Most of the fire on the working table can be extinguished by throwing sand on them.

(iii) If any wooden structure has caught fire it is put up by throwing water on it.

(iv) *Never throw water on burning oil or spirit:* Since it will only spread the fire. Throwing of a mixture of sand and sodium bicarbonate on the fire is most effective.

First Aid Box

A first aid box should be provided in every laboratory. It should contain the following things:

Bandages (3-4 rolls of different sizes), gauze, lint, cotton wool, leucoplast.

A pair of forceps, a pair of scissors, safety pins.

Glass dropper, two eye-glasses.

Vaseline, boric acid powder, sodium bicarbonate powder, a tube of Burnol.

Sarson oil, olive oil, glycerine.

Picric acid solution, Tannic acid solution, 1% acetic acid, 1% boric acid, 1% sodium bicarbonate, saturated solution of sodium carbonate.

Methylated spirit, rectified spirit, Dettol.

Storage of Chemicals

In storage of chemicals the following methods are normally adopted :

(i) Grouping the chemicals in a systematic way.

(ii) Arranging the elements in alphabetic order.

(iii) Arranging the elements and their components in which they occur in periodic table.

(iv) Grouping all elements and their similar components together.

(v) Numbering each bottle and jar and keeping an index book.

(vi) Keeping reagent bottles indefinite places on the bench and the cupboard.

(vii) Storing similar types of solutions at one place.

(viii) Using coloured bottles or bottles with spots of coloured paint.

(ix) Using same type of bottles for a particular type of reagent.

(x) Always store large bottles on floor and not on shelves.

(xi) While storing Winchester bottles of concentrated acids, they be kept in brackets with sand.

(xii) Bottles containing inflammable liquids be stored in a cool place outside the laboratory.

(xiii) White phosphorus be stored under water and sodium be stored under kerosene oil.

(xiv) Hydrogen peroxide be stored in an air tight tin.

Laboratory Assistant

Each laboratory be provided with a laboratory assistant to perform the following duties :

(i) Keeping benches and laboratory clean.

(ii) Oiling benches with linseed oil.

(iii) To draft orders for chemicals and apparatus.

(iv) To receive the supplies of chemicals and apparatus after proper checking.

(v) To prepare solutions for volumetric analysis.

(vi) To prepare the solution for reagents shelf and to keep the reagent bottles full.

(vii) To set up apparatus for demonstration and experiments.

(viii) To maintain apparatus (burette, pipette etc.) in proper working conditions.

(ix) Keeping reagent bottles and chemicals at proper places.

(x) Periodic cleaning of iron stands, balances etc.

(xi) Keeping the first aid box replenished.

(xii) For repair of apparatus and glassware.

(xiii) Periodic checking of chemistry books in library and reference books in the laboratory.

Reference Books

Books containing following types of details be kept in the chemistry laboratory as reference books :

(i) Books containing physical constants of common substances.

(ii) Books which give the details of preparation of solutions for reagent bottles as also for volumetric analysis.

(iii) Recipes for cleaning glass ware and metals, removing stains, freeing glass stoppers, fire proofing etc.

The Discipline

Maintaining discipline in laboratory is more difficult as compared to maintaining discipline in the class-room. This is so because, pupils doing the same work wish to talk and discuss with others. Modest talking is inevitable in the laboratory. Yet talking and walking in the laboratory may cause accidents. Following roles will help to avoid any such accidents.

1. Admission to the laboratory in the absence of teacher should be avoided.
2. Teacher should not be late unduly.
3. Students should silently go to their places after entering the laboratory.

4. Before beginning his lesson teacher should wait for silence.
5. The teacher should address the whole class.
6. Teacher should see that a complete silence is observed during his talk.
7. Teacher should change his pitch at times to add interest to his talk.
8. Teacher should make adequate preparation to keep class busy.

The Equipment

The list of equipment for each laboratory as recommended at the Tara Devi (Simla) seminar is given below:

Science Room

Science room should be provided with :

(i) Galleried seats.

(ii) One demonstration table (8' x 4') having cupboards, gas and water fittings.

(iii) A black board or wall board.

(iv) Black curtains for covering doors, windows and ventilators.

General Science Laboratory

It must have the following equipment:

(i) Working tables (ordinary) with drawers.

(ii) Demonstration table (8' x 4') provided with gas and water points.

(iii) A minimum of two sinks be provided in the corner of the laboratory.

(iv) A wall board or black board.

(v) Stools (in two sizes).

(vi) Almirahs (wooden or steel).

Chemistry Laboratory

The equipment for chemistry laboratory is as under:

(i) Almirahs (wooden and steel).

(ii) Wall board or blackboard.

(iii) Demonstration table (8* x 4') with cupboards, water and gas points.

(iv) Working tables with cupboards, shelves, water and gas points.

(v) Balance room should be attached to the laboratory.

(vi) Sinks on each working table or at least two large sinks at the corners of the laboratory.

(vii) A cupboard.

(viii) A wooden box half filled with sand for use as waste material box.

(ix) Acid proof drainage system.

(x) Shelves for reagent bottle on each working table and wall shelves for storage of reagent bottles.

Physics Laboratory

Physical laboratory should have the following equipment:

(i) Working tables (ordinary) with teak wood top.

(ii) At least one table having gas point fitted to it. This may be used for experiments on heat.

(iii) Projected platforms for balances.

(iv) Almirahs.

(v) Demonstration table having drawers, water and gas points.

(vi) Wall board or blackboard.

(vii) Two large sinks at the comers of the laboratory.

(viii) Stools (in two sizes).

(ix) Physics laboratory should have an attached dark room.

Planning

Teacher should be very careful while planning the purchase of equipment for the laboratory. He should carefully weigh each item to be purchased with its educational worth. He may classify his requirements as under:

(i) Apparatus required for laboratory work.

(ii) Apparatus required for demonstration purposes.

(iii) Apparatus required for general use.

While determining the quantity of apparatus to be purchased, he should keep the following points in mind :

(i) Financial resources at his disposal.

(ii) Demonstration and laboratory work that has to be done during the year.

(iii) Scheme of work including the method of teaching to be used.

(iv) Storage facilities available.

Before making actual purchases a list be prepared of experiments to be informed by students and principles to be demonstrated by the teacher. For demonstration only one set will do but for experiments to be carried out by the students the number of sets required will be equal to the number of students working at a time. Some additional sets be purchased to cover up for the breakages etc., only such articles which are really required should be purchased.

If only limited funds are available then the purchases of beakers, flasks, funnels, files etc. should be accorded first priority. These are the articles which are required by students while doing experiments. When ample store of such articles has been made then only the apparatus needed for demonstration be purchased. Another important point which must be considered is that there is enough accommodation for the proper storage of articles likely to be purchased. While ordering for purchases scheme of teaching, method of teaching and knowledge and ability of teacher must also be given due consideration.

Keeping in view the points discussed above the teacher should prepare a list of articles to be purchased. While selecting apparatus teacher must not be tempted by attractive descriptions given in catalogue. While preparing an indent the teacher should give full specifications of the article required. In the absence of such specifications it is just possible that you make purchase of items which you never intended to purchase. For selecting a good firm the list of apparatus with complete specification be sent to some competing and reputed firms and they be asked to quote their lowest rates. A specimen for inviting quotation is shown below.

After receiving quotations a reliable firm quoting the lowest rate be asked to make the supplies.

The Unesco designed apparatus for tropical schools is very satisfactory. The Government of India is considering an arrangement for the manufacture of such instruments and making supplies of these to schools in lieu of cash grants.

S.No.	*Articles*	*Quality*	*Size*	*Quantity*
1.	R.B. Flasks	Pyrex glass	250 ml	10 doz.
2.	Titration flasks	Pyrex glass	100 ml	10 doz.
3.	Troughs	Pneumatic glass	12" dia	2 doz.
4.	Nitric acid	Commercial	51	
5.	Sulphuric add	B.D.H.	11	

Chemistry teacher should carefully check the items received and then arrange them properly after making entries in the stock register.

The Method of Procurement

After preparing the list of items to be purchased the chemistry teacher should make purchases from the firms approved by the controller of stores or from some other approved source. However, if no such source is available then he should send a list of his requirements to reputed firms for quotations. After receiving quotations, the teacher can select the dealers and firms for placing orders — the criterion being lower price and better quality.

. It is desirable to patronise local and neighbouring firms. This provides the teacher a chance to select personally the items required and get them packed in his presence. Many a time, it is better to go to a firm of repute and make the selection and purchase, and have the apparatus packed in one's presence. It is always wise to get insured against breakage and loss of the fragile apparatus ordered from out station firms.

On receiving the apparatus it should be carefully unpacked and after proper checking all the items of the purchase be catalogued and recorded in stock register; then the goods received be properly stocked.

Arrangement and Care

The apparatus received be arranged in almirahs provided with glass fronts and preferably be fitted with mortise locks to avoid dust getting in. Apparatus should be arranged in such a way that each and every item could be easily located. Items which are frequently required be stored at such places that they are readily available. The apparatus should be arranged in one deep of shelf; several rows of same articles may be placed on one shelf. The apparatus may be arranged either subject wise or alphabetically. If we arrange the apparatus subject-wise we find that some articles fall under more than one heading and if we arrange them alphabetically we find that glass and metal articles are coming together in which there is more likelyhood of breakage. Thus, it is always better to reserve a few almirahs for apparatus required for individual practical work in which the apparatus be arranged alphabetically. The chemicals can also be stored alphabetically.

A list be pasted on the almirahs showing the names of articles stored in them.

The apparatus needed only for demonstration purposes may be stored in separate almirahs subject-wise.

Chemicals can be stored even on open shelves. For this purpose two open shelves can be provided on either side of the recess for balances. However, dangerous and costly chemicals like phosphorus or sodium or salts of mercury, bismith or cadmium be stored separately in an almirah. The containers or bottles containing chemicals should be neatly labelled.

To effect economy in space some items of common use such as stands, holders, clamps etc., many be stored outside almirahs. Two possible arrangements for storage of iron stands are shown on next page.

Care of Equipments and Apparatus

Care of equipment and apparatus is one of the important functions of the chemistry teacher. For this the apparatus kept in almirahs must be checked at regular intervals. During this checking operation the apparatus should not only be inspected but it should also be dusted, cleaned and polished if necessary. If proper care is taken the life of the apparatus will increase. For proper upkeep and maintenance the following points be kept in mind :

(i) After use the apparatus should be propery cleaned before it is returned to its proper place. Never return dirty apparatus to its proper place. This is specially applicable in case of glass apparatus used inchemistry laboratory. For proper cleaning of glass articles we can make use of soap, hot alkali solution, acidified potassium dichromate solution etc.

(ii) For cleaning items *made of brassware use Brasso. Brasso be* applied to the article with finger covered with a piece of muslin, allowed to dry and then rubbed off with a clean duster.

(iii) Iron articles are generally polished. For polishing such articles use Black Japan thinned with a little turpentine or kerosene oil. Aluminium paint can also be used. If the article to be painted has any rust it should be removed by rubbing with an emery paper, before painting the article. Use of kerosene oil can also be made for removal of rust. Take care to apply vaseline on screws and hinges of iron articles during rainy season.

(iv) Wooden articles be left in the sun after being polished with spirit polish. Spirit polish can be made by dissolving shellac in methylated spirit. One or two coatings of it are then applied on the article.

(v) The top of each laboratory table is unpolished but it should be waxed (specially in case of chemistry laboratory) to avoid the action of acids. For waxing either paraffin wax or candles can be used. Wax is coated over the table with the help of painters brush and is then spread over and smoothened using the hot iron of washerman. It is then allowed to dry and any excess of eax is scarped off with a blunt knife. It is then polished with a coarse duster.

(vi) Special attention be paid to keep sinks clean. For cleaning sinks use *vein* powder or some other cleaning powder. Use special chemicals for removal of stains if they persist.

(vii) In chemistry laboratory special attention be paid to the fact that stoppers of bottles are not lost or get changed. For this they should be tagged to the bottle either using a copper wire or a rubber band.

(viii) The apparatus which is frequently used by students may go out of its proper adjustment and a good chemistry teacher must find time for its proper adjustment and must also be able to carry out minor repairs. For this the chemistry laboratory must be equipped with a tool kit containing usual hammer, wrenches, pliers, screw drivers, forceps etc.

(ix) Glass panes of almirahs should also be cleaned occasionally. For cleaning glass panes use monkey brand soap. Rub a wet sponge over the soap and then over the pane and clean off with a duster. Pumice stone dipped in water is in methylated spirit and rubbed over the panes will remove all dirt.

(x) For cleaning of glass apparatus in general and burette and pipette in particular, use a solution of potassium dichromatic acidified with dilute sulphuric acid.

Record

Maintainancc of a proper record of the apparatus, material etc., in the laboratory is one of the important duties of the science master. For this after receipt of articles they should be thoroughly checked and then they be entered in the stock register. A specimen page from a stock register is shown on next page.

Separate stock register be maintained for consumable and non-consumable items, permanent articles, glass articles etc. Following stock registers are generally maintained in schools:

(i) Stock register for non-breakable articles.

(ii) Stock register for breakable articles.

(iii) Stock register for consumable articles.

(iv) Stock register for permanent articles.

In addition to various stock registers following registers should also be maintained :

Order Register : This register is meant for orders sent for the purchase of new apparatus. Entries in this registger should indicate the serial number and date of the order, name of the firm to whom the order has been placed, details of articles ordered, articles received, cost of articles received. For convenience a copy of the order be posted on the left hand page of this register and a copy of supply order be pasted on the right hand page.

Requirement Register : This register if maintained makes the task of placing orders easier. Teacher will enter in this register the items whose absence is felt by the teacher at the time of demonstration of the experiment or during the practical class. If such entries are not made them there is every likelihood that some of the items needed by the teacher may be left out while placing the order for purchase of material and equipment. The requirement register should invariably be consulted by the teacher whenever be places orders for the purchase of materials or other requirements of the laboratory.

Specimen Page from

Stock Register

Stock Register of..............................Department

Name of the article........................

Month & Date	Particulars (Name of the Firm, Bill No. and Date)	Receipt	Consumed/ written	Balance	Initials of Tr. incharge
		Qt. Rate Amount	Qty. Amount Qty.	Amount	

Stock Register for Science Club : Organising science clubs is quite useful in creating a scientific atmosphere and each secondary school is expected to have a science club. For organising various activities of science club the teacher needs different types of apparatus, equipment and materials. It is desirable to maintain a separate stock register for the science club. In this register all the apparatus meant for science club be entered. Entries of models, charts and collections made by students should also be made in this register.

Maintenance of Stock Registers : Following points should be given due consideration while maintaining any stock register:

(i) The outer cover of the stock register should indicate the name of the register, name of the school, date of opening and closing of the register, etc.

(ii) A certificate be given on the first page of the register indicating the total number of pages in the register. All the pages be numbered serially and the above certificate be countersigned by the head of the institution.

(iii) Either separate stock registers be maintained or the same stock register be divided into a number of portions under various heads such as Mechanics, Heat, Light, Sound, Electricity, Magnetism etc.

(iv) An effort be made to make entries alphabetically.

(v) An Index be given at the beginning of the stock register.

(vi) Each receipt entry should be entered with date of receipt and the items consumed or broken be shown in the columns meant for this purpose. All these entries be initialled by chemistry teacher and countersigned by head of institution.

Home Made Apparatus

It is expected that science teacher is capable of devising and making apparatus for some simple experiments, modify apparatus and carry out simple repairs. The apparatus devised and made in school workshop or laboratory by the teacher or student is known as home-made apparatus. A science teacher with a little thought and ingenuity can make a number of valuable and serviceable models making use of cheap materials such as Jam-Jars, bits of wire, corks, motor parts etc. Some of the advantages of using home-made apparatus are as under :

(i) Such an apparatus is economical.

(ii) Use of such an apparatus makes more obvious the application of science to life and things around us.

(iii) It provides an encouragement to the student to make such an apparatus and adopt it as a hobby.

(iv) It helps to correlate science with manual training.

(v) It creates extra interest in the subject.

(vi) It provides training in manual skill, resourcefulness and ingenuity. These qualities arc quite useful for life.

A word of caution for teacher in using house-made apparatus is that he must not sacrifice efficiency just for his over enthusiasm for using house-made apparatus.

Locally Produced Low Cost Equipment

Such equipment can be made by individual teachers for their own use in schools or made available from a production centre. This type of equipment can serve the needs of the teacher, the student and the curriculum more effectively. As already pointed out such an equipment can be produced by individual teachers or can be procured from production centres.

Equipments made in Schools

The *Unesco source book for Science Teaching* contains a number of suggestions for simple teacher-made equipment in addition to a wide variety of experiments. One chapter has been specially devoted, in *Unesco Handbook for Science Teachers,* to facilities, equipment and materials. The *Guidebook to Constructing Inexpensive Science Teaching Equipment,* which have been produced at the university of Maryland (United States).

A pamphlet has been produced by the Junior Engineers, Technicians, Scientists (JETS) based in the school of Engineering, University of Zambia. It is intended to help schools produce equipments such as wooden racks and stands for pipettes, burettes and test-tubes, and metal clamps, clamp holders and retort stands.

In India similar work has been undertaken by the National Council for Educational Research and Training (NCERT). Details for a mobile laboratory unit has been published in India.

The *Manual de quimica experimental,* produced in Bolivia contains a number of experiments which illustrate most of junior secondary level chemistry course e.g., preparation and properties of common gases; acids, bases and salts; laws of chemical composition. In this manual instructions arc written for teachers with little or no workshop experience, on how to make simple balances, various supports, an alcohol burner and some items of electrochemical equipment. It also provides a list of chemicals that can be procured locally from market or pharmacy.

Equipments made in Production Centres

The production of equipments by teachers in their own schools and its advantages were taken up in the previous section. However, many a teacher find it burdensome because of the fact that they are faced with day-to-day difficulties of teaching. Really speaking it is too much to expect teachers to be the sole providers of equipment. From their efforts we can develop local production units and the teachers can then be expected to maintain the equipment supplied to them. Warren and Lowe's. *The Production of School Science Equipment* provides an insight into developments in various countries. A summary of experience in Bangla Desh, Fizi, Pakistan, India, Hongkong, Japan, Indonesia, Philippines, Singapore, Vietnam and Republic of Korea has also been published.

There are some large-scale projects, in developing countries, for production of locally based equipments. The concept of centres is not new, a prototype being set up in Chile in 1964. Other production centres are NCERT (New Delhi), IPTST (Bangkok), the Science Education Production Unit (SEPU) in Kenya and the National Educational Equipment Centre (NEEC) in Pakistan.

NCERT (New Delhi) makes batches of 1500 lots for primary and middle schools and is under contract to UNICEF for 50,000 kits.

SEPU produces teaching aids (e.g. Slides and Photographs) and chemistry, biology and physics kits for secondary schools which are designed to meet all the practical requirements associated with East African Certificate of Education. Kits are accompanied by manuals for teachers and students. The emphasis is on pupil participation and small-scale experiments thus the kits are not suitable for demonstration work.

Some of the most essential points that must be kept in mind while establishing production centres for low-cost equipment are summarised below:

(i) The centre must have expertise in design, in management and distribution.

(ii) To overcome the *shortage of technicians,* the training of management staff and training of technicians is of vital importance. The committee on the Teaching of Science of International Council of Scientific Unions (ICSU — CTS) in conjunction with Unesco, is endeavouring to discover the extent of the shortages and find ways of alleviating them.

(iii) *Realistic budgeting* : The production centre must work to realistic budgeting. To lower the cost of production the production centre must be cost-concious. Making as large a range of apparatus as possible from a given item of equipment will help to lower production costs.

(iv) *Effective marketing and distribution:* For effective marketing and distribution it is essential to make an infrastructure between the production centre and the educational establishments. In small countries production centres may be set up to serve both the schools and the institution of higher studies.

(v) *Cooperation with teachers and curriculum designers* : The production centres should design the equipment, to be produced, in conjunction with teachers and curriculum designers and only such equipment as needed in view of the requirements of prevailing text-books be only produced.

(vi) *Quality control:* Before supplying the equipment to schools it must be checked for the quality including reliability. Only good quality equipment be marketed.

(vii) *Facility for repairs and maintenance:* The production centre must have an efficient system for repairs and maintenance.

The Chemicals

It is possible to reduce the cost of teaching a laboratory-based chemistry curriculum by using small scale techniques. It is also important to consider how much and what chemicals are to be used. Small-scale techniques are generally more safe and they also help to improve the manipulative skills of the students. Texts indicating how small-scale work can be used through out a school course have been published in many a countries.

To further reduce the cost of materials it is desirable that locally available chemicals are put to maximum use e.g., geochemical minerals, disused dry cells, scrap metal, vegetable oils, orange peel, root extracts, soap and baking powder.

In Thailand, IPTST has produced a detailed list of chemicals readily available in local markets. The production of similar lists by institutions in other countries would be of much use.

Use of Computers

We find that in new programmes in teaching the computers are used increasingly. Many articles that have appeared in literature also point to the increased use of computers in teaching. The applications of micro-computers in school can be classified as under:

> *Direct Teaching* : In this type are included the use of computers for simulations, instructional games, revision questions and exercises.
>
> *Data Handling* : This includes word processing, data base management and data collection and display in the laboratory.
>
> *Computer Assisted Learning* : From the survey of literature we can easily find that most commonly the micro-computers are used in teaching of chemistry are used for handling of experimental data, e.g., interfacing with a gas chromatograph, monitoring and controlling clock reactions and the calculations of numerical constants.

Though micro-computers are quite expensive yet their education potential is considerable and they offer chemistry teachers an opportunity to experiment with imaginative and innovative ways of teaching chemistry.

Charts, Diagrams and Pictures

Charts, diagrams, pictures etc., if displayed in the laboratory provides right scientific atmosphere to the place. Various details about these have been discussed in chapter on *Teaching Aids*. Here the topic is discussed just as a reference.

Charts : An all out effort be made to avoid display of printed charts available in the market because these charts are quite costly and are not fully representative. Such charts are also sacrifice simplicity and directness to details.

Following type of charts be preferred for display in chemistry room:

(i) Charts showing diagrammatic sketches of different pieces of apparatus generally used by students in their practical work, e.g., beaker, flask, gas-jar, retort, spirit lamp etc.

(ii) Charts depicting diagrammatic sketches of different important experiments from various branches of chemistry e.g., chart showing the preparation of oxygen, hydrogen, carbon dioxide etc. Such a chart should be fully labelled and should be drawn in lead pencil.

(iii) Some charts for use in demonstration lessons.

(iv) A progress chart depicting the progress of each student be prominently displayed. Such a chart should show the complete record of work of the student.

(v) Some important do's and don'ts be also displayed on a chart placed at some prominent place in the laboratory.

(vi) A chart of common accidents and first aid be also depicted in the laboratory.

In addition to various types of charts given above, the following types *of pictures and illustrations* are quite useful if depicted in the laboratory :

(i) Portraits of great Indian and world chemists.

(ii) Pictures of scientific interest e.g., pictures of Nangal Fertilizer Project.

(iii) Pictures showing progress of chemistry, e.g., pictures of atomic power stations.

(iv) Maps indicating sources of ores of metals and chemical products.

(v) Weather charts,,maps and graphs prepared by students after observing and collecting data from weather reports.

(vi) Various types of demonstration models preferably prepared by students.

Bulletin Boards

Each laboratory is expected to have at least three boards to be used as bulletin boards. These are to be used as under:

(i) One of the boards is reserved for display of newspaper cuttings, sciences news and pictorial illustrations of scientific interest.

(ii) One of the boards is reserved for putting up notices about science club activities.

(iii) One of the boards may be used for indicating the assignments.

Improvised Apparatus

For teaching of chemistry availability of good apparatus and well-equipped laboratories is a must. However, it should lead us to a wrong conception that teaching of science cannot be carried out in the absence of expensive apparatus. One of the reports by NCERT observed that from among various factors that stand in the way of science education in our country one is lack of adequate resources for laboratory building, purchase of good and adequate apparatus and equipment. This lack of funds and resources makes improvisation of apparatus almost a necessity in India.

Need for Improvisation : India is a poor country and so we have only limited financial resources. For imparting effective and efficient science education, due to this financial constraint we require the production of improvised and inexpensive learning aids. A teacher with some ingenuity and manual skill can make a number of valuable and serviceable articles from discarded things all around him. For this purpose every science room should be equipped with a work bench and a kit of tools that may be used by students and teacher in making and improvising equipment for chemistry teaching.

Definition of Improvisation : Some of the definitions of improvisations are given below :

It refers to a make shift arrangement for accomplishing the intended learning task. It refers to contrived situation that is created from reading available material for sake of convenience.

It refers to a stimulating situation for demonstrating and imparting learning is respect of controls and operations making use of low cost materials.

It refers to those learning aids which are prepared from simple and readily available cheap material by students and teacher.

Significance of Improvisation : Improvisation is quite significant and has many values as the process of improvisation needs resourcefulness and ingenuity on the part of the chemistry teacher. It is based on the concept of solving some problem by a make shift or alternate arrangement given below arc some significant values attached with the process of improvisation :

(i) It splashes the cost of apparatus and is quite helpful in making the school self-reliant.

(ii) It has instructional value as well. When we are carrying out any improvisation we do get a proper feeling for the scientific process and designing. Thus we learn by doing.

(iii) It help develop the dignity of labour and also satisfies the urge of creative production.

(iv) It helps to develop the habit of cooperation and coordination.

(v) It provides training in thinking skills through the

process of looking for low-cost substitutes or alternatives.

Process of Improvisation : It refers to a systematic way of constructing a piece of apparatus or designing an experiment. It involves the following steps :

(i) Making a careful study of the conventional apparatus or experiment.

(ii) Thinking of some low cost substitute that may be available in the market.

(iii) Designing the improvised apparatus or experiment.

(iv) Putting the improvised apparatus or experiment to test.

(v) Making further improvements in the improvised apparatus keeping the test results in mind.

(vi) Making use of the improvised apparatus in the laboratory for demonstration or practical work.

Examples of Improvised Apparatus : Some examples of improvised apparatus are given below :

Simple Tripod Stand : To make a simple tripod stand we have only to cut away A or V shaped piece from the sides of a discarded tin can. We can remove the lid and bottom of the tin can completely or we can simply make holes in the bottom. If holes are made it also serves the purpose of wire gauze.

Fig. Tripod stand (improvised).

Beehive Shelf : An improvised beehive shelf can be obtained from empty tin can. The tin can to be used for the purpose should
be rust free and its inner and outer surfaces are either galvanised or vanished. To make a beehive shelf drill a hole of 1/2" diameter in the centre of the bottom of tin can and cut a V-shaped notch on one side of it.

Distillation Plant : The design of a distillation plant is shown in Fig.

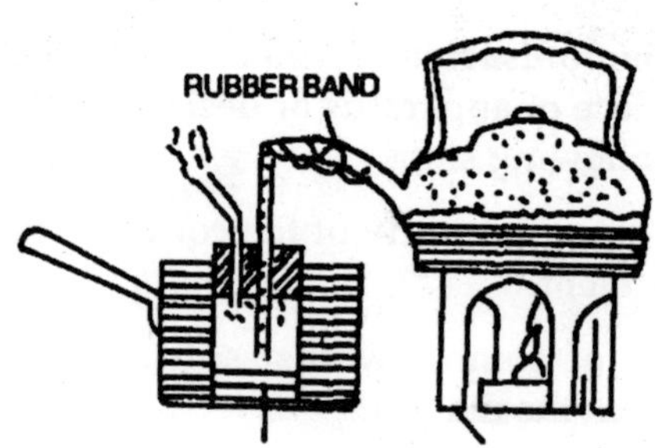

Fig. JAMJAR SIMPLE TRIPOD

In this boiling water from a kettle is allowed to condense in a jam jar which is immersed in a pan containing ice cold water. A simple glass tube fitted with a rubber tubing can be fitted to the mouth of the kettle and another glass tube is fitted to serve as outlet for condensed steam.

There are many more such items which can be easily obtained. Some such items are:

(i) Spring balance.

(ii) Spirit lamp.

(iii) Water voltameter.

(iv) Fire extinguisher.

Advantages of Improvised Apparatus : Some of the advantages of improvised apparatus are :

(i) These are quite cheap and economical.

(ii) They have great educational value. While devising such apparatus students gains more familiarity with the underlying principles of the apparatus.

(iii) It helps to develop the creative and constructive instructs of the child.

(iv) It inspires young students to explore and invent new things.

(v) It develops the lower of initiative and resourcefulness in the student.

(vi) It helps to develop power of scientific thinking.

(vii) It helps to inculcate the habit of diligency in the students.

(viii) It galvanises dignity of labour.

(ix) It solves problem of leisure time.

Examples of Improvisation for Physics Experiments

Experiment	*Conventional apparatus parts*	*Improvised apparatus parts*
1. Beam bending	(a) Steel strip	(a) Wooden scale as beam
	(b) Spherometer	(b) Wooden scale for depression measurements
	(c) Slotted weights	(c) Discarded cells and weights.
2. Terminal velocity	(a) Glass tubes	(a) Discarded fluorescent tubes
	(b) Glycerin	(b) Water or oil
	(c) Ball bearings	(c) Sealing wax balls
	(d) Iron stands	(d) Mounting on the wall

Following is the example of an improvised experiment:

Showing Self-inductions : To demonstrate self-induction we need a choke or primary coil of a step transformer, a neon taster and a battery of 4 cells (6V dry cell battery) complete the circuit as shown in the diagram. When we tap the key flashes can be observed by neon tester which show flashes. This is because of production of high induced e.m.f. in the same inductive circuit every time tile circuit is broken.

Examples of Improvised Apparatus : Some examples of improvised apparatus are given below:

Simple Tripod Stand : To make a simple tripod stand we have only to cut away A shaped pieces from the sides of a discarded tin can. We can remove the lid and bottom of the tin can completely or we can simply make holes in the bottom. If holes are made it also serves the purpose of wire gauze.

Fig. Tripod stand (Improvised).

Gold Leaf Electroscope : For obtaining an improvised gold leaf electroscope we can take a wide mouthed bottle and fix a waxed coil in its mouth. Insert an L-shaped brass or copper wire into the cork and attach the gold leaf at its end.

Davy's Safety Lamp : To get a simple model of Davy's safety lamp we only need a wire gauze. Cut the wire gauze of the shape as shown and put it round a candle.

Beehive Shell : An improvised beehive shelf can be obtained from empty tin can. The tin can to be used for the purpose should be rust free and its inner and outer surfaces are either galvanised or varnished. To make a beehive shelf drill a hole of 1/2" diameter in the centre of the bottom of tin can and cut a V-shaped notch on one side of it. This can now be used as a beehive shelf.

Fig. Davy's Safety Lamp.

Distillation Plant : The design of a distillation plant is shown in Fig.

In this boiling water from a kettle is allowed to condense in a jam jar which is immersed in a pan containing ice cold water. A simple glass tube fitted with a rubber tubing can be fitted to the mouth of the kettle and another glass gube is fitted to serve as outlet for condensed steam.

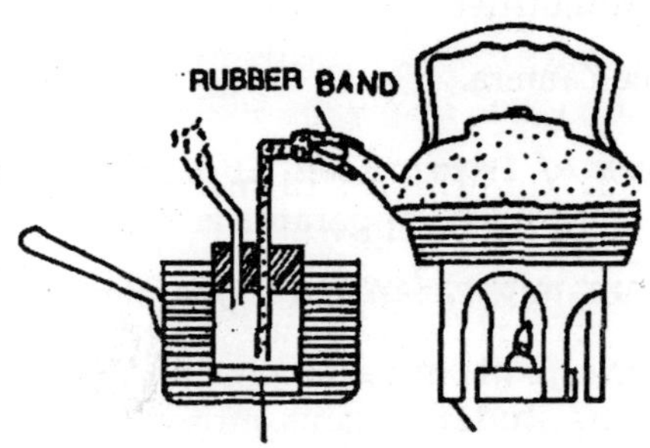

JAM JAR SIMPLE TRIPOD

Fig. Distillation Plant (Improvised).

Hydrometer : Broken pipettes can be used to prepare a hydrometer. It is sealed below its bulb and then appropriate quantity of small lead shots are inserted into it. After this the stem of the broken pipette is calibrated to get an improvised hydrometer.

There are many more such items which can be easily obtained. Some such items are :

(i) Aneroid Barometer.

(ii) Mariner's Compass.

(iii) Directing Needle.

(iv) Spring balance.

(v) Lactometer.

(vi) Spirit lamp.

(vii) Model of water pump.

(viii) Model of syringe pump.

(ix) Ingenhouz apparatus.

(x) Telescope.

(xi) Electric bell.

(xii) Periscope.

(xiii) Water voltameter.

(xiv) Fire extinguisher.

(xv) Pin hole camera.

Advantages of Improvised Apparatus **:** Some of the advantages of improvised apparatus are :

(i) These are quite cheap and economical.

(ii) They have great educational value. While devising such apparatus students gains more familiarity with the underlying principles of the apparatus.

(iii) It helps to develop the creative and constructive instructs of the child.

(iv) It inspires young students to explore and invent new things.

(v) It develops the lower of initiative and resourcefulness in the student.

(vi) It helps to develop power of scientific thinking.

(vii) It helps to inculcate the habit of diligency in the students.

(viii) It galvanises dignity of labour.

(ix) It solves problems of the use of leisure time.

Questions

1. Bring out the need and importance of laboratories in the teaching of physical sciences.
2. Discuss the plan of a combined lecture and laboratory room for a class of 40 students in lecture and 20 students in practical work.
3. What type of laboratory would you suggest for teaching physical sciences for a small high school in your state ?
4. List the various points to be kept in mind while arranging equipment and material for science laboratory,

5. What is a first-aid box ? Is it essential to keep it in the laboratory, if yes, why?
6. Write short notes on the following :
   (i) Care and maintenance of laboratory material.
   (ii) Safety measures in science laboratory.
   (iii) Keeping laboratory registers.

15

Science Club

For supplementing the teaching of science in class-room and to widen the knowledge of his students a good science teacher can involve his students in a number of co-curricular activities such as the *science club, scientific hobbies, visits of places of scientific interest, broad-cast talks, gramophone lectures* etc. Though there is no limit to such extracurricular activities and teacher is free to undertake one or more such activities in his school for the benefit of his students.

Some of these activities, their organisational and other aspects, are taken up in the next few pages.

Science Club

To channelise the energies of students and to make proper use of talent of the students science clubs may be organised in schools. Such a club then forms the backbone of the co-curricular activities in the school. Such clubs, if properly organised, will be of great help to create interest in teaching of science and so now the importance and educational value of such clubs is duly recognised. Such clubs provide better chances to acquaint the students with various facts and principles of science. Students can take up any project of a scientific hobby of his choice while participating in a science club activity. Such a participation of a student in science club activities helps to link his theoretical knowledge to the outside world and he gets more opportunities for self-expression and creativity.

Participation in various activities of science club also helps to develop manual skills of the student and he gets interested in learning of science.

The importance of science clubs in schools in words of Dr. W. Davis is, *"If the future belongs to youth and to science, then there is a vastly more important place for science clubs, in the scheme of things."*

Mckown has opined as follows while stating the advantages of science clubs over usual class-room teaching.

"The club offers the pupil an opportunity for specialisation which he does not have in the class-room. In the class-room his work is formal; in the club it is informal; in the class-room he is told what to do, in the club he chooses, in the class-room his method of dealing with a topic is clearly outlined by teacher imposed restrictions, in the club programme the method is of his own desiring; in the class he tries to please the teacher, in the club he works for his own and his club s interest and for the joy of doing his works; in the class-room he confirms to a system, in the club he suits his own convenience."

From the views expressed above we can clearly see that there is complete freedom for the student to pursue his interests in a science club and he can choose his own project and also his own method to pursue the project so chosen. This atmosphere that prevails in a science club is totally different from the one that prevails in a class-room. The club represent freedom and expression whereas the class-room represents conformity and repression.

Types of Science Clubs

Broadly speaking science clubs can be classified as

The Specialised Interest Science Clubs : In this catagory the clubs take up such projects which deal with some specialised subject. Such clubs are radio club, photographic club, nature study club, aviation club, astronomical club, etc.

General Science Club : These clubs take up any type of science activity and such clubs are generally known as chemical society, zoological society, botany club, physics association etc.

Though both types of clubs have their advantages but experience has shown that specialised clubs are only short-lived and so a sciene teacher should prefer general science club. He can undertake some specialised activity as a part of programme of such a general science club for a short duration of time.

Aims of Science Club : The major aims of science club can be summarised as under:

(i) To make proper use of leisure time.

(ii) To develop individual and group initiative.

(iii) To create students' interest in his everyday experiences and his environment.

(iv) To develop scientific attitude among students and to inculcate a training in scientific methods and to broaden his scientific outlook.

(v) Provide the student with opportunity to develop his explorative, creative and inventive faculties.

(vi) To develop a habit of cooperation in the students.

(vii) To encourage students participation in teaching-learning process.

(viii) To provide encouragement to club members for undertaking some difficult, complicated and even risky experiments which are not permitted to be undertaken in regular class.

(ix) To allow opportunities to young students to learn applications of science.

(x) To identify and nurture the would be scientists of the country.

(xi) To familiarise the students with recent advances in science.

(xii) To provide students vocational and educational guidance.

(xiii) To exchange information with other science clubs.

Organisation

A science club, if properly organised, will be a great help in enlivening the teaching of science. Such a club should be run by the students under the guidance and supervision of the teacher. For proper running of a club the most important thing is the preparation of a draft constitution of the club. This draft be prepared by the science teacher in consultation with the head of the institution. This draft constitution should provide all important details about the name of the club, aims and objectives of the club, details regarding membeiship and the fees etc., to be paid by members, purposes for which the expenditure can be incurred and the person competent to approve such an expenditure. Various offices available to members and the procedure for filling up such offices. Any other relevant details.

For efficient and successful working of science clubs an expert body has suggested the organisation as under

(i) Such a club should have the head of institution as its pattern.

(ii) One of the senior science teachers be asked to be the sponsor of the club.

(iii) Membership of the club be open to all the science students of the school.

(iv) Associate-membership may be allowed to some other students interested in science.

(v) The club may have an elected executive committee. The members of executive should include the following and should be elected or nominated from amongst the students.

(a) Chairman

(b) Secretary

(c) Asstt. Secretary

(d) Treasurer

(e) One or two class representatives from each class.

The executive committee may also include a librarian, a store keeper and a publicity officer.

(vi) Only a nominal membership fee be charged from the members.

(vii) The club members be asked to tap other resources and carry out the club activities in their own locality.

Assignment of Duties

For a cohesive and efficient functioning of a club, there must be a clear demarcation of duties to be assigned to its office bearers. Following suggestions have been made in this regard.

Patron: He is expected to take a keen interest in all the activities of the club and to extend all the possible facilities to the club.

Sponsor: He is the main force to start the club and he has to take initiative to start such a club and made it a hub of activities. His role should be that of an advisor, guide and supervisor and he should refrain from becoming a dictator. He should always be alert to avoid any mishap. He should keep a strict watch on the activities of the club members.

Chairman : He being the elected representative of the student should be asked to preside over all the formal functions organised by the club. He has also the convene and preside over the meetings of the executive committee of the club.

Secretary : He is also an elected member and is to look after and maintain a proper record of various activities of the club. He should call a meeting of the executive committee in consultation with the chairman and in accordance with the constitution of the club. He should keep a true record of the meetings of the executive committee. He is also responsible to carry out all correspondence on behalf of the club and to extend invitations to speakers and guests for various functions of the club.

Asstt. Secretary : His main role is to assist the secretary in performance of his duties. In the absence of secretary he has to carry out all the functions of the secretary.

Treasurer : He is the person who is responsible for collection of subscriptions/membership fee for the club. He has also to maintain a proper account of receipts and expenditure of the club. He must present his accounts to the executive for audit and scrutiny at least once a year.

Members of Executive Committee : A member of executive committee is expected to extend his active cooperation and participate actively in formation of club's policy and programme. He should use his contacts and influence to make the programmes of the club a success.

Suggested Activities

(i) Interesting experiments may be undertaken in the club to enable students to develop skills and abilities for research work.

(ii) Club members may be asked to make collections of specimen, prepare charts and models etc.

(iii) Club can arrange excursions to places of scientific interest.

(iv) Science clubs may be asked to arrange science fairs and science exhibitions.

(v) Under the aegis of the club some quiz contest, paper reading contest, essay competition and some such other competitions can be arranged.

(vi) Science clubs must celebrate science days. On such occasions they should put up tabuleaux and plays.

(vii) Some eminent scholars be invited to deliver extention lectures.

(viii) Science clubs can render school service in health and sanitation.

(ix) Members of the club can also render community service in realm of public health.

(x) If possible a science club should take initiative to organise a camp in which participants be educated to actively participate in national programme of health and family planning. They may be asked to inculcate sound health habits.

(xi) The club can take up the production of some common things like ink, soap, phenyl, shaving cream, boot polish, nail polish etc.

Science Club and Class-room Teaching

The activities of science club are a supplement to class-room teaching. Such clubs play an important role in making science education more meaningful and effective. Various charts, models, improvised apparatus prepared by members of the club can be used as important teaching aids for teaching of science in the class-room. References could be made to various science projects undertaken by the club members and the club members may be asked to explain their projects in the class. The explanation of a project by a student in a class may then be put to open discussion in the class which would make other students more interested in learning science.

To make best use of the trips and excursions arranged by the science club, the students be given a questionnaire so that students may be more attentive to provide their answeis. Answers given by the students may then be discussed in the class-room and teacher can coordinate all the facts observed by the students into a complete lesson.

Some methods can be used to correlate and coordinate various club activities with class-room teaching.

There is no doubt about the fact that if the club activities are organised properly they will never interfere with class-room teaching. Various activities of the club are expected to develop the skill of the student, his power of reasoning, understanding, his power to distinguish between relevant and irrelevant etc.

Evaluation

To find out the extent to which a club has succeeded in achieving its stated objectives it is necessary to cany out regular periodical evaluation of the activities of the club. Such an evaluation may be external or internal or it may be a mixture of both. For internal evaluation the views of patron, sponsor about the activities of the club may be obtained. They should express their views along with their suggestions for improvement in the working of the club. For external evaluation the sponsor of some other nearby science club be asked to visit the club activities and express his opinion. He may also be asked to give suggestions for improvement. An effort be then made to further improve the working of the club in the light of suggestions given for improvement

Scientific Hobbies

Scientific hobbies can also be undertaken as a part of activities of science club. Now that more and more attempts are being made to give a technical bias to our education and hobbies with a scientific basis are becoming more and more popular, the science master can make a valuable contribution by encouraging a number of hobbies that bear directly on education in science, students will be found only too enthusiastic and even willing to spend money in addition to their time to pursue such bobbies if the science teacher is keen and knows the particular hobbies he is going to start. In the beginning an attempt be made with one or two simple and less expensive hobbies. There is a large number of such hobbies having a scientific basis e.g., ink making, soap making, making hair oils and face creams, phenyl making, preparation of James and Jellys, achars and chutneys etc. The list can be enlarged to include gardening, making of charts and models, rendering Gist aid etc.

Use of Hobby Classes

A hobby class provides the student the best way of utilizing his leisure time and as such a hobby class fulfills one of the chief aims of education i.e. to train the child to use his leisure time properly. The students get a good opportunity to keep himself busy in a constructive way by attending such hobby classes. It helps the students to keep himself away from adolescent disturbances that helps him to adjust in later years of life. Hobby classes also provide the students a knowledge of technical side of science and also helps in correlating the teaching of science with the everyday life and environment.

Questions

1. What is a science club ? Discuss its need in teaching of physical sciences.
2. Discuss the objectives likely to be achieved by organising science clubs in schools.
3. How and for what ends would you sponsor a school science club ?
4. What are scientific hobbies ? Discuss their educational utility.
5. Name various scientific hobbies that you would like to start in a middle/ secondary school.
6. Discuss the role of science teacher in organising scientific hobbies.
7. Write short notes on the following:
   (i) Organisation of science clubs.
   (ii) Scientific hobbies.

Additional Reading

Bhaskara Rao, Digumarti (1994). *Scientific Aptitude,* New Delhi: Ashish Publishing House. ISBN 81-7024-658-X.

Bhaskara Rao, Digumarti (1995). *Animal Kingdom.* New Delhi: Discovery Publishing House. ISBN 81-7141-274-2.

Bhaskara Rao, Digumarti (1995). *Batracology.* New Delhi: Discovery Publishing House. ISBN 81-7141-279-3.

Bhaskara Rao, Digumarti (1997), *Scientific Attitude.* New Delhi: Discovery Publishing House. ISBN 81-7141-308-0.

Bhaskara Rao, Digumarti (1996). *Scientific Attitude vis-à-vis Scientific Aptitude.* New Delhi: Discovery Publishing House. ISBN 81-7141-308-0.

Bhaskara Rao, Digumarti, Editor (1996). *Encyclopaedia of Education for All,* 5 Volumes. New Delhi: APH Publishing Corporation. ISBN 81-7024-759-4 (set).

Vol. I *Education for All: The World Conference.* ISBN 81-7024-760-8.

Vol. II *Education for All: The EPA-9 Summit.* ISBN 81-7024-761-6.

Vol. III *Education for All: Quality Education for All.* ISBN 81-7024-762-6.

Vol. IV *Education for All: Planning and Monitoring.* ISBN 81-7024-763-4.

Vol. V *Education for All: The Indian Scenario.* ISBN 81-7024-764-0.

Bhaskara Rao, Digumarti, Editor (1996). *Global Perceptions on Peace Education,* 3 Volumes. New Delhi: Discovery Publishing House. ISBN 81-7141-319-6.

Bhaskara Rao, Digumarti, Editor (1996). *National Policy on Education*. 2 Volumes. New Delhi: Anmol Publications Pvt. Ltd. ISBN 81-7488-323-1.

Bhaskara Rao, Digumarti, Editor (1997). *Care the Child*, 2 Volumes. New Delhi: Discovery Publishing House. ISBN 81-7141-394-3.

Bhaskara Rao, Digumarti, Editor (1997). *Education for the 21st Century*. New Delhi: Discovery Publishing House. ISBN 81-7141-389-7.

Bhaskara Rao, Digumarti, Editor (1997). *Reflections on Scientific Attitude*. New Delhi: Discovery Publishing House, ISBN 81-7141-319-6.

Bhaskara Rao, Digumarti, Editor (1997). *Success Story of a Primary Education Project*. New Delhi: APH Publishing Corporation. ISBN 81-7024-850-7.

Bhaskara Rao, Digumarti, Editor (1997). *World Food Summit*. New Delhi: Discovery Publishing House. ISBN 81-7141-386-2.

Bhaskara Rao, Digumarti, Editor (1998). *Adolescence Education*. New Delhi: Discovery Publishing House. ISBN 81-7141-432-X.

Bhaskara Rao, Digumarti, Editor (1998). *Community and School Nutrition Education*. New Delhi: Discovery Publishing House. ISBN 81-7141-435-4.

Bhaskara Rao, Digumarti, Editor (1998). *District Primary Education Programme*. New Delhi: Discovery Publishing House. ISBN 81-7141-396-X.

Bhaskara Rao, Digumarti, Editor (1998). *Earth Summit*, 2 Volumes. New Delhi: Discovery Publishing House. ISBN 81-7141-435-4.

Bhaskara Rao, Digumarti, Editor (1998). *National Policy on Education: Towards an Enlightened and Humane Society*, New Delhi: Discovery Publishing House. ISBN 81-7141-426-5.

Bhaskara Rao, Digumarti, Editor (1998). *Reforming School Education*. New Delhi: Discovery Publishing House. ISBN 81-7141-403-6.

Bhaskara Rao, Digumarti, Editor (1998). *Teacher Education in India*. New Delhi: Discovery Publishing House. ISBN 81-7141-406-0.

Bhaskara Rao, Digumarti, Editor (1998). *World Summit for Social Development*. New Delhi: Discovery Publishing House. ISBN 81-7141-420-6.

Bhaskara Rao, Digumarti, Editor (2000). *Education for All: Achieving the Goal*, 3 Volumes, New Delhi: APH Publishing Corporation. ISBN 81-7648-152-1.

Vol. I *The Global Consensus*. ISBN 81-7648-155-6.

Vol. II *Mid-Decade Review Reports of Regional Seminars*. ISBN 81-7648-154-8.

Vol. III *Issues and Trends*. ISBN 81-7648-155-6.

Bhaskara Rao, Digumarti, Editor (2000), *International Encyclopaedia of AIDS*, 11 Volumes in 13 Parts. New Delhi: Discovery Publishing House. ISBN 81-7141-6 (Set).

Vol. 1 *Introduction to HIV/AIDS*. ISBN 81-7141-523-7.

Vol. 2 *HIV/AIDS—Issues and Challenges*, 2 Parts. ISBN 81-7141-524-5.

Vol. 3 *HIV/AIDS—Socio Economic Realities*. ISBN 81-7141-524-3.

Vol. 4 *HIV/AIDS—Law Ethics and Human Rights*, 2 Parts. ISBN 81-7141-526-1.

Vol. 5 *AIDS and NGOs*. ISBN 81-7141-527-X.

Vol. 6 *AIDS and Home Care*. ISBN 81-7141-528-8.

Vol. 7 *STD Case Management*. ISBN 81-7141-529-6.

Vol. 8 *HIV/AIDS Prevention and Care—Teaching Modules for Nurses and Midwives*. ISBN 81-7141-530-X.

Vol. 9 *HIV Prevention Education for Education for Educational Institutions*. ISBN 81-7141-531-8.

Vol. 10 *Instructional Modules for AIDS Education*. ISBN 81-7141-532-6.

Vol. 11 *School Health Education to Prevent AIDS and STD—A Package for Curriculum Planners*. ISBN 81-7141-5338-4.

Bhaskara Rao, Digumarti, Editor (2000). *International Encyclopaedia of Science and Technology Education*, 11 Volumes. New Delhi: Discovery Publishing House. ISBN 81-7141-548-2 (Set).

Vol. 1 *Science and Technology Education*. ISBN 81-7141-568-7.

Vol. 2 *Science Education in Developing Countries*. ISBN 81-7141-570-9.

Vol. 3 *Organisational Structure of Science*. ISBN 81-7141-570-9.

Vol. 4 *Science Education in Asia and the Pacific*. ISBN 81-7141-571-7.

Vol. 5 *Science and Technology Education for All*. ISBN 81-7141-572-5.

Vol. 6 *Values, Ethics, Talent and Girls in Science and Technology Education*. ISBN 81-7141-573-3.

Vol. 7 *Popularization of Science and Technology Education*. ISBN 81-7141-574-1.

Vol. 8 *Science, Power and Society*. ISBN 81-7141-575-X.

Vol. 9 *Information Technology*. ISBN 81-7141-576-8.

Vol. 10 *Teacher Training in Science and Technology Education*. ISBN 81-7141-577-6.

Vol. 11 *Teacher Training in Science and Technology: A Curriculum Framework*. ISBN 81-7141-578-4.

Bhaskara Rao, Digumarti, Editor (2001). *Distance Education in Different Countries*. New Delhi: APH Publishing Corporation. ISBN 81-7648-229-3.

Bhaskara Rao, Digumarti, Editor (2001). *Decentralised Management of Education (Management of Education in Panchayati Raj and Municipal Bodies)*. New Delhi: Discovery Publishing House. ISBN 81-7141-617-9.

Bhaskara Rao, Digumarti, Editor (2001). *Electrochemistry for Environmental Protection*. New Delhi: Discovery Publishing House. ISBN 81-7141-619-5.

Bhaskara Rao, Digumarti, Editor (2001). *Global Educational Studies*. New Delhi: Discovery Publishing House. ISBN 81-7141-616-0.

Bhaskara Rao, Digumarti, Editor (2001). *Global Synthesis of Educational Assessment*. New Delhi: Discovery Publishing House. ISBN 81-7141-613-6.

Bhaskara Rao, Digumarti, Editor (2000). *International Encyclopaedia of Human Rights*. 7 Volumes in 13 Parts. New Delhi: Discovery Publishing House. (Royal Size). ISBN 81-7141-567-9 (Set).

Vol. 1 *International Instruments of Human Rights*, 2 Parts. ISBN 81-7141-595-4.

Vol. 2 *Regional Instruments of Human Rights*. ISBN 81-7141-604-7.

Vol. 3 *Human Rights and the United Nations*, 2 Parts. ISBN 81-7141-605-5.

Vol. 4 *Fact Files of Human Rights*, 3 Parts. ISBN 81-7141-605-3.

Vol. 5 *Study Stories of Human Rights*, 3 Parts. ISBN 81-7141-607-3.

Vol. 6 *International Meetings on Human Rights*, 2 Parts. ISBN 81-7141-608-X.

Vol. 7 *Professional Training in Human Rights*. ISBN 81-7141-609-8.

Bhaskara Rao, Digumarti, Editor (2001). *Jomtein Decade of Education*. New Delhi: Discovery Publishing House. ISBN 81-7141-618-7.

Bhaskara Rao, Digumarti, Editor (2001). *Nuclear Materials: Issues and Concerns*, 2 Volumes. New Delhi: Discovery Publishing House. ISBN 81-7141-611-X.

Bhaskara Rao, Digumarti, Editor (2001). *World Conference on Education for All*. New Delhi: APH Publishing Corporation. ISBN 81-7141-274-9.

Bhaskara Rao, Digumarti, Editor (2001). *World Conference on Higher Education*, New Delhi: Discovery Publishing House. ISBN 81-7141-610-1.

Bhaskara Rao, Digumarti, Editor (2001). *World Conference on Science*. New Delhi: Discovery Publishing House. ISBN 81-7141-612-8.

Bhaskara Rao, Digumarti, Editor (2003). *Inspiring Experience in Teacher Education*. New Delhi: Discovery Publishing House. ISBN 81-7141-656-X.

Bhaskara Rao, Digumarti, Editor (2003). *International Studies in Education*, 3 Volumes, New Delhi: Discovery Publishing House. ISBN 81-7141-647-0.

Bhaskara Rao, Digumarti, Editor (2003). *Military Conversion: Impact on Science and Technology*, New Delhi: Discovery Publishing House. ISBN 81-7141-578-4.

Bhaskara Rao, Digumarti, Editor (2003). *United Nations Millennium Summit*. New Delhi: Discovery Publishing House. ISBN 81-7141-632-2.

Bhaskara Rao, Digumarti, Editor (2003). *World Assembly on Aging*. New Delhi: Discovery Publishing House. ISBN 81-7141-637-3.

Bhaskara Rao, Digumarti, Editor (2004). *World Conference on Human Rights*. New Delhi: Discovery Publishing House. ISBN 81-7141-661-6.

Bhaskara Rao, Digumarti, Editor (2003). *World Education Forum*. New Delhi: Discovery Publishing House. ISBN 81-7141-639-X.

Bhaskara Rao, Digumarti, Editor (2004). *Education Employment and Human Resource Development*. New Delhi: Discovery Publishing House. ISBN 81-7141-681-0.

Bhaskara Rao, Digumarti, Editor (2004). *Successfully Schooling*. New Delhi: Discovery Publishing House. ISBN 81-7141-677-2.

Bhaskara Rao, Digumarti, Editor (2004). *European Education and Teachers*. New Delhi: Discovery Publishing House. ISBN 81-7141-702-7.

Bhaskara Rao, Digumarti, Editor (2004). *Teachers in a Changing World*. New Delhi: Discovery Publishing House. ISBN 81-7141-694-2.

Bhaskara Rao, Digumarti, Editor (2004). *Learning to Live Together*, 4 Volumes. New Delhi: Discovery Publishing House.

Vol. 1 *International Conference on Learning to Live Together.*

Vol. 2 *Globalisation and Living Together.*

Vol. 3 *Curriculum for Learning to Live Together.*

Vol. 4 *Science Education for the Contemporary Society.*

Bhaskara Rao, Digumarti (2004). *International Guidelines on Open and Distance Education*, New Delhi: Discovery Publishing House.

Bhaskara Rao, Digumarti, Editor (2004). *Adult Learning in the 21st Century*. New Delhi: Discovery Publishing House.

Bhaskara Rao, Digumarti, Editor (2004). *Educational Practices: Research and Recommendations*. New Delhi: Discovery Publishing House.

Bhaskara Rao, Digumarti, Editor (2004). *Chernobyl: Never Again*. New Delhi: APH Publishing Corporation.

Bhaskara Rao, Digumarti, Editor (2004). *Virology and Immunology*. New Delhi: APH Publishing Corporation.

Bhaskara Rao, Digumarti, C.A.P. Swami and B.S.V. Dutt (1997). *Self-Evaluation in Student Teaching*. New Delhi: Discovery Publishing House. ISBN 81-7141-374-9.

Bhaskara Rao, Digumarti and B.S.V. Dutt, Editors (2003). *Education: Programmes and Policies*. New Delhi: APH Publishing Corporation. ISBN 81-7648-470-9.

Bhaskara Rao, Digumarti and D. Naresh Kumar (2004). *School Teacher Effectiveness*. New Delhi: Discovery Publishing House.

Bhaskara Rao, Digumarti and D. Sridhar (2002). *Job Satisfaction of School Teachers*. New Delhi: Discovery Publishing House. ISBN 81-7141-652-7.

Bhaskara Rao, Digumarti and Digumarti Pushpa Latha (1994). *Achievement in Biology*. New Delhi: Discovery Publishing House. ISBN 81-7141-264-5.

Bhaskara Rao, Digumarti, C. Sridevi and K. Vijaya (1995). *Achievement in Social Studies*. New Delhi: Discovery Publishing House. ISBN 81-7141-281-5.

Bhaskara Rao, Digumarti and Digumarti Pushpa Latha (1995). *Achievement in English*. New Delhi: Discovery Publishing House. ISBN 81-7141-283-1.

Bhaskara Rao, Digumarti and Digumarti Pushpa Latha (1994). *Achievement in Science*. New Delhi: Discovery Publishing House. ISBN 81-7141-280-70.

Bhaskara Rao, Digumarti and Digumarti Pushpa Latha (1995). *Achievement in Mathematics*. New Delhi: Discovery Publishing House. ISBN 81-7141-278-5.

Bhaskara Rao, Digumarti and Digumarti Pushpa Latha, Editors (1998). *International Encyclopaedia of Women*. 5 Volumes. New Delhi: Discovery Publishing House. ISBN 81-7141-410-9.

Vol. 1 *Status of World's Women*. ISBN 81-7141-494-X.

Vol. 2 *Women, Education and Empowerment*. ISBN 81-7141-498-1.

Vol. 3 *Women Challenges and Advancement*. ISBN 81-7141-497-4.

Vol. 4 *Women and Family Health*. ISBN 81-7141-497-4.

Vol. 5 *Women and International Action*. ISBN 81-7141-498-2.

Bhaskara Rao, Digumarti, Digumarti Pushpa Latha and Digumarti Harshitha, Editors (2001). *Biological Warfare*. New Delhi: Discovery Publishing House. ISBN 81-7141-597-0.

Bhaskara Rao, Digumarti, Digumarti Pushpa Latha and Digumarti Harshitha, Editors (2001). *Women as Educators*. New Delhi: Discovery Publishing House. ISBN 81-7141-602-0.

Bhaskara Rao, Digumarti and Digumarti Harshitha, Editors (2001). *Education in India*. New Delhi: APH Publishing Corporation. ISBN 81-7141-207-2.

Bhaskara Rao, Digumarti, Digumarti Pushpa Latha and Digumarti Harshitha, Editors (2001). *Assessing Learning Achievement*. New Delhi: Discovery Publishing House. ISBN 81-7141-601-2.

Bhaskara Rao, Digumarti, Digumarti Pushpa Latha and Digumarti Harshitha, Editors (2001). *Energy Security*. New Delhi: Discovery Publishing House. ISBN 81-7141-598-9.

Bhaskara Rao, Digumarti, Digumarti Harshitha and K.R.S.S. Rao, Editors (1999). *Advanced Biotechnology*. New Delhi: Discovery Publishing House. ISBN 81-7141-516-4.

Bhaskara Rao, Digumarti and K.R.S. Sambhasiva Rao, Editors (1996). *Current Trends in Indian Education*. New Delhi: Discovery Publishing House. ISBN 81-7141-311-0.

Bhaskara Rao, Digumarti and K. Vijaya (1995). *A Text Book of Evaluation*. Ambala Cantt: The Associated Publishers.

Bhaskara Rao, Digumarti and N.V.M. Mohana Rao (2002). *Problems of Mentally Handicapped Children*. New Delhi: Discovery Publishing House. ISBN 81-7141-645-4.

Bhaskara Rao, Digumarti and S. Chandra Mohan (2002). *Sports Management*. New Delhi: APH Publishing Corporation. ISBN 81-7648-467-9.

Bhaskara Rao, Digumarti and Sk. Johni Basha (2004). *Teachers' Population Education Awareness*. New Delhi: APH Publishing Corporation.

Bhaskara Rao, Digumarti, V.V. Rao, V.V. Lakshmi and V.V. Krishna, Editors (1999). *Status and Advancement of Women*. New Delhi: APH Publishing Corporation. ISBN 81-7648-169-6.

Babu, P.C., Author and Digumarti Bhaskara Rao, Editor (2004). *Flowers of Wisdom*. New Delhi: Discovery Publishing House. ISBN 81-7141-695-0.

Bhagya Lakshmi, Lingineni, Author and Digumarti Bhaskara Rao, Editor (2000). *Reading and Comprehension*. New Delhi: Discovery Publishing House. ISBN 81-7141-543-1.

Bhuvaneswara Lakshmi, Gadde, Author and Digumarti Bhaskara Rao, Editor (2000). *Attitude Towards Science*. New Delhi: Discovery Publishing House. ISBN 81-7141-541-6.

Devraj, T.A.S., Author and Digumarti Bhaskara Rao, Editor (1997). *Trace Analysis of Uranium and Thorium*. New Delhi: Discovery Publishing House. ISBN 81-7141-375-7.

Durga Rani, K., Author and Digumarti Bhaskara Rao, Editor (2000). *Educational Aspirations and Scientific Attitudes*. New Delhi: Discovery Publishing House. ISBN 81-7141-555-55.

Dutt, B.S.V. and Digumarti Bhaskara Rao (2001). *Empowering Primary Teachers*. New Delhi: Discovery Publishing House. ISBN 81-7141-615.2.

Ediger, Marlow and Digumarti Bhaskara Rao (1996). *Science Curriculum*. New Delhi: Discovery Publishing House. ISBN 81-7141-321-8.

Ediger, Marlow and Digumarti Bhaskara Rao (2000). *Teaching Mathematics Successfully*. New Delhi: Discovery Publishing House. ISBN 81-7141-552-0.

Ediger, Marlow and Digumarti Bhaskara Rao (2001). *Teaching Science Successfully*. New Delhi: Discovery Publishing House. ISBN 81-7141-600-4.

Ediger, Marlow and Digumarti Bhaskara Rao (2001). *Teaching Social Studies Successfully*. New Delhi: Discovery Publishing House. ISBN 81-7141-596-2.

Ediger, Marlow and Digumarti Bhaskara Rao (2002). *Philosophy and Curriculum*. New Delhi: Discovery Publishing House. ISBN 81-7141-631-4.

Ediger, Marlow and Digumarti Bhaskara Rao (2002). *Improving School Administration*. New Delhi: Discovery Publishing House. ISBN 81-7141-633-0.

Ediger, Marlow and Digumarti Bhaskara Rao (2002). *Elementary Curriculum*. New Delhi: Discovery Publishing House. ISBN 81-7141-658-6.

Ediger, Marlow and Digumarti Bhaskara Rao (2003). *Language Arts Curriculum*. New Delhi: Discovery Publishing House. ISBN 81-7141-657-8.

Ediger, Marlow and Digumarti Bhaskara Rao (2004). *Teaching Language Arts Successfully*. New Delhi: Discovery Publishing House. ISBN 81-7141-678-0.

Ediger, Marlow and Digumarti Bhaskara Rao (2004). *Teaching Mathematics in Elementary Schools*. New Delhi: Discovery Publishing House. ISBN 81-7141-687-X.

Ediger, Marlow and Digumarti Bhaskara Rao (2004). *Teaching Science in Elementary Schools*. New Delhi: Discovery Publishing House. ISBN 81-7141-709-4.

Ediger, Marlow and Digumarti Bhaskara Rao (2004). *School Curriculum and Administration*. New Delhi: Discovery Publishing House. ISBN 81-7141-709-4.

Ediger, Marlow and Digumarti Bhaskara Rao (2004). *Modern Elementary School*. New Delhi: Discovery Publishing House.

Ediger, Marlow and Digumarti Bhaskara Rao (2004): *Relevancy in Elementary Curriculum*. New Delhi: Discovery Publishing House. ISBN 81-7141-751-5.

Ediger, Marlow and Digumarti Bhaskara Rao, (2004). *Teaching Social Studies in Elementary Schools*. New Delhi: Discovery Publishing House.

Ediger Marlow, B.S.V. Dutt and Digumarti Bhaskara Rao (2004). *Teaching English Successfully*. New Delhi: Discovery Publishing House. ISBN 81-7141-707-8.

Harshitha, Digumarti and Digumarti Bhaskara Rao, Editors (2004). *Educational Innovations*. New Delhi: Discovery Publishing House.

Indira Devi, Author and J. Prasanth Kumar and Digumarti Bhaskara Rao, Editors (2004). *Values in Language Text Books*. New Delhi: Discovery Publishing House.

Jayasree, Kandi, Author and Digumarti Bhaskara Rao, Editor (1999). *Correlates of Socialisation*. New Delhi: Discovery Publishing House. ISBN 81-7141-517-2.

John Babu, Chikati, Author and T.J.R. Prasad, G.M. Madhukar and Digumarti Bhaskara Rao, Editors (1996). *Problem Solving in Mathematics*. New Delhi: APH Publishing Corporation. ISBN 81-7648-273-0.

Lalitha, T., Author and K.S. Prabhakaram, D.S.N. Sastry and Digumarti Bhaskara Rao, Editors (2004). *Educational Philosophic Beliefs*. New Delhi: Discovery Publishing House. ISBN 81-7141-765-5.

Madhu Bala, Jampala, Author and Digumarti Bhaskara Rao, Editor (2004). *Adjustment Problems of Hearing Impaired*. New Delhi: Discovery Publishing House.

Marja, Talvi and Digumarti Bhaskara Rao, Editors (1996). *Educational Leadership and Social Changes*. New Delhi: Discovery Publishing House. ISBN 81-7141-320-X.

Nirmala Jyothi, M., Author and Digumarti Bhaskara Rao, Editor (2003). *Non-detention Systems in School Education*. New Delhi: Discovery Publishing House. ISBN 81-7141-654-3.

Prabhakaram, K.S., Author and Digumarti Bhaskara Rao, Editor (1998). *Concept Attainment Model in Mathematics Teaching*. New Delhi: Discovery Publishing House. ISBN 81-7141-424-9.

Prasanth Kumar, J., Author and Digumarti Bhaskara Rao, Editor (1998). *Effectiveness of Distance Education System*. New Delhi: Discovery Publishing House. ISBN 81-7141-437-0.

Prasanth Kumar, J., Author and G. Sundara Rao and Digumarti Bhaskara Rao, Editors (2000). *Open University Student Support Services*. New Delhi: Discovery Publishing House. ISBN 81-7141-550-4.

Ramatulasamma, K., Author and Digumarti Bhaskara Rao, Editor (2002). *Job Satisfaction of Teacher Educators*, New Delhi: Discovery Publishing House. ISBN 81-7141-655-1.

Rama Krishnaiah, D., Author and Digumarti Bhaskara Rao, Editor (1998). *Job Satisfaction of College Teachers*, New Delhi: Discovery Publishing House. ISBN 81-7141-438-9.

Rama Kumar Ratnam, M., Author and Digumarti Bhaskara Rao, Editor (1998). *Dukka: Suffering in Early Buddhism*. New Delhi: Discovery Publishing House. ISBN 81-7141-653-5.

Rathaiah, Lavu and Digumarti Bhaskara Rao, Editors (1996). *International Innovations in Education*. New Delhi: Discovery Publishing House. ISBN 81-7141-359-5.

Ramesh, Ganta and Digumarti Bhaskara Rao, Editors (1998). *Environmental Education: Problems and Prospects*. New Delhi: Discovery Publishing House. ISBN 81-7141-423-0.

Rathaiah, Lavu and Digumarti Bhaskara Rao (1997). *Achievement Correlates*. New Delhi: Discovery Publishing House. ISBN 81-7141-385-4.

Reddy, Sudhakar Y., Author, and Digumarti Bhaskara Rao, Editor (2003). *Creativity in Adolescents*. New Delhi: Discovery Publishing House. ISBN 81-7141-659-4.

Reddy, M.S., Author and Digumarti Bhaskara Rao, Editor (2004). *Creativity in College Students*. New Delhi: Discovery Publishing House. ISBN 81-7141-697-7.

Radramamba, B., Author and Digumarti Bhaskara Rao, Editor (2003). *Problems of Teaching*. New Delhi: APH Publishing Corporation. ISBN 81-7648-462-8.

Sanjeeva Rao, P.C., Author and Digumarti Bhaskara Rao, Editor (1996). *A Text Book of Geology*. New Delhi: Discovery Publishing House. ISBN 81-7141-313-7.

Satya Narayana V., Author and Digumarti Bhaskara Rao, Editor (2001). *Physical Education, Social Attitudes and Leadership Qualities*. New Delhi: Discovery Publishing House. ISBN 81-7141-593-8.

Srinivasulu Reddy, M., and K.R.S. Sambasiva Rao, Authors and Digumarti Bhaskara Rao, Editor (1999). *A Text Book of Aquaculture*. New Delhi: Discovery Publishing House. ISBN 81-7141-482-6.

Srinivasa Rao, Mandalapu, Author and Digumarti Bhaskara Rao, Editor (2004). *Achievement Motivation and Achievement in Mathematics*. New Delhi: Discovery Publishing House. ISBN 81-7141-674-8.

Vanaja, M. Author and Digumarti Bhaskara Rao, Editor (1999). *Inquiry Training Model*. New Delhi: Discovery Publishing House. ISBN 81-7141-515-6.

Vanaja. M. and N. Sneha Latha, Authors and Digumarti Bhaskara Rao, Editor (2004). *Student Shyness*. New Delhi: APH Publishing Corporation.

Valeri V. Koustiouk, Author and Digumarti Bhaskara Rao, Editor (2002). *A Text Book of Cryogenics*. New Delhi: Discovery Publishing House. ISBN 81-7141-642-X.

Valeri V. Koustiouk, Author and Digumarti Bhaskara Rao, Editor (2004). *Refrigeration and Environment*. New Delhi: APH Publishing Corporation.

Veena Kumari, Balusu and Digumarti Bhaskara Rao (1996). *Operation Black Board*. New Delhi: Ashish Publishing Corporation. ISBN 81-7024-711-X.

Veena Kumari, Balusu, Author and Digumarti Bhaskara Rao, Editor (2000). *Psycho-Social Correlates of Achievement*, New Delhi: Discovery Publishing House. ISBN 81-7141-547-4.

Vanaja, M., Author and Digumarti Bhaskara Rao, Editor (1999). *Inquiry Training Model*. New Delhi: Discovery Publishing House. ISBN 81-7141-515-6.

Venkata Rao, P. and Digumarti Bhaskara Rao (1989). *A Text Book of Zoology—Junior Intermediate*. Guntur: Vignan Publishers.

Venkata Rao, P. and Digumarti Bhaskara Rao (1989). *A Text Book of Zoology—Senior Intermediate*. Guntur: Vignan Publishers.

Venugopala Rao, K., Author and Digumarti Bhaskara Rao, Editor (2000). *Teacher Morale in Secondary Schools*. New Delhi: Discovery Publishing House. ISBN 81-7141-551-2.

Vidya, C., Author and Digumarti Bhaskara Rao. Editor (1996). *A Text Book of Nutrition*. New Delhi: Discovery Publishing House. ISBN 81-7141-309-9.

Vidya Bharathi, D., Author and Digumarti Bhaskara Rao, Editor (2000). *Educational Philosophies of Swami Vivekananda and John Dewey*. New Delhi: APH Publishing Corporation. ISBN 81-7648-309-9.

Books in Telugu Language

Bhaskara Rao, Digumarti (1986). *Dhrushya Sravana Bodhanapakaranalu* (Audio Visual Teaching Aids). Guntur: Nagarjuna Publishers.

Bhaskara Rao, Digumarti (1993). *Jeevasashtra Bodhana* (Teaching of Biology). Guntur: Nagarjuna Publishers.

Bhaskara Rao, Digumarti (1995). *Vignanasasthra Bodhana* (Teaching of Science) Guntur: Nagarjuna Publishers.

Bhaskara Rao, Digumarti (1997). *Vidya Manovignana Seshtram* (Educational Psychology). Guntur: Creative Press.

Bhaskara Rao, Digumarti (1998). *DSC Study Material*. Guntur: Nagarjuna Publishers.

Bhaskara Rao, Digumarti (1998). *Upadhyayudu Vidya*. (Teacher and Education). Guntur: Nagarjuna Publishers.

Bhaskara Rao, Digumarti (1998). *Vidya Drukpadalu* (Prespectives of Education). Guntur: Nagarjuna Publishers.

Bhaskara Rao, Digumarti (1999). *EdCET Teaching Aptitude*. Guntur: Nagarjuna Publishers.

Bhaskara Rao, Digumarti (2001). *Bharata Samajamulo Upadyayudu Vidya* (Teacher and Education in Emerging Indian Society). Guntur: Nagarjuna Publishers.

Bhaskara Rao, Digumarti (2001). *Bhoutika Sastra Bodhana Paddathulu* (Methods of Teaching Physical Science). Guntur: Nagarjuna Publishers.

Bhaskara Rao, Digumarti (2001). *Jeeva Sastra Bodhana Padhathulu* (Methods of Teaching Biology). Guntur: Nagarjuna Publishers.

Bhaskara Rao, Digumarti (2001). *Vidya Manovignana Sastram* (Educational Psychology). Guntur: Nagarjuna Publishers.

Bhaskara Rao, Digumarti (2003). *Patsala Yajamanyam/Paripalana* (School Management and Administration). Guntur: Nagarjuna Publishers.

Bhaskara Rao, Digumarti (2004). *Vidya Sanketika Sastram mariyu Computer Vidya* (Educational Technology and Computer Education). Guntur: Nagarjuna Publishers.